T5-BBB-539

SOVIET COMMUNISM:
PROGRAMS AND RULES

Chandler Publications
in Political Science

Victor Jones, Editor

SOVIET COMMUNISM: PROGRAMS and RULES

OFFICIAL TEXTS OF

1919

1952(1956)

1961

Edited by

JAN F. TRISKA
Stanford University

CHANDLER PUBLISHING COMPANY   San Francisco

Copyright © 1962 by Chandler Publishing Company

Library of Congress Catalog Card No. 61-18483

Printed in the United States of America

LIBRARY
ALMA COLLEGE
ALMA, MICHIGAN

PREFACE

✦✦✦✦✦✦✦✦✦✦✦✦✦✦✦✦✦✦✦✦✦✦✦✦✦✦✦✦✦✦✦✦✦

This volume is a product of the Stanford University STUDIES IN INTERNATIONAL CONFLICT AND INTEGRATION. The subject represents one of several research undertakings, and the primary sources contained in it are the basis for several methodological types which this project supports and fosters.

In February 1960, the Ford Foundation awarded Stanford University funds in order to enlarge the research and teaching program in progress under its STUDIES IN INTERNATIONAL CONFLICT AND INTEGRATION. Already under way on an exploratory basis, this project had been applying techniques from several disciplines to the study of international relations.

As developed since that time, the STUDIES IN INTERNATIONAL CONFLICT AND INTEGRATION have become a systematic inquiry into the nature, processes and effects of conflict and integration in international relations.

Investigations currently in progress under this program include:

Factors Contributing to the Outbreak of War in 1914

The Bosnian Crisis of 1908–1909

The Arab-Israeli Conflict: Selected Phases

Conflictual and Cohesive Elements in the Sino-Soviet Alliance: 1960–1961

Communication and Control in Recent Soviet Disarmament Negotiations

Individual Personality and Attitudes toward International Affairs

Decision-making in Crises

Background of the Japanese Decision to Attack Pearl Harbor

Treaties, Charters, Constitutions and Other Contracts as Integration Instruments

A Cross Cultural Inquiry into the Operational Behavior of Underground Movements

☆ **v** ☆

PREFACE

The documents in this volume, and in particular the 1961 Program and Rules of the Communist Party of the Soviet Union—important contemporary primary sources of Soviet communism—alledgedly mark the beginning of a new era in the development of the USSR, the Communist Bloc, and world communism. Under the Soviet leadership, we are told, communism has come of age. But communism has become a world of paradox of its own which merits the closest scrutiny. We on the STUDIES IN INTERNATIONAL CONFLICT AND INTEGRATION consider the careful investigation, study and analysis of Soviet, Chinese, Yugoslav, Polish, Albanian and other varieties of communism—and principally of its primary basic sources such as the Program and the Rules of the Communist Party of the Soviet Union—of utmost significance in order to meet its ways and means with intelligence, imagination and wisdom. For the same reason, we make these documents widely available in this edition for all who, like us, wish to scrutinize them, compare them with their respective antecedents, and derive from them the lesson which they contain.

ROBERT C. NORTH
JAN F. TRISKA

Stanford, California
October, 1961

ACKNOWLEDGMENTS

I am grateful to the staff of the Hoover Institution on War, Revolution and Peace, and in particular to Mr. Karol Maichel, the Assistant Curator of East European Collections, for their kind assistance in preparation of this volume. Without the efficient ministration of my secretary, Mrs. Lydia Teichner, moreover, this manuscript would not have reached the publisher's desk on time.

I also wish to acknowledge permission to reprint material the copyright for which is held by The George Wahr Publishing Company in Ann Arbor, Michigan.

Professor John N. Hazard kindly traded with me information on the final version of the Party Rules when we both were most pressed for time.

JAN F. TRISKA

CONTENTS

★★★★★★★★★★★★★★★★★★★★★★★★★★★★★★★★

OUTLINES OF THE DOCUMENTS
★★★★★★★★★★★★★★★★★★★★★★★★★★★★★★★★

The 1961 Programme of the Communist Party of the Soviet Union

The 1919 Program of the All-Russian Communist Party (Bolsheviks)

The Rules of the Communist Party of the Soviet Union

☆ x ☆

SOVIET COMMUNISM: PROGRAMS AND RULES

English Versions of CPSU Documents— a Publisher's Note

In this book the publisher offers to readers an opportunity to make comparisons of two kinds: (1) of current documents with their analogs of earlier date; (2) of draft versions with final versions of current documents.

The draft versions and the finally adopted versions of the 1961 Programme and Rules are especially convenient for comparison. The final versions, where they differ from the draft versions, are indicated by interlinear insertions. The draft versions, which were released by official Soviet sources some weeks before the Congress, were set in type early in October, 1961. Then, as soon as the Russian texts of the documents became available after their final adoption on October 31 when the Congress adjourned, the Russian texts were compared with the English texts of the drafts. Changes and discrepancies were noted by Dr. Triska and translated by him into English for the interlinear additions.

It is to be emphasized that the language of the 1961 draft versions is faithful—in every detail of spelling, word order, and punctuation—to the officially released English text. Inasmuch as such details are normally subjected by the Party to close scrutiny for both political and literary exactness, the details may be significant, and in this book they are in no way distorted by intended "corrections."

The 1919 and 1952-1956 documents are likewise offered without any "corrections" of the language in the supposed interest of idiom or consistency.

INTRODUCTION

★★★★★★★★★★★★★★★★★★★★★★★★★★★★★★★

This introduction is a brief review of the Program and Rules of the Communist Party of the Soviet Union approved and adopted at the Twenty-second Congress of the Communist Party of the Soviet Union on October 31, 1961, and also a comparison of these documents with the superseded 1919 Party Program and the 1952 Party Rules. All of these four documents are included in this volume.

Program of the Communist Party of the Soviet Union

The 1961 Program of the Communist Party of the Soviet Union is historically the third program of the Russian Party since the beginning of the century.

The first Party Program, adopted at the Second Congress in Brussels in 1903—and in part reprinted in the introductory portion of the second Party Program because it "correctly characterizes the nature of capitalism and of bourgeois society" (although it used "the incorrect designation of the party as the Social-Democratic Party")—began with an assertion of the growing contradiction between the exploiting capitalism and the exploited masses in bourgeois societies. It stated that this contradiction could be resolved only by a social revolution carried out by the proletariat. However, dictatorship of the proletariat was a "necessary condition" for such revolution in order that the resistance of the exploiting capitalism could be effectively and rapidly crushed. In Russia, the immediate aim of the Party, according to the Program, was the overthrow of the autocracy and its replacement by a democratic republic. This democratic republic was to bring about a series of reforms: political and civil freedoms, universal education, self-determination for all nationalities, election of judges, separation of church and state, and a militia in place of a standing army. In addition, the 1903 Program stipulated that the conditions of industrial work would be improved and that concessions would be made to the peasants "in the interests of the free development of class war in the villages."

This Program, endorsed by a few dozen angry radicals, revolutionaries, and refugees, remained largely irrelevant for many years. When it became relevant, after the successful Bolshevik revolution in Russia, it ceased to fit the new conditions. Consequently the Seventh Party Congress, which met in March, 1918, appointed a committee (composed of Lenin, Bukharin, Zinoviev, Trotsky, Stalin, Sokolnikov, and Smirnov) to elaborate a new program which would either "revise the theoretical part [of the 1903 Program] or supplement it with material relating it to the epoch of imperialism and the new era of the international socialist revolution."

The committee presented the draft program to the Eighth Party Congress a year later, in March, 1919, a few days after the foundation in Moscow of the Third International (the Comintern) and at a time when the civil war was still in progress and many of the borderlands were still outside of Bolshevik control. It was adopted by the Congress as a new, second Party Program. Essentially the Program was a restatement of the theory of communism and an experiment in applying it to the tasks of effective communist rule in Russia.

In particular, the 1919 Party Program proclaimed, first, that with the successful Bolshevik revolution in Russia as a "foundation of communist society" there had begun "the era of a world-wide proletarian communist revolution." Like the Comintern, the Party Program anticipated "the growth of the revolutionary movement of the proletariat in all advanced countries, the spreading of the Soviet form of this movement," and the outbreak of communist revolutions everywhere. Second, the Program reprinted verbatim the 1903 Program's plank on the "inherent contradictions in bourgeois society," repeating that only "social revolution . . . will liberate all oppressed humanity" and summoning again "the toiling and the exploited masses" to join the ranks of "the Communist Party." Third, the Program stated that in "the period of imperialism," wars were "inevitable." Under these conditions, the Program sternly warned, "the watchwords of pacifism, international disarmament, courts of arbitration, etc., are not merely reactionary utopias, but deception of the toiling classes . . . Only the proletarian revolution is able to lead humanity out of the blind alley . . . [of] wars." Fourth, the Program attacked "the bourgeois perversion of socialism" by Social-Democratic and socialist parties, condemning them for "opportunism" and attempts "to revise the bankrupt Second International." Fifth, it praised the brand new Third Communist International, "cleansed of all bourgeois-opportunistic perversion"; one of its "sections" was now the All-Russian Communist Party.

With reference to the immediate *tasks* of the All-Russian Communist Party, the Program stated the following:

In the field of *political organization*, the Soviet state must become

"the highest type of democracy" in the world, "explaining that deprivation of political rights and any kind of limitation of freedom are necessary as temporary measures in order to defeat the attempts of exploiters
to retain or to reestablish their privileges." The Party must liberate
women "from all the burdens of antiquated methods of housekeeping,
by replacing" such methods "by house-communes, public kitchens, central laundries, nurseries, etc." Factories and mills, rather than territorial
districts, must form "electoral units and units of state." The Program
conferred privileges upon "the industrial proletariat" but not on "the
more scattered petty-bourgeois masses in the village." And it promised
to "overcome the evil . . . of bureaucratism" by "inducing . . . all the
working masses to take part in the work of the state administration."

In the field of *nationality policy,* the Program's watchwords were
equality, respect for national feelings, the possibility of political separation, and "a federative combination of all states organized on the
Soviet basis."

In *military affairs,* the Program promised, in the long run, "national
socialist militia"; in the short run, it found it "necessary to attract
military specialists who have gone through the training of the old army."

With regard to the *judicial system,* the Program provided for a
"simplified, uniform system of Peoples' Courts . . . freed of all useless
formalities of procedure," "comradely tribunals," and forced labor for
prisoners.

In the field of *education,* the 1919 Program promised to make
schools instruments "for a communist regeneration of society" with the
regime's whole-hearted support.

In the field of *religion,* it promised to liberate the minds of the toiling masses "from religious superstition."

In the future Soviet *economic organization,* the Program foresaw
the need for a general economic plan. To this end, it stressed the necessity of "utilization of small-scale and handicraft industry to the widest
extent," of freeing the trade unions "from their narrow guild outlook,"
of "a maximum utilization of labor," of developing the "comradely discipline of toilers," of "placing the bourgeois experts in a setting of
comradely common effort," and of "increasing the productive forces of
the country." However, it rejected, "at the moment," "equal remuneration of labor." It considered abolition of "the opposition between the
town and village" as one of its "principal tasks" but promised "a resolute struggle" against "the rural bourgeois elements." It hoped "to
replace private trade by a systematic distribution of products on a national scale." Recognizing that it was "impossible to abolish money" as
yet, the Program promised to do so in the long run. It stipulated that
"the system of levies imposed on the capitalist" would be replaced by

"the progressive income and property tax." It decreed future "abolition of inadequate housing," promised a "six-hour working day as a maximum without a reduction of wages" ("but on the condition that all workers must devote two hours overtime without pay to the study of the theory of trade and industry, to practical training for state administration and to military drill"), and guaranteed by every means the protection of public health in Soviet Russia.

This visionary, mystical, revolutionary Party Program—a romantic extravaganza, really, considering the state in which Soviet Russia was in March of 1919—became largely irrelevant, impractical, and obsolete almost as soon as it was published. If it were not for its admitted propaganda value, the document would have been rapidly forgotten.

Afterward, individual high Party meetings called for amendments at least of the 1919 Program to take account of the new conditions and developments of the time. Stalin, however, managed to prevent action on all such requests.

Twenty years after the adoption of the 1919 Party Program, at the Eighteenth Party Congress in 1939, a new committee was appointed with Stalin as Chairman to rewrite the archaic 1919 Party Program. However, nothing more is known of the work of the committee. Malenkov did mention a new Party program, together with new Party rules, at the conference which founded the Cominform in the fall of 1947. He did not spell out any details, however, concerning either of the alleged documents.

The Nineteenth Party Congress, which met in 1952, concerned itself anew with the revision of the 1919 Party Program. Having resolved that "fundamental changes have taken place both in the sphere of international relations and in the sphere of the construction of socialism in the USSR, in which connection many of the propositions set forth in the Program and tasks of the Party expounded therein . . . no longer correspond to modern conditions and the Party's new tasks," the Congress decided that the 1919 Party Program ought to be revised and the new draft submitted to the next, the Twentieth, Party Congress for approval and adoption. In particular, the Nineteenth Party Congress "unanimously" voted

To consider it necessary and timely to institute a revision of the existing Party Program.

In revising the program, to be guided by the fundamental theses of Comrade Stalin's work *Economic Problems of Socialism in the USSR.*

To entrust the work of revising the program to a commission composed of the following members: J. V. Stalin, Chairman of the Commission, and L. P. Beria, L. M. Kaganovich, O. V. Kuusinen,

G. M. Malenkov, V. M. Molotov, D. N. Pospelov, A. M. Rumyantsev, M. Z. Saburov, D. I. Chesnokov and P. F. Yudin.

To submit the draft revised Party Program for consideration to the next Congress of the Communist Party of the Soviet Union.

However, the Commission lost its Chairman Stalin, who died March 3, 1953; Beria, who was executed; Chesnokov, who was dropped from the Central Committee; and Yudin, who was sent to Communist China as the new Soviet Ambassador. Hence the Commission failed again, as Khrushchev had to admit at the Twentieth Party Congress in 1956. Presiding at the final meeting of the Twentieth Congress, Khrushchev proposed therefore that a new draft program be prepared for the approval of the next Party Congress to replace the antiquated 1919 Party Program. "We will have a large task in drafting the new Party program, which is, for the present, not prepared," he reported, adding that the design for the new Party platform would have to be developed in accordance with long-range designs for several five-year plans. TASS reported that the new Party Program was to be "based on the main tenets of Marxist-Leninist theory, constructively developed on a foundation of the historical experience of our Party, the experience of fraternal parties of socialist countries, and the experience and achievements of the whole international Communist and Workers' movement." Apparently, a new committee was appointed to draft the new program; this time, however, the names of the members who worked under Khrushchev's guidance were not disclosed.

The 1961 Party Program constitutes, then, the culmination and fulfillment, long overdue, of a prolonged effort on the part of the Soviet Communist Party.

Compared with the 1919 Party platform, the new Party Program is sheer heresy. It does not reject coexistence with imperialism, as Lenin did at the Eighth Party Congress, but advocates it. It no longer considers Communist revolutions abroad to be the necessary means of change. Wars are viewed as no longer inevitable. The new Program advocates, rather than condemns, pacifist movements and disarmament, and it views patriotism as a fine thing. Neutrality abroad is now fully embraced. The 1961 Program borrows ideas from socialists everywhere; grants considerable "rights" to all Soviet peoples; does not even mention, in view of its huge armed forces, a "national socialist militia"; nor does it mention moneyless economy. Formalities of judicial procedure are now significant rather than "useless." The 1961 Program advances new, fresh ideas on education; it aims at economic reorganization which has little to do with the Bolshevik dreams of 1919; it has no patience with "factories and mills" as electoral units; and the CPSU certainly is no longer "a section" of the Comintern, which has disappeared along the way.

Is Khrushchev, the undisputed father of the new Soviet Party Program, hereby parting ways with the early Soviet period, with Lenin, and with the Marxist-Leninist-Stalinist doctrinal heritage? Or is he merely bringing Marx, Engels, Lenin & Co. up to date? Let us see.

The 1961 Party Program first and appropriately pays its respects to Marx and Engels, "the Paris Commune," the October (Bolshevik) Revolution, the Chinese Communist Revolution, "the brilliant genius of Lenin," the Party and its first and second Program, socialism in the USSR, and "the establishment of the world Socialist system" embracing "one-third of mankind." It restates the introductory portion of the 1919 Party Program on the fundamental contradiction in capitalism and "its final stage, the stage of monopoly capitalism, of imperialism," and "the anarchy" which results from it. (The Program attacks here, however, nineteenth-century capitalism rather than twentieth-century reality.)

Second, the new Program describes the significance and the merits of the Bolshevik revolution in Russia; of "socialism in one country"; of the wisdom of Lenin and the Party and their victory over "skeptics and capitulators," "Trotskyists," "Right opportunists," "national deviators and other hostile groups"; of the Soviet "Socialist democracy" with its "political freedoms," economic rights, and "social justice"; of the Soviet conquest of outer space; of the enlightened Soviet nationality policy; and of the general glorious "Soviet experience," which it predicts "soon" to share with "all the people."

Third, the new Party Program describes "the socialist camp" ("or, which is the same thing, the world community of socialist countries") and its eleven members' "people's democracy, a variety of the dictatorship of the proletariat," and condemns Yugoslavia, whose "leaders by their revisionist policy contraposed Yugoslavia to the socialist camp." It predicts that the socialist camp, with the assistance of the USSR, "will shortly surpass the world capitalist system in aggregate industrial and agricultural production." The socialist camp, the Program states, "is a prototype of new society, of the future of all mankind"; imperialism, on the other hand, "has entered the final period of decline and collapse."

Fourth, because of this crucial change in the world, violence is no longer inevitable; frankly, the Marxist-Leninist parties "prefer to achieve the transfer of power from the bourgeoisie to the proletariat by peaceful means, without civil war." As a matter of fact, the bourgeoisie may "agree to the means of production being purchased from it and for the proletariat to 'pay off' the bourgeoisie" (sic!).

Fifth, the Program explains the dangers of revisionism, dogmatism, and sectarianism to world communism and to the individual Communist

Parties and recommends struggle against these deviations from the true course as "a necessary condition for the further strengthening of the unity of the world Communist movement." The CPSU now promises to see to it that such dangers in "the ranks of the great army of Communists of all countries" are eliminated.

Sixth, the underdeveloped, uncommitted countries ought to "put an end to their economic dependence on imperialism" for their own good. (To be sure, "U.S. imperialism is the chief bulwark of modern colonialism.") Once unshackled, they should choose socialism over capitalism because, the Program explains in great detail, they may miss their great opportunity to join the winning trend in the world.

Seventh, analyzing modern capitalism, the Program carefully explains that the so-called "free world" is "a world of obscurantism and political reaction," "fascism," "chauvinism," "anti-Semitism," "racial discrimination," "clericalism," "anti-communism," "militarism" and, of course, "imperialism."

Eighth and finally, advocating "peace," "equality," "self-determination of nations," "respect for the independence and sovereignty of all countries," "general and complete disarmament under strict international control," and "peaceful coexistence," the Program promises that the CPSU would "use . . . every means of preventing war," to stop "the cold war," to disband "all military blocs," to abolish "bases on foreign territory," and to support "neutralist and pacifist movements." The resumption of nuclear tests by the USSR is not mentioned in the new document.

This first part of the 1961 Program, which constitutes almost half of the new platform, corresponds roughly to the brief introductory part in the 1919 Program. What follows, in the 1961 Program as well as in the 1919 Program, is the description of the *future tasks* of the Party: quite general, brief, and immediate in the 1919 document but most detailed and long-range here.

In its Part Two, the 1961 Party Program explains what communism—the Khrushchevian version—is: A classless social system of "equality of all members of society," without difference between town and country and between mental and physical labor, which provides all people "with material and cultural benefits according to their growing needs," where all "work willingly," with "high standards of organization, precision and discipline," and where family relationships are based on "mutual love and friendship." The Program foresees, however, that rather than "overnight," communism will arrive in the USSR in three successive stages: In the current decade (1961-1970) the USSR "will surpass . . . the U.S.A. in production per head of population," and will achieve a correspondingly high standard of living. In the next decade

(1971-1980) "Soviet society will come close to a stage where it can introduce the principle of distribution according to needs." And, "The construction of communist society will be fully completed in the subsequent period." (The state will disappear only *after* the complete victory of communism.) Communism, however, as Khrushchev remarked in a speech, will mean no wallowing in luxuries, but enjoyment of "the sound, reasonable requirements of perfectly developed persons."

In the field of *economic development,* the Program promises "within 20 years" to have completed "on the whole" the electrification of the USSR; the mechanization of production with a high degree of automation; considerably increased development of the Soviet chemical industry; large-scale use of cybernetics, computers, and control systems; fusion of science and production; accelerated development of all transport facilities and means of communication; modernization of the building industry; enlargement of the role of science; and utilization of atomic power and construction of atomic power stations. In particular, the Program foresees 150 per cent increase in the total Soviet industrial output "within the current 10 years" and 500 per cent increase "within 20 years."

With reference to agricultural production, it predicts that the 10-year and 20-year increase will be 150 per cent and 250 per cent respectively, through extensive application in agriculture of the biological sciences and microbiology; by means of future development and improvement of both collective farms and state farms; through development of community services—such as bakeries, laundries, clubs, libraries, sports grounds, and the like—on the collective farms, thereby releasing new labor forces for the farms; and by increase in pay and by introduction of pensions, holidays, social security, and the like.

As for planning and economic management, the Program calls for "the most rational and effective use of the material, labor and financial resources and natural wealth and . . . the elimination of excessive expenditure, . . . the highest results at the lowest cost." In view of the projected rapid expansion of the Soviet economy, this improvement must be achieved, and more, and certainly not in heavy industry alone; otherwise, the projected economic goals will remain largely unfulfilled.

As regards the *standard of living,* the 1961 Program stipulates "rapid improvement" in the future and promises "nearly 150 per cent" increase in the national income "in the next ten years" and "about 400 per cent in twenty years" (which is interpreted to mean an increase in the "real income per head of population" by "more than 250 per cent in twenty years"). This increased income will purport, according to the Program, "high-quality and varied foodstuffs," "attractive clothes, footwear," "comfortable modern furniture," extended production of "motor-cars for the population," "good shopping facilities," and other benefits. "The second decade will see an abundance" of those things, and what is more, "every family, including newlyweds [sic!], will have a comfortable flat," and public transportation will be "free" as will housing, water, gas and heating. The work week will be shortened, vacations lengthened, free medical services improved, free care for children extended, and education at all educational establishments made free.

With reference to the *Soviet state organization,* the Party Program stipulates that the state will be "necessary" and will "survive until the complete victory of communism," whenever that may be. In the meantime, the Soviets, "which combine the features of a government body and a social organization," "will grow as communist construction progresses." In order "to bring a wider range of able persons into [leading bodies] and "rule out abuses of authority by individual government officials," the Party "considers systematic renewal" necessary—at least one-third of the deputies should be elected anew in each election. "As a rule," deputies should not be elected "for more than three consecutive terms"; but like the 1961 Party Rules, the new Program permits gifted individuals to be excepted from this rule if "no less than three quarters of the votes are cast in his favor." (Social organizations—the trade unions; consumer, housing and other cooperatives; collective farms; the various professional societies; sports organizations, and the like—should not elect their leading officials "for more than two consecutive terms.") However, as this innovation applies, in the realm of the Soviet political reality, to bodies and organs other than the ruling oligarchy, its meaning is limited. Furthermore, the Program promises gradual increase in the responsibility and jurisdiction of deputies on all levels and corresponding decrease in the responsibility and jurisdiction of the departments and executive agencies; increase in the use of referenda for "important draft laws"; "rigid enforcement of law, legality and order" against abuse of power by officials, as well as general "strict observance of socialist legality . . . eradication of all violation of law and order . . . abolition of crime and the removal of all the causes of crime," and strict observance of "all the norms of judicial procedure."

As for the Soviet *Armed Forces,* the Party sees it as the Soviet Union's "internationalist duty to guarantee . . . the reliable defense and security of the entire socialist camp."

In the field of *national relations,* the Party now stresses "internationalism" in relations of nationalities in the USSR, "proletarian internationalism" within the socialist camp, and "patriotism"—which means "love for one's country" but not "the reactionary ideology of bourgeois nationalism, racism and cosmopolitanism" elsewhere.

In the field of *ideology, education, science and culture,* indoctrination toward "devotion to communism," "the moulding of the new man," comes first. Then come principles, in part reprinted in the Party Rules—among others: "humane relations and mutual respect between individuals—man is to man a friend, comrade and brother; honesty and truthfulness, moral purity, modesty, and unpretentiousness in social and private life; mutual respect in the family, and concern for the upbringing of children"; "friendship and brotherhood among all peoples of the USSR; intolerance of national and racial hatred." What a difference from the 1919 Party Program! The Party is now concerned with the "all-round and harmonious development of the individual," "equal opportunities," "personal dignity," and "free choice of occupation." Is this, or is it not, communist language? The Program has the answer to this query: The language may not be communist, but the meaning is: this Soviet individual, "the new man," will be imbued with "*communist* morality, which is the noblest and most just morality," rejecting "the class morality" and "the perverse, selfish views and morals of the old world."

The new Program promises the introduction of universal compulsory secondary education in the USSR, much improved higher education, emphasis on theoretical research in science, and a wider role for scientists. In the field of cultural development, the Program foresees "the closing stage of a great cultural revolution" both at home and in relations "with all other countries."

In the *Socialist Bloc,* the Party expects growth of "common basic objective laws for communist construction," modified, however, by "due allowance . . . for the historical and national peculiarities of each country." Unlike Stalin, Khrushchev knows now that "It is in the best interest of socialist and communist construction that each socialist country combine the effort to strengthen and develop its national economy with the effort to expand economic co-operation of the socialist camp as a whole."

And finally, *The Party* itself, "the brain, the honor and the conscience of our epoch," must increase its creative activity among the masses; further develop propaganda and indoctrination; improve its own organization and the forms and methods of its work; serve constantly as an example in the difficult period ahead of transition to communism; and observe the principles of collectivism, responsibility to the rank and file, accountability at all levels, criticism and self-criticism, inner-Party democracy, socialist legality, "regular renewal" of the officials in all Party organs and restriction on their tenure in office (see below in 1961 Party Rules), struggle against the cult of the individual and against all manifestations of factionalism, and service to "all the people." (All these "principles" are made functional in the 1961 Party Rules.) On this basis, the Program concludes: "The Party solemnly proclaims: the present generation of Soviet people shall live under communism." It is not stipulated here whether this will be the first, the second, or the third stage of communism.

The new Party Program is a remarkable, fascinating document. It mixes fact and fancy with the greatest of facility. It is repetitious though not really redundant. It brings communism up to date and yet postpones it again. In it, Marx is Marx, Engels is Marx's collaborator, Lenin is Lenin—but Stalin is "the people," "the Party," or both; he is not mentioned by name at all. For that matter, neither is Khrushchev; and yet he should have signed the Program. It is his document.

There is no doubt that Khrushchev's stature abroad was considerably enhanced by this historic communist manifesto. In the Communist Bloc, it successfully challenged Khrushchev's ideological senior, the chairman of the Chinese Communist Party and Stalin's political contemporary, Mao Tse-tung (whose name is not mentioned in the Program). Fortunately for Khrushchev, Mao faces at the present time a grave economic crisis at home; and rather than replying to the challenge, he may have to do some ideological retooling of his own.

The Program is not a repudiation of the past, however, not even of the heritage left by Stalin. Rather, in terms of the projected short-range goals, it is an ambitious revision, possibly the most radical one, of Marxism since the early period of Bolshevism—one which hopefully establishes Khrushchev as the ideological leader of world communism.

In terms of its long-range objectives, on the other hand, the Program is a sober and restrained document. In view of the much debated and publicized official Soviet thinking on the subjects of the transition to communism in the USSR and to world communism, and especially when compared with the utopian, anarchic 1919 Party Program of Lenin, the new document must appear, at least to some Party members, as leaving much to be desired.

The Party Program is a Soviet document; as such, it is Khrushchev's sharp and clear reply to the patched-up Moscow Manifesto of the 81 Communist Parties' leaders of November, 1960, which was designed to pacify all but which satisfied no one. It is a Soviet guide for the members of the Communist bloc whom it counsels how to build their own communist societies.

The Party Program is a first-rate propaganda weapon. The image of communism which it projects abroad, and principally in the less developed countries, must appear most attractive. The time element—the distance of twenty and more years before it all happens—may easily seem less significant than the carefully spelled out appealing details.

In this sense, the Program is a true political platform. It appeals to so many and promises so much that the issue of fulfillment is questionable also on the ground of the Program's own tactical flexibility and unrestrained ambivalence.

However, the Program is also an important statement of Soviet national purpose. As such, it is a significant 1961 blueprint, in which the present substance and technique of Soviet social engineering are perhaps even more important than the promises, goals, and assurances of the glorious future. It may be well to remember that in addition to its propaganda value abroad and the needed strengthening of Khrushchev's position in the Communist Bloc, the Program is also a considered response to the present hopes, expectations, and demands of the Soviet people. A shrewd and sensitive strategist, Khrushchev knows that almost five decades after the Bolshevik revolution, he had better motivate the long-neglected Soviet masses by promising them what they want and need most rather than by obsolete, revolutionary slogans and some unspecified communist heaven in the distant future. Right now, Khrushchev needs the labor, productivity, efficiency, and good will of all Soviet citizens; otherwise, he will never be able to accomplish what he set out to accomplish—namely, to make the USSR the strongest power on earth. Soviet citizens, having enjoyed some improvement of their lot recently, demand more. Judging from the Program, they demand by now much more, even possibly the luxury of stability on which to plan their own individual lives. In this respect the affluent, advanced, prestigious, and status-oriented Soviet society of the future (that description sounds much like the capitalist society of the United States, which attained these achievements for the most part many years ago) may be less significant than the actual effect these optimistic promises will have *now* on the mood of the Soviet people.

Rules of the Communist Party of the Soviet Union

The 1961 Rules of the Communist Party of the Soviet Union, the sixth version of the Soviet Union's Party Rules to date, represent the most thorough revision of this constitution of the Soviet Communist Party since the adoption of the first all-Union Party Rules by the Fourteenth Party Congress in 1925.

The 1925 Party Rules translated into practical Party language and organizational system the (second) Party Program, approved at the Eighth Party Congress in 1919. The Party Program restated the doctrine of communism in Soviet Russia; the Party Rules were the reflection of the Program in terms of distribution of functions within the all-Union organizational structure and over-all responsibilities of the Party. While the Program recorded the principal doctrinal developments as well as the brave hopes for the Soviet future, the Rules represented the Party's concrete ways and means of dealing with everyday reality in the USSR.

Although the 1919 Party Program was not changed until 1961, the Party Rules have been altered frequently. Every regular Party Congress which met after 1925 revised or amended the Party Rules. It is true that some of the changes were only minor; the Twentieth Party Congress which met in 1956, for example, introduced only a few amendments to the Party Rules adopted in 1952.* The fact remains, however, that the changing realities of Soviet life had to be dealt with by and through the

---

* First, the 1952 Rules were modified so that more than three secretaries of Party committees could be appointed. This amendment confirmed the prevailing practice of appointing five secretaries. The number of secretaries was not determined in the Party Rules, however, as such determination was considered "inexpedient." This measure was adopted in spite of the overt emphasis at the Twentieth Party Congress on the reduction of the size of the Party apparatus. Second, the 1952 stipulation of Article 35, Paragraph c, empowering the Committee of Party Control to have its own representatives "independent of local Party bodies" in republics, territories, and provinces was abrogated. As Khrushchev pointed out, "experience has demonstrated that there is no need for this institution of plenipotentiaries." It seems that this step was taken in order to streamline the Party's punitive chain of command. Third, the frequency of committee plenary sessions was reduced. While the 1952 Rules provided for province and territory committees and union republic Central Committees to hold plenary sessions "at least every two months," the amendment called for meetings "at least every four months." (Plenary sessions of regional, city and district Party Committees were now scheduled to meet "at least once every three months.") Local Party conferences and congresses were to be held at least every eighteen months under the 1952 Rules; the Twentieth Party Congress amended this provision by stipulating that congresses and conferences of Party organizations in union republics, territories, provinces, regions, and cities having boroughs were to be held every two years, while congresses of Party organizations in union republics having provinces (Ukraine, Byelorussia, Kazakhstan and Uzbekistan) were to be held every four years. Frequent conferences, congresses, and committee plenary sessions probably stood in the way of rapid "socialist construction." Fourth, shop Party organizations could now be established—again with the sanction of the district or city Party committees or the appropriate political departments—in primary organization numbering 50 (rather than 100) members. And fifth, all references to political departments in transportation were now eliminated.

Party. For this purpose, the Party Rules have been more appropriate, useful, and effective vehicles than the lofty Party Program.

Compared with the 1952 Party Rules, amended in 1956, the 1961 Party Rules are a fair reflection of the principal issues of the post-Stalin era. Like the new Program, the new Rules bear the heavy imprint and seal of Khrushchev, the Soviet Party and government leader. As formulated in 1961, the Party Rules, like the Party Program, present to us the widely proclaimed "new" Communist Party of the USSR, the heart of the allegedly "new" Soviet Union. What actually emerges is a fascinating combination of something old and something new, with the old prevailing. Let us briefly analyze the more significant innovations and changes contained in the 1961 Party Rules.

Unlike the 1952 Rules—but like the 1939 version—the 1961 Rules start with an *introduction* (called Preamble in the 1939 Rules), almost twice as long as the corresponding Article 1 in the 1952 document. Here the new emphasis is on the experience ("tried and tested") of the Party, its service to "the people as a whole," its adherence to "the principle of collective leadership," its rejection of "factionalism and group activity" and "revisionism and dogmatism," its "creative development of Marxism-Leninism," and its adherence to "proletarian internationalism" and "unity of the international communist movement" abroad. In this new introduction, Lenin is mentioned twice and Marxism-Leninism three times; Stalin, by omission, is in effect denounced.

With reference to the *duties* of Party members, the new Rules lay emphasis on work "for the creation of the material and technical basis of communism," "the initiative in all that is new and progressive," the support for "advanced methods," and the raising of "labor productivity." The new Rules are less conspiratorial than the 1952 Rules and stress productive work, equality of all Party members ("the Party has one discipline [and] one law for all communists, irrespective of their past services or the positions they occupy"), and "considerate" assistance "to the people."

With reference to the Party members' *rights,* the new Rules stipulate that "those who commit the offense of suppressing criticism or victimizing anyone for criticism are responsible to and will be penalized by the Party, to the point of expulsion from the CPSU." This provision echoes Khrushchev's secret speech at the Twentieth Party Congress in 1956.

Article 5, Paragraph d of the 1952 Rules, which dealt with the *admission of new members,* stipulated: "Former members of other parties are admitted to the Party on the recommendation of five Party members: three of ten years' Party standing and two of prerevolutionary Party standing"; this provision has been deleted in the 1961 Party

Rules as obsolete. The corresponding Article 4, Paragraph (C) now stipulates that "former members of other parties are admitted to membership of the CPSU in conformity with the regular procedure, except that their admission must be endorsed by the regional or territorial committee of the Central Committee of the Communist Party of a union republic."

With reference to the *expulsion of members* from the Party, Article 8 of the new Rules is more liberal than the corresponding Article 9 of the 1952 Rules. The 1952 Rules provided that Party members or candidate members who failed to pay their membership dues for three months in succession without sufficient reason "automatically dropped out of the Party." The new Rules now stipulate that in these cases "the matter shall be discussed by the primary Party organization." Only if it is found that the member or the candidate member "has virtually lost contact with the Party organization" is such member or candidate member regarded "as having ceased to be a member of the Party."

Unlike the 1952 Rules, the new Rules provide in Article 11 that members or alternate members of the Central Committee of the Communist Party of a union republic, of a territorial, regional, area, city or district Party committee, or of an auditing commission, may be called to account before the Party. Party organizations may now not only discuss the issues involved, but may make decisions imposing penalties on members or alternate members of these Party bodies. Under the 1961 Rules, just as under the 1952 Rules, however, primary Party organizations have no right to expel members of those bodies; only the plenary meetings of these bodies may do so.

Article 26 of the 1952 Rules presumed that voting on individual candidates in the *election of Party bodies* would be unanimous; no qualifying majority for the election of individual members to Party bodies was admitted. The 1961 Rules provide in Article 24 that "a candidate is considered elected if more than one-half of those attending the meeting, conference or congress has voted for him."

Article 25 of the new Rules—a stipulation missing in the 1952 Rules—provides for "the principle of *systematic renewal of the composition of Party bodies and of continuity of leadership.*" In particular, this significant new provision means that "at each regular election, not less than one-quarter of the composition of the Central Committee of the Party and its Presidium shall be renewed." And for the first time in the history of the Communist Party, "members of the Presidium shall not, as a rule, be elected for more than three successive terms." An ironic twist is added by this escape clause: "Particular Party officials may, by virtue of their generally-recognized prestige and high political, organizational and other qualities, be successively elected to leading bodies for a longer period." In that case, however, "a candidate is considered elected if not less than three-quarters of the votes are cast for him by secret ballot." Apparently, Khrushchev is quite certain by now of his position within the Party apparatus.

Article 25 of the new Rules further stipulates that at least one-third of the membership of the Central Committees of the Communist Parties of the union republics and of the territorial and regional Party committees must be renewed at each regular election, while the area, city, and district Party committees and the committees or bureaus of primary Party organizations must be renewed at least by one-half. Members of those Party bodies may be elected successively for "not more than three terms" (and the secretaries of primary Party organizations "for not more than two terms"). A particular official may be elected for a longer period if at least three-quarters of the attending members vote for him.

Equally significant, and by implication anti-Stalinist, is the new Article 26. It provides ways and means *for removing from the Central Committee of the Party a member or an alternate member* who does not "justify the great trust placed in him by the Party" or who does not "uphold his honor and dignity" as a member of the Party. (The same provision applies to the members and candidate members of the Central Auditing Commission, the Central Committees of the Communist Party of the union republics, territorial, regional, area, city, or district Party committees, and the auditing commissions of republican, territorial, regional, area, city, or district Party organizations.)

The last principle discussed in this section of the Rules is *collectivism,* "the highest principle of Party leadership." Collective leadership is now considered in the Party Rules "an absolute requisite for the normal functioning of the Party organizations." "The cult of the individual" is rejected as not only "incompatible with the Leninist principles of Party life," but also as a cause of "violations of inner-Party democracy." A corollary to this principle, which provides that "collective leadership does not exempt persons in office from their responsibility for the job entrusted to them," is now added.

According to Article 33, Paragraph (C) of the new Rules, the Party congress now "determines the line of the Party in matters of domestic and foreign policy," not "the *tactical* line" as provided in Article 31, Paragraph c of the 1952 Rules.

Under Article 39 of the new Rules, the Central Committee of the Party now "elects" a Presidium and a Secretariat. Under the 1952 Rules it "set up" a Presidium and a Secretariat.

The Central Committee of the CPSU also now establishes "a *bureau of the Central Committee of the CPSU for the Russian Soviet*

Federative Socialist Republic (RSFSR)." The meaning of this provision is not entirely clear: The bureau, originally established in 1956, created for the first time in the history of the Party a separate Party administration for the RSFSR, probably as an attempt to introduce a measure of decentralization into the administrative apparatus of the Party. This process of administrative decentralization was not allowed to go too far, however. As a matter of fact, effective co-ordination at the center was secured, first, by making the First Secretary of the Party also the Chairman of the RSFSR bureau, and second, by permitting the existence of only one central register of Party members within the Department of Party Organs of the Central Committee. The budget of the Party remains centralized, and the Central Committee retains its authority to intervene in the affairs of the republican Party bodies when necessary.

The new Party Rules *streamline the provisions concerning organization and bodies of the Party below the Central Party organs.* The three sections of the 1952 Rules dealing with the regional, territorial, and republican organizations of the Party, area Party organizations, and city and district (rural and urban) organizations have now been integrated into one section called "Republican, Territorial, Regional, Area, City and District Organizations of the Party." The functions of these organizations are much the same as before, although the emphasis is now again on production, "promotion of the communist awareness of the working people," and "solicitude for the steady improvement of the material and cultural standards of the working people."

Article 45 of the new Rules does not prescribe any more that the regional and territorial committees and the Central Committees of the Communist Parties of union republics "each elect an executive body, consisting of not more than 11 persons," as did Article 42 of the old Rules. Article 45 now provides that these executive bodies—the bureaus—must be elected, but it does not stipulate the minimum or maximum number of members.

The new Rules omit Article 53 of the 1952 Rules on the establishment of borough organizations, which used to be subordinate to the city committees in large cities.

Under the new Rules, Article 56 provides that in addition to a secretary, "a *deputy secretary*" should be elected by the primary, shop, and departmental Party organizations with less than fifteen members.

Significantly at variance with the 1952 Party document, the 1961 Rules, referring to (a) all Party organizations below the Central organs, (b) rank-and-file Communists, and (c) Party organizations in the Soviet Armed Forces, respectively, provide that they "take guidance from ("observe in [their] own life") the Program and the Rules of the CPSU." It is true, however, that the new Rules at the same time again admonish those concerned to follow closely also the directives of the Central Party organs, in particular of the Central Committee of the CPSU.

Among the more surprising innovations in the new Rules are the new *duties of individual Communists* which the primary Party organizations are directed to enforce upon the rank-and-file members and candidate members of the Party. Unlike the 1952 Party Rules, and in addition to the more mundane duties enumerated both in the 1952 and the 1961 Rules, the new provisions include the following: "collectivism and comradely mutual assistance: one for all, and all for one; — humane relations and mutual respect among people: Man is to man a friend, comrade and brother; — honesty and truthfulness, moral purity, unpretentiousness and modesty in public and personal life; — mutual respect in the family circle and concern for the upbringing of children; — intolerance of injustice . . ; — friendship and fraternity among all peoples of the USSR, intolerance of national and racial hostility; . . . fraternal solidarity with the working people of all countries, with all peoples."

Compared with the five previous editions and amendments of the Party Rules, respectively adopted in 1925, 1934, 1939, 1952, and 1956, these new provisions are, to put it mildly, unusual. They signify a major breakthrough into a new dialectic stage. It cannot be emphasized enough, however, that these admirable principles must be viewed as an integral part of a specific Soviet semantic system, wholly different from our own. It would be entirely misleading to perceive them in the frame of reference of nineteenth-century Western liberalism. "Peace," "justice," "freedom," "equality" and "democracy," terms which crop up frequently in the Soviet official literature, have particular communist connotation, borne out by communist ideology. It may help to insert the adjective "communist" before such significant nouns as "people," "man," and "family" in order to understand better the meaning of these new "duties" of the Party members. This semantic qualification does not suggest that Khrushchev does not mean what he says here, but rather that what he says should be interpreted in the light of communist experience and objectives. The fact that these humanitarian statements appear at all indicate an advance for the Soviet Union, however—one leaving other communist states, especially Communist China, far behind.

The new Party Rules concerning the Young Communist League define and spell out the purposes, functions, and principal activities of the Young Communist League—another innovation absent in the 1952 Rules. The same innovation—a definition of purposes, functions and activities—is employed now in the section on the Party organizations within the Soviet Army. (The 1952 Rules dealt in this section with Party organizations in the Soviet Army and Navy and in the Transport Services; the Twentieth Party Congress in 1956 eliminated all references to transport services.) What is meant, however, as Article 65 points out, is the Armed Forces as a whole. The heading reflects the old Soviet preference for and emphasis on the Army over the Navy. (The Air Force is part of the Soviet Army.)

The last difference between the 1961 and 1952 Party Rules concerns the Party funds. First, because of the recent change from the old to the new ruble (worth 10 old rubles), the monthly earnings upon which Party dues are based have been correspondingly reduced. Second, Party members and candidate members who earn less than 50 new rubles a month do not pay as their dues ½ per cent of their income as prescribed in the 1952 Rules, but only 10 kopeks a month.

The above comments concern only the major differences between the new and the old Party Rules. These differences are significant: they make the 1961 Party Rules anti-Stalinist in spirit, broaden what the communists call "the inner-Party democracy," de-emphasize the authoritarian role of the top Party bodies and limit their members' tenure in office, somewhat encourage criticism from below, and make the Party seem less conspiratorial and absolutist. In that part which deals with the primary Party organizations and the rank-and-file communists, the Rules appear, certainly to the uninitiated, more liberal and more humanitarian. Also, the over-all emphasis is now even more than previously on diligence, industry, and productivity.

However, all the innovations in the 1961 Party Rules must be read against the context of the new Party Rules as a whole. On review, it becomes clear that at least as many of the provisions of the 1952 Rules were left unchanged as were rewritten, omitted, or added. It is true that the organization of the Party in the new Rules is streamlined, but the purpose is to make the Party demonstrably more efficient and effective. It is also true that the Party officials, including the members of the Party Presidium, are now subject to limitations, the most important of which restricts their tenure of office to three successive terms. First of all, however, "highly respected" Party officials may be elected "for a longer period"; second, as one observer pointed out, this new provision may very well have been intended by Khrushchev to serve as a periodical, institutionalized, legitimate purge of his actual or potential rivals in the Party; and third, the lower down on the Party pyramid, the more restrictive these limitations are. Moreover, some of the innovations, such as the emphasis on "creatively developing Marxism-Leninism" while vigorously combating "all manifestations of revisionism and dogmatism," have been incorporated into the 1961 Rules for reasons which have little to do with greater inner-Party democracy, criticism from below, or any other lofty objective of enlightened Party rule.

In the context of actual Soviet practice, the Party remains what it has always been in the past, only more so. It is the supreme instrumentality and tool of Soviet power and a means of implementing decisions made at the top as rapidly, effectively, efficiently, and universally as possible. The effective control and authority, however, remain with the top Party elite—with Khrushchev, the First Secretary of the Central Committee of the Party, Member of the Party Presidium, and Chairman of the Council of Ministers; with his colleagues, Secretaries of the Communist Party, several of whom are also Members of the Party Presidium; and with the other assorted Members and Candidate Members of the Party Presidium and Secretaries. This is not to suggest that Soviet decision-making is truly collective, nor that it is shared on an equal basis among the top members of the Soviet oligarchy, nor that Khrushchev cannot or does not impose his will on his colleagues. What it means is that Khrushchev's temperament, style, and methods differ by a great deal from those of his predecessors, and that times have changed. Unwilling to employ Stalinist methods and unable to copy Lenin, Khrushchev's choice of means is also greatly conditioned by the hopes, expectations, and demands of the Soviet people. Khrushchev's responsibilities, moreover, are incomparably greater now than they were ever before in the history of Soviet Russia; the communist camp, we know, creates not only advantages but problems, too, for the Soviet leadership.

The new Rules, then, should be understood for what they are: an up-to-date Party document which formulates, orders, and organizes the Soviet Party organization, a document which is as much Khrushchev's as the 1952 Party Rules were Stalin's. The structure of power in the Soviet Union has not changed; only the ways and means of applying that power are somewhat altered.

1961

PROGRAMME OF THE
COMMUNIST PARTY
OF THE SOVIET UNION*

★★★★★★★★★★★★★★★★★★★★★★★★★★★★★★★★

Introduction

The Great October Socialist Revolution ushered in a new era in the history of mankind, the era of the downfall of capitalism and the establishment of communism. Socialism has triumphed in the Soviet Union and has achieved decisive victories in the People's Democracies; socialism has become a cause of practical significance to hundreds of millions of people, and the banner of the revolutionary movement of the working class throughout the world.

More than a hundred years ago Karl Marx and Frederick Engels, the great teachers of the proletariat, wrote in the Communist Manifesto: *"A spectre is haunting Europe, the spectre of communism."* The courageous and selfless struggle of the proletarians of all countries brought mankind nearer to communism. First dozens and hundreds of people, and then thousands and millions, inspired by the ideals of communism, stormed the old world. The Paris Commune, the October Revolution, the socialist revolutions in China and in a number of European and Asian countries are the major historical stages in the heroic battles fought by the international working class for the victory of communism. A tremendously long road, a road drenched in the blood of fighters for the happiness of the people, a road of glorious victories and temporary reverses, had to be traversed before *communism, which had once seemed a mere spectre,*
        . . . which once was a mere dream, *became . . .*†

* The basis of this text is the Draft version which appeared as a supplement to *Moscow News*, No. 31 (554), August 5, 1961. Changes made at the Twenty-second Congress of the CPSU on October 31, 1961, are those reported in *Izvestiia*, November 2, 1961, pp. 1 ff. and translated by the Editor of this book for incorporation into this text.

        † Interlinear passages give the changes from the draft version of the Programme.

☆ **23** ☆

became the greatest force of modern times, a society that is being built up over vast areas of the globe.

In the early twentieth century the centre of the international revolutionary movement shifted to Russia. Russia's heroic working class, led by the Bolshevik Party headed by Vladimir Ilyich Lenin, became its vanguard. The Communist Party inspired and led the socialist revolution; it was the organizer and leader of the first workers' and peasants' state in history. The brilliant genius of Lenin, whose name will live for ever,

. . . Lenin, *the great teacher of the working people of the whole world,* whose . . .

illumines mankind's road to communism.

On entering the arena of political struggle, the Leninist Communist Party raised high the banner of revolutionary Marxism over the world. Marxism-Leninism became a powerful ideological weapon for the revolutionary transformation of society. At every stage of historical progress,

. . . At every *historical stage,* the . . .

the Party, taking guidance from the theory of Marx-Engels-Lenin, accomplished the tasks scientifically formulated in its Programmes.

In adopting its *first Programme* at its Second Congress in 1903, the Bolshevik Party called on the working class and all working people of Russia to fight for the overthrow of the tsarist autocracy and then of the bourgeois system and for the establishment of the dictatorship of the proletariat. In February, 1917 the tsarist regime was swept away. In October 1917 the proletarian revolution abolished the capitalist system so hated by the people. *A socialist country came into being for the first time in history. The creation of a new world began.*

The first Programme of the Party had been carried out.

Adopting its *second Programme* at its Eighth Congress in 1919, the Party promulgated the task of building a socialist society. Treading on unexplored ground and overcoming difficulties and hardships, the Soviet people under the leadership of the Communist Party put into practice the plan for socialist construction drawn up by Lenin. *Socialism triumphed in the Soviet Union completely and finally.*

The second Programme of the Party had likewise been carried out.

The gigantic revolutionary exploit accomplished by the Soviet people, has roused and inspired the masses in all countries and continents. A mighty purifying thunderstorm marking the spring-time of mankind is raging over the earth. *The socialist revolutions in European and Asian countries have resulted in the establishment of the world socialist system.* A powerful wave of national-liberation revolutions is sweeping away the colonial system of imperialism.

One-third of mankind is building a new life under the banner of scientific communism. The first contingents of the working class to shake off capitalist oppression are facilitating victory for fresh contingents of their class brothers. The socialist world is expanding; the capitalist world is shrinking. Socialism will inevitably succeed capitalism everywhere. Such is the objective law of social development. Imperialism is powerless to check the irresistible process of emancipation.

Our epoch, whose main content is the transition from capitalism to socialism, in an epoch of struggle between the two opposing social systems, an epoch of socialist and national-liberation revolutions, of the breakdown of imperialism and the abolition of the colonial system, an epoch of the transition of more and more peoples to the socialist path, of the triumph of socialism and communism on a world-wide scale. The central factor of the present epoch is the international working class and its main creation, the world socialist system.

Today the Communist Party of the Soviet Union (C.P.S.U.) is adopting its third Programme, a programme for the building of communist society. The new Programme is a constructive generalisation of the experience of socialist development, it takes account of the experience of the revolutionary movement throughout the world and, giving expression to the collective opinion of the Party, defines the main tasks and principal stages of communist construction.

The supreme goal of the Party is to build a communist society on whose banner will be inscribed: "From each according to his ability, to each according to his needs". The Party's motto, "Everything in the name of man, for the benefit of man", will be put into effect in full.

The Communist Party of the Soviet Union, true to proletarian internationalism, always follows the militant slogan "Workers of all countries, unite!" *The Party regards communist construction in the U.S.S.R. as the Soviet people's great internationalist task,* in keeping with the interests of the world socialist system as a whole, and with the interests of the international proletariat and all mankind.

Communism accomplishes the historic mission of delivering all men from social inequality, from every form of oppression and exploitation, from the horrors of war, and proclaims Peace, Labour, Freedom, Equality, and Happiness for all peoples of the earth.

ity, *Brotherhood* and Happiness . . .

Part One

THE TRANSITION FROM CAPITALISM TO COMMUNISM IS THE ROAD OF HUMAN PROGRESS

I. The Historical Necessity of the Transition from Capitalism to Socialism

The epoch-making turn of mankind from capitalism to socialism, initiated by the October Revolution, is a natural result of the development of society. Marxism-Leninism discovered the objective laws of social development and revealed the contradictions inherent in capitalism, the inevitability of their bringing about a revolutionary explosion and of the transition of society to communism.

Capitalism is the last exploiting system. Having developed its productive forces to an enormous extent, it became a tremendous obstacle to social progress. Capitalism alone is responsible for the fact that the twentieth century, a century of colossal growth of the productive forces and of great scientific progress, has not yet put an end to the poverty of hundreds of millions of people, has not provided an abundance of material and spiritual values for all men on earth. The growing conflict between productive forces and production relations imperatively demands that mankind should break the decayed capitalist shell, release the powerful productive forces created by man and use them for the good of society as a whole.

Whatever the specific character of the rise and development of capitalism in any country, that system has everywhere common features and objective laws.

The development of world capitalism and of the revolutionary struggle of the working class has fully confirmed the correctness of the Marxist-Leninist analysis of capitalism and its highest stage, imperialism, given in the first and second Programmes of the Party. The basic propositions of this analysis are also given in the present Programme.

Under capitalism, the basic and decisive means of production belong to the numerically small capitalist class, while the vast majority of
. . . class *and landlords,* while the . . .
the population consists of proletarians and semi-proletarians, who own no means of production and are therefore compelled to sell their labour-power and by their labour create profits and riches for the ruling classes of society. The bourgeois state, whatever its form, is an instrument of the domination of labour by capital.

The development of large-scale capitalist production—production for profit, for the appropriation of surplus value—leads to the elimination of small independent producers, makes them wholly dependent on capital. Capitalism extensively exploits female and child labour. The economic laws of its development necessarily give rise to a huge reserve army of unemployed, which is constantly replenished by ruined peasants and urban petty bourgeoisie. The exploitation of the working class and all working people is continuously increasing, social inequality is becoming more and more marked, the gulf between the haves and have-nots is widening, and the sufferings and privations of the millions are growing worse.

Capitalism, by concentrating millions of workers in its factories, socialising the process of labour, imparts a social character to production; nevertheless it is the capitalists who appropriate the fruits of labour. This fundamental contradiction of capitalism—the contradiction between the social character of production and the private-capitalist form of appropriation—manifests itself in production anarchy and in the fact that the purchasing power of society falls short of the expansion of production and leads periodically to destructive economic crises. Crises, and periods of industrial stagnation, in turn, are still more ruinous to small producers, increase the dependence of wage-labour on capital and lead more rapidly to a relative, and sometimes an absolute, deterioration of the condition of the working class.

The growth and development of the contradictions of bourgeois society are accompanied by the growing discontent of the working people and the exploited masses with the capitalist system, by an increase in the number of proletarians and their greater unity, and by a sharpening of their struggle against the exploiters. At the same time there is an accelerated creation of *the material conditions that make possible the replacement of capitalist by communist production relations, that is, the accomplishment of the social revolution which is the aim of the Communist Party, the politically conscious exponent of the class movement of the proletariat.*

The working class, which is the most consistent revolutionary class, is the chief motive force of the revolutionary transformation of the world. In the course of class struggles it becomes organised, sets up its trade unions and political parties, and wages an economic, political and theoretical struggle against capitalism. In fulfilling its historic mission as the revolutionary remaker of the old society and creator of a new system, the working class has become the exponent not only of its own class interests, but of the interests of all working people. It is the natural leader of all forces fighting against capitalism.

The dictatorship of the proletariat and the leadership of the Marxist-Leninist party are indispensable conditions for the triumph of the socialist revolution and the building of socialism.

. . . socialism. [ADDED:] *The highest principle of the dictatorship of the proletariat is a stable alliance between the working class and the laboring peasant masses under the leadership of the working class.*

The process of concentration and centralisation of capital, while destroying free competition, led in the early twentieth century to the establishment of powerful capitalist monopoly associations—syndicates, cartels, and trusts—which acquired decisive importance in the economy, led to the merging of bank capital and immensely concentrated industrial capital, and to intensive export of capital. The trusts, which encompassed entire groups of capitalist powers, began the economic division of a world already divided territorially among the wealthiest countries. Capitalism had entered its final stage, the stage of monopoly capitalism, of imperialism.

The period of a more or less smooth spread of capitalism all over the globe gave way to spasmodic, cataclysmic development causing an unprecedented growth and aggravation of all the contradictions of capitalism—economic, political, class, and national. The imperialist powers' struggle for markets, for spheres of capital investment, for raw materials and labour, and for world domination became more intense than ever. In an epoch of the undivided rule of imperialism, that struggle necessarily led to devastating wars.

Imperialism is decaying and moribund capitalism; it is the eve of the socialist revolution. *The world capitalist system as a whole is ripe for the social revolution of the proletariat.*

The exceedingly high degree of development of world capitalism in general; the replacement of free competition by state-monopoly capitalism; the establishment, by banks as well as associations of capitalists, of machinery for the social regulation of production and the distribution of products; the growing cost of living and the oppression of the working class by the syndicates, connected with the growth of capitalist monopolies; the enslavement of the working class by the imperialist state, and the growing difficulty of the economic and political struggle of the proletariat; and the horrors, hardships, and ruination brought about by imperialist war have all made inevitable the downfall of capitalism and the transition to a higher type of social economy.

The revolutionary defeat of imperialism does not take place all over the world simultaneously. The uneven character of the economic and political development of the capitalist countries under imperialism leads to revolutions occurring at different periods in different countries. V. I. Lenin developed the theory of the socialist revolution in new historical conditions, elaborated the theory of the possibility of socialism triumphing first in one capitalist country taken singly.

Russia was the weakest link in the imperialist system and the focal point of all its contradictions. On the other hand, she had all the condi-
. . . had *a pool of* all the conditions necessary for the victory of socialism. Her working class was the most revolutionary and best organised in the world and had considerable experience of class struggle. It was led by a Marxist-Leninist party armed with an advanced, revolutionary theory and steeled in class battles.

The Bolshevik Party brought together in one revolutionary torrent the struggle of the working class for socialism, the country-wide peace movement, the peasants' struggle for land, and the national-liberation movement of the oppressed peoples of Russia, and directed these forces to the overthrow of capitalism.

II. The Historic Significance of the October Revolution and of the Victory of Socialism in the U.S.S.R.

The Great October Revolution breached the imperialist front in Russia, one of the world's largest countries, firmly established the dictatorship of the proletariat and created a new type of state—the Soviet state—
. . . Soviet *Socialist* state—
and a new type of democracy—democracy for the working people.

Workers' and peasants' power, born of the revolution, took Russia out of the bloodbath of the imperialist war, saved her from the national catastrophe to which the exploiting classes had doomed her, and delivered her peoples from the danger of enslavement by foreign capital.

The October Revolution undermined the economic basis of a system of exploitation and social injustice. Soviet power nationalised industry, the railways, banks, and the land. It abolished landed proprietorship and fulfilled the peasants' age-long dream of land.

The October Revolution smashed the chains of national oppression; it proclaimed and put into effect the right of nations to self-determination, up to and including the right to secede. The Revolution completely abolished the social-estate and class privileges of the exploiters. For the first time in history, it emancipated women and granted them the same rights as men.

The socialist revolution in Russia shook the entire structure of world capitalism to its very foundations; the world split into two opposing systems.

For the first time there emerged in the international arena a state which put forward the great slogan of peace and began carrying through new principles in relations between peoples and countries. Mankind acquired a reliable bulwark in its struggle against wars of conquest, for peace and the security of the peoples.

The October Revolution led the country on to the road of socialism. The path which the Soviet people were to traverse was an unexplored and arduous one. The reactionary forces of the old world did all they could to strangle the Soviet state at its birth. The young Soviet Republic had to cope with intervention and civil war, economic blockade and disruption, conspiracies, sabotage, subversion, terrorism, and numerous other trials. Socialist construction was rendered incredibly difficult by the socio-economic, technical and cultural backwardness of the country. The victorious workers and peasants lacked knowledge of state administration and the experience necessary for the construction of a new society. The difficulties of socialist construction were greatly increased by the fact that for almost thirty years the U.S.S.R. was the world's only socialist state, and was subjected to incisive attacks by the hostile capitalist environment. The class struggle in the period of transition from capitalism to socialism was therefore acute.

The enemies of Leninism maintained that Russia was not mature enough for a socialist revolution, that it was impossible to build socialism in one country. But the enemies of Leninism were put to shame.

A wise, discerning policy, the greatest staunchness, organisation, and deep faith in their own strength and in the strength of the people were required of the Party and the working class. It was necessary to steer the right course in socialist construction and ensure the victory of socialism, despite the highly complicated international situation and a relatively weak industrial basis, in a country whose economy had been badly ravaged by war and where small-commodity production was overwhelmingly predominant.

The Party proved equal to that historic task. Under the leadership of Lenin it worked out a plan for the radical transformation of the country, for the construction of socialism. On the basis of a thorough scientific analysis, Lenin elaborated the policy of the proletarian state for the entire period of transition from capitalism to socialism. He evolved the New Economic Policy (NEP), designed to bring about the victory of socialism. The main elements of the Lenin plan for the building of a socialist society were industrialisation of the country, agricultural co-operation, and the cultural revolution.

The Party upheld that plan in an acute struggle against sceptics and capitulators, against the Trotskyists, Right opportunists, nationalist-deviators, and other hostile groups. It rallied the whole of the Soviet people to put Lenin's programme into practice.

The point at issue at the time was: either perish or forge full steam ahead and overtake the capitalist countries economically.

The Soviet state had first of all to solve the problem of *industrialisation*. In a historically brief period, without outside help, the Soviet Union built up a large-scale modern industry. By the time it had fulfilled three five-year plans (1929-41) the Soviet Union had become a mighty industrial power that had achieved complete economic independence from the capitalist countries. Its defence capacity had increased immeasurably. *The industrialisation of the U.S.S.R. was a great exploit performed by the working class and the people as a whole,* for they spared no effort or means, and consciously made sacrifices to lift the country out of its backward state.

The destiny of socialism in a country like the U.S.S.R. largely depended on the solution of a most difficult problem, namely, the transition from a small-scale, dispersed peasant economy to *socialist co-operation*. Led by the Party, aided and fully supported by the working class, the peasantry took the road of socialism. Millions of small individual farms went into voluntary association to form collective farms. A large number of Soviet state farms and machine and tractor stations were established. The introduction in the Soviet countryside of large-scale socialist farming, meant *a far-reaching revolution in economic relations, in the entire way of life of the peasantry*. Collectivisation forever delivered the countryside from kulak bondage, from class differentiation, ruin, and poverty. The real solution of the eternal peasant question was provided by the Lenin co-operative plan.

To build socialism it was necessary to raise the cultural level of the people; that task too was accomplished. A *cultural revolution* was carried out in the country. It freed the working people from spiritual slavery and ignorance and gave them access to the cultural values accumulated by mankind. The country, the bulk of whose population had been illiterate, made breath-taking progress in science and culture.

Socialism, which Marx and Engels scientifically predicted as inevitable and the plan for the construction of which was mapped out by . . . construction which Lenin mapped out, has . . . Lenin, has become a reality in the Soviet Union.

Socialism has done away for ever with the supremacy of private ownership of the means of production, that source of the division of society into antagonistic classes. Socialist ownership of the means of production has become the solid economic foundation of society. Unlimited opportunities have been afforded for the development of the productive forces.

Socialism has solved a great social problem—it has abolished the exploiting classes and the causes engendering the exploitation of man by man. There are now two friendly classes in the U.S.S.R.—the working class and the peasantry. And these classes, furthermore, have changed. The common character of the two forms of socialist property has brought the working class and the collective-farm peasantry close together; it has strengthened their alliance and made their friendship indestructible. A new intelligentsia, coming from the people and devoted to socialism, has emerged. The one-time antithesis between town and countryside, between labour by hand and by brain, has been abolished. The indestructible socio-political and ideological unity of the Soviet people has been built on the basis of the common vital interests of the workers, peasants and intellectuals.

The socialist principle "From each according to his abilities, to each according to his work" has been put into effect in the Soviet Union. This principle ensures that the members of society have a material interest in the fruits of their labour; it makes it possible to harmonise personal and social interests in the most effective way and serves as a powerful stimulus for increasing productivity of labour, developing the economy and raising the people's standard of living. The awareness that they work for themselves and their society and not for exploiters inspires the working people with labour enthusiasm; it encourages their effort for innovation, their creative initiative, and mass socialist emulation. Socialism results from the creative effort of the working masses. The growing ac-
. . . The *growth of* activity of the people in the building of a new life is a law of the socialist epoch.

The aim of socialism is to meet the growing material and cultural requirements of the people ever more fully by continuously developing and improving social production.

The entire life of socialist society is based on the principle of broad *democracy*. Working people take an active part, through the Soviets, trade unions, and other mass organisations, in managing the affairs of the state and in solving problems of economic and cultural advancement. Socialist democracy includes both political freedoms—freedom of speech, of the press and of assembly, the right to elect and to be elected, and also social rights—the right to work, to rest and leisure, to education, to
. . . leisure, to *free education and medical services,* to material security in old age and in case of illness or disability; equality of citizens of all races and nationalities; equal rights for women and men in all spheres of political, economic and cultural activity. Socialist democracy, unlike bourgeois democracy, does not merely proclaim the rights of the people, but makes it really possible for the people to exer-
. . . but *guarantees their real exercise.* Soviet . . .
cise them. Soviet society ensures the real liberty of the individual. The highest manifestation of this liberty is man's emancipation from exploi-

tation, which is what primarily constitutes genuine social justice.

Socialism has created conditions for the rapid progress of science.

   . . . created *the most favorable* conditions . . .

The achievements of Soviet science clearly show the superiority of the socialist system and testify to the unlimited possibilities of scientific progress and to the growing role of science under socialism. It is only logical that the country of victorious socialism should have ushered in the era of the utilisation of atomic energy for peaceful purposes, and that it should have blazed a trail into outer space. The man-made satellites of the earth and the sun, powerful space rockets and interplanetary spaceships, atomic power stations and the first triumphal orbiting of the

     . . . triumphal *orbitings* of . . .

globe, accomplished by a Soviet citizen, which are a source of pride to all mankind, have become symbols of the creative energy of ascendant communism.

The solution of the *national question* is one of the greatest achievements of socialism. This question is of especial importance to a country like the Soviet Union, inhabited by more than a hundred nations and nationalities. Socialist society has not only guaranteed the political equality of nations, but has also abolished the economic and cultural back-

. . . nations *and created a Soviet national statehood,* but . . .

wardness inherited from the old system. With reciprocal fraternal assistance, primarily from the great Russian people, all the Soviet non-Russian republics have set up their own modern industries, trained their own national working class and intelligentsia and developed a culture that is national in form and socialist in content. Many nations which in the past were backward have achieved socialism, by-passing the capitalist stage of development. The union and consolidation of equal peoples on a voluntary basis in a single multinational state—the Union of Soviet Socialist Republics—their close co-operation in state, economic and cultural development, their fraternal friendship and a flourishing economy and culture constitute the most important result of the Leninist national policy.

The Soviet people were destined by history to start on a new road, to blaze a new path of social development. This required special efforts of them, a continuous quest for forms and methods of building the new society that had to be tested in the crucible of practice. For nearly two out of little more than four decades, the Soviet people were compelled to devote their energies to the repulsion of invasions by the imperialist powers and to postwar economic rehabilitation. The Soviet system was put to a particularly severe test during the Great Patriotic War, the most trying war in history. By winning that war, the Soviet people proved that there are no forces in the world capable of stopping the progress of socialist society.

What are the principal lessons to be learned from the experience of the Soviet people?

Soviet experience has shown that the peoples are able to achieve socialism only as a result of *the socialist revolution and the establishment of the dictatorship of the proletariat.* Despite certain specific features due precisely to the historical conditions of socialist construction in the Soviet Union, then in a hostile capitalist encirclement, this experience has fully confirmed the fundamental principles of socialist revolution and socialist construction, principles which are of universal significance.

Soviet experience has shown that socialism alone can put an end to the exploitation of man by man, production anarchy, economic crises, unemployment and the poverty of the people, and ensure planned, continuous and rapid development of the economy and steady improvement of the people's standard of living.

Soviet experience has shown that the working class can fulfil its historic mission as the builder of a new society only in a sound *alliance with the non-proletarian working masses,* primarily the peasantry.

Soviet experience has shown that the victory of the socialist revolution alone provides all possibilities and conditions for the abolition of all national oppression, *for the voluntary union of free and equal nations and nationalities in a single state.*

Soviet experience has shown that *the socialist state* is the main instrument for the socialist transformation of society. The state organises and unites the masses, exercises planned leadership of economic and cultural construction, and safeguards the revolutionary gains of the people.

Soviet experience has shown that *socialism and peace are inseparable.* The might of socialism serves peace. The Soviet Union saved mankind from fascist enslavement. The Soviet state, which champions peace and implements the Leninist principle of peaceful coexistence, is a mighty . . . coexistence *of states with different social systems,* is . . . barrier to imperialist aggression.

Soviet experience has fully borne out the Marxist-Leninist theory that *the Communist Party plays a decisive role* in the formation and development of socialist society. Only a party that steadfastly pursues a class, proletarian policy, and is equipped with progressive, revolutionary theory, only a party solidly united and closely linked with the masses, can organise the people and lead them to the victory of socialism.

Soviet experience has shown that fidelity *to the principles of Marxism-Leninism, of proletarian internationalism,* their firm and unswerving implementation and defence of those principles against opportunists and all other enemies, are imperative conditions for the victory of socialism.

The world's greatest revolution and the socialist reorganisation of society, which has attained unprecedented heights in its development and prosperity, have confirmed in practice *the historical truth of Leninism* and have delivered a crushing blow to social-reformist ideology.

As a result of the devoted labour of the Soviet people and the theoretical and practical activities of the Communist Party of the Soviet Union, *there exists in the world a socialist society that is a reality and a science of socialist construction that has been tested in practice. The highroad to socialism has been paved.* Many peoples are already marching along it, and it will be taken sooner or later by all peoples.

III. The World Socialist System

The Soviet Union is not pursuing the tasks of communist construction alone but in fraternal community with the other socialist countries.

The defeat of German fascism and Japanese militarism in the Second World War, in which the Soviet Union played a decisive part, created favourable conditions for the overthrow of capitalist and landlord rule by the peoples in a number of European and Asian countries. The peoples of Albania, Bulgaria, China, Czechoslovakia, the Democratic Republic of Vietnam, the German Democratic Republic, Hungary, the Korean People's Democratic Republic, Poland and Rumania, and still earlier the people of the Mongolian People's Republic, adopted the path of socialist construction and, together with the Soviet Union, have formed the socialist camp. Yugoslavia likewise took the socialist path. But the Yugoslav leaders by their revisionist policy contraposed Yugoslavia to the socialist camp and the international Communist movement, thus threatening the loss of the revolutionary gains of the Yugoslav people.

The socialist revolutions in Europe and Asia dealt imperialism a further powerful blow. The victory of the revolution in China was of special importance. The revolutions in European and Asian countries are the biggest event in world history since October 1917.

A new form of political organisation of society, *people's democracy,* a variety of the dictatorship of the proletariat, emerged. It reflected the distinctive development of socialist revolution at a time when imperialism had been weakened and the balance of forces had tilted in favour of socialism. It also reflected the distinctive historical and national features of the countries concerned.
of the *various countries.*

There emerged a world socialist system, a social, economic and political community of free sovereign peoples pursuing the socialist and communist path, united by common interests and goals and the close bonds of international socialist solidarity.

In the People's Democracies socialist production relations are dominant and the socio-economic possibility of capitalist restoration has been eliminated. The successes of these countries have conclusively proved that true progress in all lands, irrespective of the level of their economic development, their area and population, is feasible only under socialism.

The combined forces of the socialist camp guarantee each socialist country against encroachments by imperialist reaction. The consolidation of the socialist countries in a single camp, its increasing unity and steadily growing strength, ensure the complete victory of socialism

. . . socialism *and communism* within . . .

within the framework of the system as a whole.

The countries of the socialist system have accumulated considerable collective experience in the remodelling of the lives of hundreds of millions of people and have contributed many new and specific features to the forms of political and economic organisation of society. This experience is a most valuable asset to the international revolutionary movement.

It has been borne out in practice and recognised by all Marxist-Leninist parties that the processes of socialist revolution and construction are founded on a number of *basic objective laws* applicable to all countries entering upon the socialist path.

The world socialist system is *a new type of economic and political relationship between countries*. The socialist countries have the same type of economic basis—social ownership of means of production; the same type of political system—rule of the people with the working class at their head; a common ideology—Marxism-Leninism; common interests in the defence of their revolutionary gains and national independence from encroachments by the imperialist camp; and a great common goal—communism. This socio-economic and political community of purpose is the objective groundwork for lasting and friendly intergovernmental relations within the socialist camp. The distinctive features of the relations existing between the countries of the socialist community are complete equality, respect for independence and sovereignty and

. . . equality, *mutual* respect . . .

fraternal mutual assistance. In the socialist camp or, which is the same thing, in the world community of socialist countries, none have, nor can have, any special rights or privileges.

The experience of the world socialist system has confirmed the need for the *closest unity* of countries that fall away from capitalism, for their united effort in the building of socialism and communism. The line of socialist construction in isolation, detached from the world community of socialist countries, is theoretically untenable because it conflicts with the objective laws governing the development of socialist society. It is harmful economically because it causes waste of social labour, retards the rates of growth of production and makes the country dependent upon the capitalist world. It is reactionary and dangerous politically because it does not unite, but divides the peoples in face of the united front of imperialist forces, because it nourishes bourgois-nationalist tendencies and may ultimately lead to the loss of the socialist gains.

As they combine their effort in the building of a new society, the socialist states give active support to and extend their political, economic and cultural co-operation with countries that have cast off colonial rule. They maintain—and are prepared to maintain—broad, mutually advantageous trade relations and cultural contacts with the capitalist countries.

The development of the world socialist system and of the world capitalist system is governed by diametrically opposed laws. The world capitalist system emerged and developed in fierce struggle between the countries composing it, through the subjection and exploitation of the weaker countries by the strong, through the enslavement of hundreds of millions of people and the reduction of entire continents to the status of colonial appendages of the imperialist metropolitan countries. The formation and development of the world socialist system, on the other hand, proceeds on the basis of sovereignty and free will and in conformity with the fundamental interests of the working people of all the countries of that system.

Whereas the world capitalist system is governed by the law of uneven economic and political development that leads to conflicts between countries, the world socialist system is governed by opposite laws, which ensure the steady and balanced growth of the economies of all countries belonging to that system. Growth of production in a country belonging to the capitalist world deepens the contradictions between countries and intensifies competitive rivalries. The development of each socialist country, on the other hand, promotes the general progress and consolidation of the world socialist system as a whole. The economy of world capitalism develops at a slow rate, and goes through crises and upheavals. Typical of the economy of world socialism, on the other hand, are high and stable rates of growth, and the common unintermittent economic progress of all socialist countries.

All the socialist countries make their contribution to the building and development of the world socialist system and the consolidation of its might. The existence of the Soviet Union greatly facilitates and accelerates the building of socialism in the People's Democracies. The Marxist-Leninist parties and the peoples of the socialist countries proceed from the fact that the successes of the world socialist system as a whole depend on the contribution and effort made by each country, and therefore consider the greatest possible development of the productive forces of their country an internationalist duty. The co-operation of the socialist countries enables each country to use its resources and develop its productive forces to the full and in the most rational manner. *A new type of international division of labour* is taking shape in the process of the economic, scientific and technical co-operation of the socialist countries, the co-ordination of their economic plans, the specialisation and combination of production.

The establishment of the Union of Soviet Socialist Republics and, later, of the world socialist system is the commencement of the historical process of an all-round association of peoples. With the disappearance of class antagonisms in the fraternal family of socialist countries, national antagonisms also disappear. The rapid cultural progress of the peoples of the socialist community is attended by a progressive mutual enrichment of the national cultures, and an active moulding of the internationalist features typical of man in socialist society.

The experience of the peoples of the world socialist community has confirmed that their fraternal *unity and co-operation* conform to the supreme national interests of each country. The strengthening of the unity of the world socialist system on the basis of proletarian internationalism is an imperative condition for the further progress of all its member countries.

The socialist system has to cope with certain difficulties, deriving chiefly from the fact that most of the countries in that system had a medium or even low level of economic development in the past, and also from the fact that world reaction is doing its utmost to impede the building of socialism.

The experience of the Soviet Union and the People's Democracies has confirmed the accuracy of Lenin's thesis that the class struggle does . . . that *in the period of the building of socialism the class struggle does not disappear.* The . . . not disappear in the period of the building of socialism. The general development of the class struggle within the socialist countries in conditions of successful socialist construction leads to consolidation of the position of the socialist forces and weakens the resistance of the remnants of the hostile classes. But this development does not follow a straight line. Changes in the domestic or external situation may cause the class struggle to intensify in specific periods. This calls for constant vigilance in order to frustrate in good time the designs of hostile forces within and without, who persist in their attempts to undermine people's power and sow strife in the fraternal community of socialist countries.

Nationalism is the chief political and ideological weapon used by international reaction and the remnants of the domestic reactionary forces against the unity of the socialist countries. Nationalist sentiments and national narrow-mindedness do not disappear automatically with the establishment of the socialist system. Nationalist prejudice and survivals of former national strife are a province in which resistance to social progress may be most protracted and stubborn, bitter and insidious.

The Communists consider it their prime duty to educate working people in a spirit of internationalism, socialist patriotism, and intolerance of all possible manifestations of nationalism and chauvinism. Nationalism is harmful to the common interests of the socialist community and, above all, the people of the country where it obtains, since isolation from the socialist camp holds up that country's development, deprives it of the advantages deriving from the world socialist system and encourages the imperialist powers to make the most of nationalist tendencies for their own ends. Nationalism can gain the upper hand only where it is not consistently combated. The Marxist-Leninist internationalist policy and determined efforts to wipe out the survivals of bourgeois nationalism and chauvinism are an important condition for the further consolidation of the socialist community. Yet while they oppose nationalism and national egoism, Communists always show utmost consideration for the national feelings of the masses.

The world socialist system is advancing steadfastly towards decisive victory in its economic competition with capitalism. It will shortly surpass the world capitalist system in aggregate industrial and agricultural production. Its influence on the course of social development in . . . production. *The influence of the world socialist system* on . . . the interests of peace, democracy and socialism is growing more and more.

The magnificent edifice of the new world being built by the heroic labours of the free peoples on vast areas of Europe and Asia is a prototype of the new society, of the future of all mankind.

IV. Crisis of World Capitalism

Imperialism has entered the period of decline and collapse. An inexorable process of decay has seized capitalism from top to bottom—its economic and political system, its politics and ideology. Imperialism has for ever lost its power over the bulk of mankind. The main content, main trend and main features of the historical development of mankind are being determined by the world socialist system, by the forces fighting against imperialism, for the socialist reorganisation of society.

The First World War and the October Revolution ushered in the general crisis of capitalism. The second stage of this crisis developed at the time of the Second World War and the socialist revolutions in a . . . revolutions *took place* in a number of European and Asian countries. World capitalism has now entered a new, third stage of that crisis, the principal feature of which is that its development was not due to a world war.

The break-away from capitalism of more and more countries; the weakening of imperialist positions in the economic competition with socialism; the break-up of the imperialist colonial system; the intensification of imperialist contradictions with the development of state-monopoly capitalism and the growth of militarism; the mounting internal instability and decay of capitalist economy evidenced by the increasing inability of capitalism to make full use of the productive forces (low rates of production growth, periodic crises, continuous undercapacity operation of production plant, and chronic unemployment); the mounting struggle between labour and capital; an acute intensification of contradictions within the world capitalist economy; an unprecedented growth of political reaction in all spheres, rejection of bourgeois freedoms and establishment of fascist and despotic regimes in a number of countries; and the profound crises of bourgeois policy and ideology—all these are

. . . ideology—[DELETION] these are manifestations of the *general crises of capitalism.*

In the imperialist stage *state-monopoly capitalism* develops on an extensive scale. The emergence and growth of monopolies leads to the direct intervention of the state, in the interests of the financial oligarchy, in the process of capitalist reproduction. It is in the interests of the financial oligarchy that the bourgeois state institutes various types of regulation and resorts to state control over some branches of the economy. World wars, economic crises, militarism, and political upheavals have accelerated the development of monopoly capitalism into state-monopoly capitalism.

The oppression of finance capital keeps growing. Giant monopolies controlling the bulk of social production dominate the life of the nation. A handful of millionaires and multimillionaires wield arbitrary power over the entire wealth of the capitalist world and make the life of entire nations mere small change in their selfish deals. The financial oligarchy is getting fabulously rich. The state is becoming a committee for the management of the affairs of the monopoly bourgeoisie. The bureaucratisation of the economy is rising steeply. State-monopoly capitalism combines the strength of the monopolies and that of the state into a single mechanism whose purpose is to enrich the monopolies, suppress the working-class movement and the national-liberation struggle, save the capitalist system, and launch aggressive wars.

The Right-Wing socialists and revisionists are making out state-monopoly capitalism to be almost socialism. The facts give the lie to this contention. State-monopoly capitalism does not change the nature of imperialism. Far from altering the position of the principal classes in the system of social production, it widens the rift between labour and capital, between the majority of the nation and the monopolies. Attempts at state regulation of the capitalist economy cannot eliminate competition and anarchy of production, cannot ensure the planned development of the economy on a nation-wide scale, because capitalist ownership and exploitation of wage-labour remain the basis of production. The bourgeois theories of "crisis-free" and "planned" capitalism have been laid in the dust by the development of contemporary capitalist economy. The dialectics of state-monopoly capitalism is such that instead of shoring up the capitalist system, as the bourgeoisie expects, it aggravates the contradictions of capitalism and undermines its foundations. State-monopoly capitalism is the fullest material preparation for socialism.

The new phenomena in imperialist development corroborate the accuracy of Lenin's conclusions on the principal objective laws of capitalism in its final stage and on its increasing decay. Yet this decay does not signify complete stagnation, a palsy of its productive forces, and does not rule out growth of capitalist economy at particular times and in particular countries.

All in all, capitalism is increasingly impeding the development of the contemporary productive forces. Mankind is entering the period of a . . . of a [DELETION] scientific . . .

great scientific and technical revolution bound up with the conquest of nuclear energy, space exploration, the development of chemistry, automation and other major achievements of science and engineering. But the relations of production under capitalism are much too narrow for a scientific and technical revolution. Socialism alone is capable of effecting it and of applying its fruits in the interests of society.

Technical progress under the rule of monopoly capital is turning against the working class. By using new forms, the monopolies intensify the exploitation of the working class. Capitalist automation is robbing the worker of his daily bread. Unemployment is rising, the living standard is dropping. Technical progress is continuously throwing more sections of small producers overboard. Imperialism is using technical progress chiefly for military purposes. It is turning the achievements of human genius against humanity. As long as imperialism exists, mankind cannot feel secure about its future.

Modern capitalism has made the *market problem* extremely acute. Imperialism is incapable of solving it, because lag of effective demand behind growth of production is one of its objective laws. Moreover, it retards the industrial development of the underdeveloped countries. The world capitalist market is shrinking relative to the more rapidly expanding production capacity. It is partitioned by countless customs barriers and restrictive fences and split into exclusive currency and finance zones.

An acute competitive struggle for markets, spheres of investment and sources of raw materials is under way in the imperialist camp. It is becoming doubly acute since the territorial sphere of capitalist domination has geen greatly narrowed.

Monopoly capital has, in the final analysis, doomed bourgeois society to low rates of production growth that in some countries barely keep ahead of the growth of population. A considerable part of the production plant stands idle, while millions of unemployed wait at the factory gates. Farm production is artificially restricted, although millions are underfed in the world. People suffer want in material goods, but imperialism is squandering them on war preparations.

. . . squandering *the material resources and labor of society* on war . . .

Abolition of the capitalist system in a large group of countries, the developing and strengthening of the world socialist system, the disintegration of the colonial system and the collapse of old empires, the commencing reorganisation of the colonial economic structure in the newly-free countries and the expanding economic connections between the latter and the socialist world—all these factors intensify *the crisis of the world capitalist economy.*

State-monopoly capitalism stimulates militarism to an unheard-of degree. The imperialist countries maintain immense armed forces even in peacetime. Military expenditures devour an ever growing portion of the state budget. The imperialist countries are turning into militarist states run by the army and the police. Militarisation pervades the life of bourgeois society.

While enriching some groups of the monopoly bourgeoisie, militarism leads to the exhaustion of nations, to the ruin of the peoples languishing under an excessive tax burden, mounting inflation, and a high cost of living. Within the lifetime of one generation imperialism plunged mankind into the abyss of two destructive world wars. In the First World War the imperialists annihilated ten million and crippled twenty million people. The Second World War claimed nearly fifty million human lives. In the course of these wars entire countries were ravaged, thousands of towns and villages were demolished and the fruits of the labour of many generations were destroyed. The new war being hatched by the imperialists threatens mankind with unprecedented human losses and destruction. Even the preparations for it bring suffering and privation to millions of people.

The progress achieved in the development of the productive forces and the socialisation of labour is being usurped by the contemporary capitalist state in the interests of the monopolies.

The monopoly bourgeoisie has become a useless growth on the social organism, one unneeded in production. The industries are run by hired managers, engineers, and technicians. The monopolists lead a parasitical life and with their menials consume a substantial portion of the national income created by the toil of proletarians and peasants.

Fear of revolution, the successes of the socialist countries, and the pressure of the working-class movement compel the bourgeoisie to make partial concessions with respect to wages, labour conditions, and social security. But more often than not mounting prices and inflation reduce these concessions to nought. Wages lag behind the daily material and cultural requirements of the worker and his family, which grow as society develops. Even the relatively high standard of living in the small group of capitalistically developed countries rests upon the poverty of the

. . . upon the plunder of . . .

Asian, African and Latin American peoples, upon non-equivalent exchange, discrimination of female labour, brutal oppression of Negroes and immigrant workers, and also upon the intensified exploitation of the working people in those countries. The bourgeois myth of "full employment" has proved to be sheer mockery, for the working class is suffering continuously from mass unemployment and insecurity. In spite of some successes in the economic struggle, the condition of the working class in the capitalist world is, on the whole, deteriorating.

The development of capitalism has dissipated the legend of the stability of small peasant farming once and for all. The monopolies have seized dominant positions in agriculture as well. Millions of farmers and peasants are being driven off the land, and their farms are being brought under the hammer. Small farms survive at the price of appalling hardships, excessive labour and the peasants' underconsumption. The

. . . underconsumption and excessive labour of peasants. . . .

peasantry is groaning under the burden of mounting taxes and debts. Agrarian crises are bringing ever greater ruin to the countryside. Unspeakable want and poverty fall to the lot of the peasantry in the colonial and dependent countries; it suffers the dual oppression of the landlords and the monopoly bourgeoisie.

The monopolies are also ruining small urban proprietors. Handicrafts are going under. Small-scale industrial and commercial enterprises are fully dependent upon the monopolies.

Life has fully confirmed the Marxist thesis of increasing proletarisation in capitalist society. The expropriated masses have no other prospect of acquiring property than the revolutionary establishment of the social ownership of means of production, that is, making them the property of the whole people.

The uneven development of capitalism alters the balance of forces between countries and makes the contradictions between them more acute. The economic and with it the political and military centre of imperialism, has shifted from Europe to the United States. U.S. monopoly

capital, gorged on war profits and the arms race, has seized the main
. . . has seized the *most important*
sources of raw materials, the markets and the spheres of investment, has
built up a covert colonial empire and become the biggest *international*
built up a *singular* colonial . . .
exploiter. Taking cover behind spurious professions of freedom and
democracy, U.S. imperialism is in effect performing the function of
world gendarme, supporting reactionary dictatorial regimes and decayed
monarchies, opposing democratic, revolutionary changes and launching
aggressions against peoples fighting for independence.

*The U.S. monopoly bourgeoisie is the mainstay of international
reaction.* It has assumed the role of "saviour" of capitalism. The U.S.
financial tycoons are engineering a "holy alliance" of imperialists and
founding aggressive military blocs. American troops and war bases are
stationed at the most important points of the capitalist world.

But the facts reveal the utter incongruity of the U.S. imperialist
claims to world domination. Imperialism has proved incapable of stem-
ming the socialist and national-liberation revolutions. The hopes which
American imperialism pinned on its atomic-weapons monopoly fell
through. The U.S. monopolies have not been able to retain their share
in the economy of the capitalist world, although they are still its chief
economic, financial and military force. The United States, the strongest
capitalist power, is past its zenith and has entered the stage of decline.
Imperialist countries such as Great Britain, France, Germany, and Japan
have also lost their former power.

The basic contradiction of the contemporary world, that between
socialism and imperialism, does not eliminate the *deep contradictions*
rending the capitalist world. The aggressive military blocs founded under
the aegis of the U.S.A. are time and again faced with crises. The international state-monopoly organisations springing up under the motto of
"integration," the mitigation of the market problem, are in reality new
forms of the redivision of the world capitalist market and are becoming
seats of acute strain and conflict.

The contradictions between the principal imperialist powers are
growing deeper. The economic rehabilitation of the imperialist countries
defeated in the Second World War leads to the revival of the old and
the emergence of new knots of imperialist rivalry and conflict. The
Anglo-American, Franco-American, Franco-German, American-German,
. . . Franco-*West*-German, American-*West*-German,
Anglo-*West*-German, . . .
Anglo-German, Japanese-American, and other contradictions are becoming especially acute. Fresh contradictions will inevitably arise and grow
in the imperialist camp.

The American monopolies and their British and French allies are openly assisting the resurgence of West-German imperialism which is . . . assisting [DELETION] West-German . . . cynically advocating aggressive aims of revenge and preparing a war against the socialist countries and other European states. A dangerous centre of aggression, imperilling the peace and security of all peoples, is being revived in the heart of Europe. In the Far East the American monopolies are reviving Japanese militarism, another dangerous hotbed . . . militarism, *which is explicitly dependent on them,* another . . . of war threatening the countries of Asia and, above all, the socialist countries.

The interests of the small group of imperialist powers are incompatible with the interests of all other countries, the interests of all peoples. Deep-rooted antagonism divides the imperialist countries from the countries that have won national independence and those that are fighting for liberation.

Contemporary capitalism is inimical to the vital interests and progressive aspirations of all mankind. Capitalism with its exploitation of man by man, with its chauvinist and racist ideology, with its moral degradation, its rampage of profiteering, corruption and crime is defiling society, the family, and man.

The bourgeois system came into being with the alluring slogans of liberty, equality, fraternity. But the bourgeoisie made use of these slogans merely to elbow out the feudal gentry and to assume power. Instead of equality a new gaping abyss of social and economic inequality appeared. Not fraternity but ferocious class struggle reigns in bourgeois society.

Monopoly capital is revealing its reactionary, anti-democratic substance more and more strikingly. It does not tolerate even the former bourgeois-democratic freedoms, although it proclaims them for its demagogic ends. In the current stage of historical development it is *hypocritical* ends . . . getting harder for the bourgeoisie to propagate, as heretofore, slogans of equality and liberty. The upswing of the international labour movement restricts the manoeuvres of finance capital. Finance capital can no longer squash revolutionary sentiments and cope with the inexorably growing anti-imperialist movement by means of the old slogans and by bribing the labour bureaucracy.

Having taken full possession of the principal material values, monopoly capital refuses to share political power with anyone. It has established a dictatorship, the dictatorship of the minority over the majority, the dictatorship of the capitalist monopolies over society. The ideologists of imperialism hide the dictatorship of monopoly capital behind specious slogans of freedom and democracy. They declare the imperialist powers to be countries of the "free world" and represent the ruling bourgeois circles as opponents of all dictatorship. In reality, however, freedom in the imperialist world signifies nothing but freedom to exploit the working class, the working people, not only at home, but in all other countries that fall under the iron heel of the monopolies.

The bourgeoisie gives extensive publicity to the allegedly democratic nature of its election laws, singing special praise to its multi-party system and the possibility of nominating many candidates. In reality, however, the monopolists deprive the masses of the opportunity to express their will and elect genuine champions of their interests. Being in control of such potent means as capital, the press, radio, cinema, television, and also of their henchmen in the trade unions and other mass . . . and *using* their . . .
organisations, they mislead the masses, imposing their own candidates upon the electorate. The different bourgeois parties are usually no more than different factions of the ruling bourgeoisie.

The dictatorship of the bourgeoisie is also manifest in the gross violation of the will of the electorate. Whenever the bourgeoisie sees that the working people are likely, by using their constitutional rights, to elect a considerable number of the champions of their interests to the legislative organs, it brazenly alters the election system and arbitrarily limits the number of working people's representatives in parliament.

The financial oligarchy resorts to the establishment of fascist regimes banking on the army, police, and gendarmerie as a last refuge from the people's wrath, especially when the masses try to make use even of the curtailed democratic rights to uphold their interests and end the all-pervading power of the monopolies. Although the vicious German and Italian fascism has crashed, fascist regimes still survive in some countries and fascism is being revived in new forms in others.

Thus, *the world imperialist system is rent by deep-rooted and acute contradictions*. The antagonism of labour and capital, the contradictions between the people and the monopolies, growing militarism, the break-up of the colonial system, the contradictions between the imperialist countries, conflicts and contradictions between the young national states and the old colonial powers, and—most important of all—the rapid growth of world socialism, are sapping and destroying imperialism, leading to its weakening and collapse.

Not even nuclear weapons can protect the monopoly bourgeoisie from the unalterable course of historical development. Mankind has learned the true face of capitalism. Hundreds of millions of people see that capitalism is a system of economic chaos and periodical crises, . . . economic *anarchy* and . . .
chronic unemployment, mass poverty, and indiscriminate waste of pro-

ductive forces, a system constantly fraught with the danger of war. Mankind does not want to, and will not, tolerate the historically outdated capitalist system.

V. The International Revolutionary Movement of the Working Class

The international revolutionary movement of the working class has achieved epoch-making victories. *Its chief gain is the world socialist system.* The example of victorious socialism has a revolutionising effect on the minds of the working people of the capitalist world; it inspires them to fight against imperialism and greatly facilitates their struggle.

Social forces that are to ensure the victory of socialism are taking shape, multiplying and becoming steeled in the womb of capitalist society. A new contingent of the world proletariat—the young working-class movement of the newly-free, dependent and colonial countries of Asia, Africa, and Latin America—has entered the world arena. Marxist-Leninist parties have arisen and grown. They are becoming a universally recognised national force enjoying ever greater prestige and followed by large sections of the working people.

The international revolutionary movement has accumulated vast experience in the struggle against imperialism and its placemen in the ranks of the working class. It has become more mature ideologically and possesses great organised strength and a militantly dynamic spirit. The trade union movement, which unites vast masses of working people, is playing an increasing role.

The capitalist countries are continuously shaken by class battles; militant actions of the working class in defence of its economic and political interests are growing in number. The working class and all working people have frequently imperilled the class rule of the bourgeoisie. In an effort to maintain its power, the finance oligarchy, in addition to methods of suppression, uses diverse ways of deceiving and corrupting the working class and its organisations, and of splitting the trade union movement on a national and international scale. It bribes the top stratum of trade unions, co-operatives and other organisations and swells the labour bureaucracy, to which it allots lucrative positions in industry, the municipal bodies and the government apparatus. Anticommunist and anti-labour legislation, the banning of Communist parties, wholesale dismissal of Communists and other progressive workers, blacklisting in industry, government employee loyalty screening, police reprisals against the democratic press, and the suppression of strikes by military force have all become routine methods of action for the governments of the imperialist bourgeoisie in its efforts to preserve its dictatorship.

The reactionary forces in individual capitalist countries can no longer cope with the growing forces of democracy and socialism. Struggle and competition between the capitalist states do not preclude, however, a certain unity among them in the face of the increasing strength of socialism and the working-class movement. The imperialists form reactionary alliances; they enter into mutual agreements and set up military blocs and bases spearheaded not only against the socialist coun-

. . . bases *directed* not . . .

tries, but also against the revolutionary working-class and national-liberation movement. The reactionary bourgeoisie in a number of European states have in peacetime opened the doors of their countries to foreign troops.

The bourgeoisie seeks to draw definite lessons from the October Revolution and the victories of socialism. It is using new methods to cover up the ulcers and vices of the capitalist system. Although all these methods render the activities of the revolutionary forces in the capitalist countries more difficult, they cannot reduce the contradictions between labour and capital.

The world situation today is more favourable to the working-class movement. The achievements of the U.S.S.R. and the world socialist system as a whole, the deepening crisis of world capitalism, the growing influence of the Communist Parties among the masses, and the ideological breakdown of reformism have brought about a substantial change in the conditions of class struggle that is to the advantage of the working people. Even in those countries where reformism still holds strong positions, appreciable shifts to the Left are taking place in the working-class movement.

In the new historical situation, the working class of many countries can, even before capitalism is overthrown, compel the bourgeoisie to carry out measures that transcend ordinary reforms and are of vital importance to the working class and the progress of its struggle for

. . . its *continuing* struggle for
the victory of the revolution and for socialism . . .

socialism, as well as to the majority of the nation. By uniting large sec-

. . . uniting *democratic and peace-loving forces,* the working . . .

tions of the working people, the working class can make ruling circles cease preparations for a new world war, renounce the idea of starting local wars, and use the economy for peaceful purposes; it can beat back

. . . purposes. *The working
class, uniting the working people and the broad national masses,*
can . . .

the offensive of fascist reaction and bring about the implementation of a national programme for peace, national independence, democratic rights, and a certain improvement of the living standard of the people.

The capitalist monopolies are the chief enemy of the working class. They are also the chief enemy of the peasants, handicraftsmen, and other small urban proprietors, of most office workers, intellectuals, and small . . . intellectuals, [DELETION] and even . . . capitalists, and even of a section of the middle capitalists.

The working class directs its main blow against the capitalist monopolies. All the main sections of a nation have a vital interest in abolishing the unlimited power of the monopolies. This makes it possible to unite all the democratic movements opposing the oppression of the finance oligarchy in a mighty *anti-monopoly torrent*.

The proletariat advances a programme for combating the power of the monopolies with due regard to the present as well as the future interests of its allies. It advocates broad nationalisation on terms most favourable to the people, control by parliament, the trade unions, and . . . people. (*control . . . state* deleted) It backs the other democratic and representative bodies over the nationalised industries and over the entire economic activity of the state. It backs the peasants' demands for radical land reforms and works for the realisation of the slogan "The land to those who till it".

The proletariat, together with other sections of the people, wages a resolute struggle for broad democracy. It mobilises the masses for effective action against the policy of the finance oligarchy, which strives to abolish democratic freedoms, restrict the power of parliament, revise the constitution with the aim of establishing the personal power of monopoly placemen, and to go over from the parliamentary system to some variety of fascism.

It is in this struggle that the alliance of the working class and all working people is shaped. The working class unites the peasantry, its chief ally, to combat the survivals of feudalism and monopoly domination. Large sections of the office workers and a considerable section of the intelligentsia, whom capitalism reduces to the status of proletarians and who realise the need of changes in the social sphere, become allies of the working class.

General democratic struggles against the monopolies do not delay the socialist revolution but bring it nearer. *The struggle for democracy is a component of the struggle for socialism.* The more profound the democratic movement, the higher becomes the level of the political consciousness of the masses and the more clearly they see that only socialism clears for them the way to genuine freedom and well-being. In the course of this struggle, Right socialist, reformist illusions are dispelled and a political army of the socialist revolution is brought into being.

Socialist revolutions, anti-imperialist national-liberation revolutions, people's democratic revolutions, broad peasant movements, popular struggles to overthrow fascist and other despotic regimes, and general democratic movements against national oppression—all these merge in a single world-wide revolutionary process undermining and destroying capitalism.

The proletarian revolution in any country, being part of the world socialist revolution, is accomplished by the working class of that country and the masses of its people. The revolution is not made to order. It cannot be imposed on the people from without. It results from the profound internal and international contradictions of capitalism. The victorious proletariat cannot impose any "felicity" on another people without thereby undermining its own victory.

Together with the other Marxist-Leninist parties, the Communist Party of the Soviet Union regards it as its internationalist duty to call on the peoples of all countries to rally, muster all their internal forces,
. . . all [DELETION] internal . . .
take vigorous action, and drawing on the might of the world socialist system, forestall or firmly repel imperialist interference in the affairs of the people of any country risen in revolt and thereby prevent imperialist export of counter-revolution. It will be easier to prevent export of counter-revolution if the working people, defending the national sovereignty of their country, strive to bring about the abolition of foreign military bases on their territory and to make their country dissociate itself from aggressive military blocs.

Communists have never held that the road to revolution lies necessarily through wars between countries. Socialist revolution is not necessarily connected with war. Although both world wars, which were started by the imperialists, culminated in socialist revolutions, revolutions are quite feasible without war. The great objectives of the working class can be realised without world war. Today the conditions for this are more favourable than ever.

The working class and its vanguard—the Marxist-Leninist parties—prefer to achieve the transfer of power from the bourgeoisie to the pro-
[REVISION AND ADDITION FOLLOW IN ITALICS]
The working class and its vanguard—the Marxist-Leninist parties—attempt to achieve socialist revolutions by peaceful means. *This would meet the interests of the working class and the people as a whole; it would accord with the national interests of the country.*

Under present conditions, it is possible for the working class, led by its advance guard and based upon the workers' and peoples' front, other potential forms of agreement, or political cooperation of different parties and social organizations, to unite the majority of the people in many capitalist countries, to win state power, and secure the transition of basic means of production into the hands of the people without civil war. . . . [CONTINUE]

letariat *by peaceful means,* without civil war. Realisation of this possibility would meet the interests of the working class and the people as a whole, it would accord with the national interests of the country.

The working class, supported by the majority of the people and firmly repelling opportunist elements incapable of renouncing the policy of compromise with the capitalists and landlords, can defeat the reactionary, anti-popular forces, win a solid majority in parliament, transform it from a tool serving the class interests of the bourgeoisie into an instrument serving the working people, launch a broad mass struggle outside parliament, smash the resistance of the reactionary forces and provide the necessary conditions for a peaceful socialist revolution. This can be done only by extending and continuously developing the class struggle of the workers and peasants and the middle strata of the urban population against big monopoly capital and reaction, for far-reaching social reforms, for peace and socialism.

Where the exploiting classes resort to violence against the people, the possibility of a *non-peaceful transition to socialism* should be borne in mind. Leninism maintains, and historical experience confirms, that the ruling classes do not yield power of their own free will. Hence, the degree of bitterness of the class struggle and the forms it takes will depend not so much on the proletariat as on the strength of the reactionary groups' resistance to the will of the overwhelming majority of the people, and on the use of force by these groups at a particular stage of the struggle for socialism. In each particular country the actual applicability of one method of transition to socialism or the other depends on concrete historical conditions.

It may well be that as the forces of socialism grow, the working-class movement gains strength and the positions of capitalism are weakened, there will arise in certain countries a situation in which it will be preferable for the bourgeoisie, as Marx and Lenin foresaw, to agree to the means of production being purchased from it and for the proletariat to "pay off" the bourgeoisie.

The success of the struggle which the working class wages for the victory of the revolution will depend on how well the working class and its party master the use of *all forms* of struggle—peaceful and non-peaceful, parliamentary and extra-parliamentary—and how well they are prepared to replace one form of struggle by another as quickly and unexpectedly as possible. While the principal law-governed processes of the socialist revolution are common to all countries, the diversity of the national peculiarities and traditions that have arisen in the course of history creates specific conditions for the revolutionary process, a variety of forms and rates of the proletariat's advent to power. This pre-determines the possibility and necessity, in a number of countries, of *transition stages* in the struggle for the dictatorship of the proletariat, and a *variety of forms* of political organisation of the society building socialism. But whatever the form in which the transition from capitalism to socialism is effected, that transition can come about only through revolution. However varied the forms of a new, people's state power in the period of socialist construction their essence will be the same—*dictatorship of the proletariat,* which represents genuine democracy, democracy for the working people.

A bourgeois republic, however democratic, however hallowed by slogans purporting to express the will of the people or nation as a whole, or extra-class will, inevitably remains in practice—owing to the existence of private capitalist ownership of the means of production—a dictatorship of the bourgeoisie, a machine for the exploitation and suppression of the vast majority of the working people by a handful of capitalists. In contrast to the bourgeoisie, which conceals the class character of the state, the working class does not deny the class character of the state.

The dictatorship of the proletariat is a dictatorship of the over-whelming majority over the minority; it is directed against the exploiters, against the oppression of peoples and nations, and is aimed at abolishing all exploitation of man by man. The dictatorship of the proletariat expresses not only the interests of the working class, but also those of all working people; its chief content is not violence but creation, the building of a new, classless society, and the defence of its gains against the enemies of socialism.

Overcoming the split in its ranks is an important condition for the working class to fulfil its historic mission. No bastion of imperialism can withstand a closely-knit working class that exercises unity of action. The Communist Parties favour co-operation with the Social-Democratic Parties not only in the struggle for peace, for better living conditions for the working people, and for the preservation and extension of their democratic rights and freedoms, but also in the struggle to win power and build a socialist society.

At the same time Communists criticise the ideological positions and Right opportunist practice of Social-Democracy and expose the Right Social-Democratic leaders, who have sided openly with the bourgeoisie and renounced the traditional socialist demands of the working class.

The Communist Parties are the vanguard of the world revolutionary movement. They have demonstrated the vitality of Marxism-Leninism and their ability not only to propagate the great ideals of scientific communism, but also to put them into practice. Today the international

Communist movement is so powerful that the combined forces of reaction cannot crush it.

The Communist movement grows and becomes steeled as it fights against various opportunist trends. Revisionism, Right opportunism, which is a reflection of bourgeois influence, is the chief danger within the Communist movement today. The revisionists, who mask their renunciation of Marxism with talk about the necessity of taking account of the latest developments in society and the class struggle, in effect play the role of pedlars of bourgeois-reformist ideology within the Communist movement. They seek to rob Marxism-Leninism of its revolutionary spirit, to undermine the faith which the working class and all working people have in the socialist cause, to disarm and disorganise

. . . in *socialism,* to . . .

them in their struggle against imperialism. The revisionists deny the historical necessity of the socialist revolution and of the dictatorship of the proletariat. They deny the leading role of the Marxist-Leninist party, undermine the foundations of proletarian internationalism, and drift to nationalism. The ideology of revisionism is most fully embodied in the programme of the League of Communists of Yugoslavia.

Another danger is dogmatism and sectarianism, which cannot be reconciled with a creative development of revolutionary theory, which lead to the dissociation and isolation of Communists from the masses,

. . . from the *broad* masses,

doom them to passive expectation or incite them to Leftist adventurist actions in the revolutionary struggle, and hinder a correct appraisal of the changing situation and the use of new opportunities for the benefit of the working class and all democratic forces. Dogmatism and sectarianism, unless steadfastly combated, can also become the chief danger at particular stages in the development of individual parties.

The Communist Party of the Soviet Union holds that an uncompromising struggle against revisionism, dogmatism and sectarianism, against all departures from Leninism, is a necessary condition for the further strengthening of the unity of the world Communist movement and for the consolidation of the socialist camp.

The Communist Parties are independent and they shape their policies with due regard to the specific conditions prevailing in their own countries. They base relations between themselves on equality and the principles of proletarian internationalism. They co-ordinate their actions, consciously and of their own free will, as components of a single international army of labour. The Communist Party of the Soviet Union, like the other Communist Parties, regards it as its internationalist duty to abide by the appraisals and conclusions which the fraternal parties have reached jointly concerning their common tasks in the struggle against imperialism, for peace, democracy and socialism, and by the Declaration and the Statement adopted by the Communist Parties at their international meetings.

Vigorous defence of the unity of the world Communist movement in line with the principles of Marxism-Leninism and proletarian internationalism, and the prevention of any action likely to disrupt that unity are an essential condition for victory in the struggle for national independence, democracy and peace, for the successful accomplishment of the tasks of the socialist revolution, for the construction of socialism and communism.

The C.P.S.U. will continue to strengthen the unity and cohesion of
 . . . continue to *direct its efforts to* the unity . . .
the ranks of the great army of Communists of all countries.

VI. The National-Liberation Movement

The world is experiencing a period of stormy national-liberation revolutions. Imperialism suppressed the national independence and freedom of the majority of the peoples and put the fetters of brutal colonial slavery on them, but *the rise of socialism marks the advent of the era of emancipation of the oppressed peoples*. A powerful wave of national-liberation revolutions is sweeping away the colonial system and undermining the foundations of imperialism. Young sovereign states have arisen, or are arising, in one-time colonies or semi-colonies. Their peoples have entered a new period of development. They have emerged as makers of a new life and as active participants in world politics, as a revolutionary force destroying imperialism.

But the struggle is not yet over. The peoples who are throwing off the shackles of colonialism have attained different degrees of freedom. Many of them, having established national states, are striving for economic and durable political independence. The peoples of those formally independent countries that in reality depend on foreign monopolies politically and economically are rising to fight against imperialism and reactionary pro-imperialist regimes. The peoples who have not yet cast off the chains of colonial slavery are conducting a heroic struggle against
 . . . are *heroically struggling* against
their foreign enslavers.

The young sovereign states do not belong either to the system of imperialist states or to the system of socialist states. But the overwhelming majority of them have not yet broken free from world capitalist economy even though they occupy a special place in it. They constitute that part of the world which is still being exploited by the capitalist monopolies. As long as they do not put an end to their economic dependence on imperialism, they will be playing the role of a "world countryside", and will remain objects of semi-colonial exploitation.

The existence of the world socialist system and the weakening of imperialism offer the peoples of the newly-free countries the prospect of a national renascence, of ending age-long backwardness and poverty, and achieving economic independence.

The interests of a nation call for the eradication of the remnants of colonialism, the elimination of the roots of imperialist power, the ousting of foreign monopolies, the founding of a national industry, the abolition of the feudal system and its survivals, the implementation of radical land reforms with the participation of the entire peasantry and in its interests, the pursuit of an independent foreign policy of peace, the democratisation of the life of society and the strengthening of political independence. All patriotic and progressive forces of the nation are interested in the solution of national problems. That is the basis on which the latter can be unified.

Foreign capital will retreat only before a broad union of patriotic, democratic forces pursuing an anti-imperialist policy. The pillars of feudalism will crumble only under the impact of a general democratic movement. Only far-reaching agrarian reforms and a broad peasant movement can sweep away those remnants of medievalism that fetter the development of the productive forces, and solve the acute food problem that faces the peoples of Asia, Africa and Latin America. Political independence can be made secure only by a nation that has won democratic rights and freedoms and is taking an active part in governing the state.

Consistent struggle against imperialism is a paramount condition for the solution of national tasks. Imperialism seeks to retain one-time colonies and semi-colonies within the system of capitalist economy and perpetuate their underprivileged position in it. *U.S. imperialism is the chief bulwark of modern colonialism.*

The imperialists are using new methods and new forms to maintain colonial exploitation of the peoples. They resort to whatever means they can (colonial wars, military blocs, conspiracies, terrorism, subversion, economic pressure, bribery) to control the newly-free countries and to reduce the independence they have won to mere form, or to deprive them of that independence. Under the guise of "aid", they are trying to retain their old positions in those countries and capture new ones, to extend their social basis, lure the national bourgeoisie to their side, implant military despotic regimes and put obedient puppets in power. Using the poisoned weapon of national and tribal strife, the imperialists seek to split the ranks of the national-liberation movement; reactionary groups of the local exploiting classes play the role of allies of imperialism.

Imperialism thus remains the chief enemy and the chief obstacle to the solution of the national problems facing the young sovereign states and all dependent countries.

A national-liberation revolution does not end with the winning of political independence. Independence will be unstable and will become fictitious unless the revolution brings about radical changes in the social and economic spheres and solves the pressing problems of national rebirth.

The working class is the most consistent fighter for the consummation of this revolution, for national interests and social progress. As industry develops, its ranks will swell and its role on the socio-political scene will increase. The alliance of the working class and the peasantry is the fundamental condition for the success of the struggle to carry out far-reaching democratic changes and achieve economic and social progress. This alliance must form the core of a broad national front. The extent to which the national bourgeoisie will take part in the anti-imperialist and anti-feudal struggle will depend in considerable measure on the solidity of the alliance of the working class and the peasantry. The national front also embraces the urban petty bourgeoisie and the
. . . embraces *the working class, the peasantry, the national* bourgeoisie and the . . .
democratic intelligentsia.

In many countries, the liberation movement of the peoples that have awakened proceeds under the flag of nationalism. Marxists-Leninists draw a distinction between the nationalism of the oppressed nations and that of the oppressor nations. The nationalism of an oppressed nation contains a *general democratic element* directed against oppression, and Communists support it because they consider it historically justified at a given stage. That element finds expression in the striving of the oppressed peoples to free themselves from imperialist oppression, to gain national independence and bring about a national renascence. But the nationalism of an oppressed nation has yet another aspect, one expressing the ideology and interests of the reactionary exploiting top stratum.

The national bourgeoisie is dual in character. In modern conditions the national bourgeoisie in those colonial, one-time colonial and dependent countries where it is not connected with the imperialist circles is objectively interested in accomplishing the basic tasks of an anti-imperialist and anti-feudal revolution. Its progressive role and its ability to participate in the solution of pressing national problems are, therefore, not yet spent.

But as the contradictions between the working people and the propertied classes grow and the class struggle inside the country becomes more acute, the national bourgeoisie shows an increasing inclination to compromise with imperialism and domestic reaction.

The development of the countries which have won their freedom may be a complex multi-stage process. By virtue of varying historical and socio-economic conditions in the newly-free countries, the revolutionary effort of the masses will impart distinctive features to the forms and rates of their social progress.

One of the basic questions confronting these peoples is which road of development the countries that have freed themselves from colonial tyranny are to take, whether the capitalist road or the non-capitalist.

What can capitalism bring them?

Capitalism is the road of suffering for the people. It will not ensure rapid economic progress nor eliminate poverty; social inequality will increase. The capitalist development of the countryside will ruin the peasantry still more. The workers will be fated either to engaging in back-breaking labour to enrich the capitalists, or to swelling the ranks of the disinherited army of the unemployed. The petty bourgeoisie will be crushed in competition with big capital. The benefits of culture and education will remain out of reach of the people. The intelligentsia will be compelled to sell its talent.

What can socialism bring the peoples?

Socialism is the road to freedom and happiness for the peoples. It ensures rapid economic and cultural progress. It transforms a backward country into an industrial country within the lifetime of one generation and not in the course of centuries. Planned socialist economy is an economy of progress and prosperity by its very nature. Abolition of the exploitation of man by man does away with social inequality. Unemployment disappears completely. Socialism provides all peasants with land, helps them to develop farming, combines their labour efforts in voluntary co-operatives and puts modern agricultural machinery and agronomy at their disposal. Peasant labour is made more productive and the land is made more fertile. Socialism provides a high material and cultural standard of living for the working class and all working people. Socialism lifts the people out of darkness and ignorance and gives them access to modern culture. The intelligentsia is offered ample opportunities for creative effort for the benefit of the people.

It is for the peoples themselves to decide which road they will choose. In view of the present balance of the world forces and the actual feasibility of powerful support from the world socialist system, the peoples of the former colonies can decide this question in their own interest. Their choice will depend on the balance of the class forces. The non-capitalist road of development is ensured by the struggle of the working class and the masses of the people, by the general democratic movement, and meets the interests of the absolute majority of the na-

. . . tion. [REMAINDER OF PARAGRAPH DELETED]

tion. This road will require concessions from the bourgeoisie, but those will be concessions in behalf of the nation. All sections of the population can find application for their energies, provided they follow the non-capitalist road of development.

Establishing and developing *national democracies* opens vast prospects for the peoples of the underdeveloped countries. The political basis of a national democracy is a bloc of all the progressive, patriotic forces fighting to win complete national independence and broad democracy, and to consummate the anti-imperialist, anti-feudal, democratic revolution.

A steady growth of the class and national consciousness of the masses is a characteristic of the present stage of social development. The imperialists persist in distorting the idea of national sovereignty, trying to rob it of its main content and to use it as a means of fomenting national egoism, implanting a spirit of national exclusiveness and increasing national antagonisms. The democratic forces establish the idea of national sovereignty in the name of equality for the peoples, of their mutual trust, friendship and assistance and of closer relations between them, in the name of social progress. The idea of national sovereignty in its democratic sense becomes more and more firmly established; it acquires increasing significance and becomes an important factor in the progressive development of society.

The Communist Parties are steadfastly carrying on an active struggle to consummate the anti-imperialist, anti-feudal, democratic revolution, to establish a state of national democracy and achieve social progress. *The Communists' aims are in keeping with the supreme interests of the nation.* The attempts of reactionary circles to disrupt the national front under the guise of anti-communism and their persecution of Communists lead to the weakening of the national-liberation movement and run counter to the national interests of the peoples; they imperil the gains achieved.

The national states become ever more active as an independent force on the world scene; objectively, this force is in the main a *progressive, revolutionary and anti-imperialist force.* The countries and peoples that are now free from colonial oppression are to play a prominent part in the prevention of a new world war—the focal problem of today. The time is past when imperialism could freely use the man-power and material resources of those countries in its predatory wars. The time has come when the peoples of those countries, breaking the resistance of the reactionary circles and those connected with the colonialists, and overcoming the vacillation of the national bourgeoisie, can put their resources at the service of universal security and become a new bulwark of peace. This is what their own fundamental interests and the interests of all peoples demand.

The joining of the efforts of the newly-free peoples and of the peoples of the socialist countries in the struggle against the war danger is a cardinal factor of world peace. This mighty front, which expresses the will and strength of two-thirds of mankind, can force the imperialist aggressors to retreat.

The socialist countries are sincere and true friends of peoples fighting for their liberation and of those that have freed themselves from imperialist tyranny, and render them all-round support. They stand for the abolition of all forms of colonial oppression and vigorously promote the strengthening of the sovereignty of the states rising on the ruins of colonial empires.

The C.P.S.U. considers fraternal alliance with the peoples who have thrown off colonial or semi-colonial tyranny to be a corner-stone of its international policy. This alliance is based on the common vital interests of world socialism and the world national-liberation movement. The C.P.S.U. regards it as its internationalist duty to assist the peoples who have set out to win and strengthen their national independence, all peoples who are fighting for the complete abolition of the colonial system.

VII. The Struggle against Bourgeois and Reformist Ideology

A grim struggle is going on between two ideologies—communist and bourgeois—in the world today. This struggle is a reflection, in the spiritual life of mankind, of the historic process of transition from capitalism to socialism.

The new historical epoch has brought the revolutionary world outlook of the proletariat a genuine triumph. Marxism-Leninism has gripped the minds of progressive mankind.

Bourgeois doctrines and schools have failed in the test of history. They have been and still are unable to furnish scientific answers to the questions posed by life. The bourgeoisie is no longer in a position to put forward ideas that will induce the masses to follow it. *Bourgeois . . . follow it. More and more people in the capitalist countries are breaking off with the bourgeois world view. Bourgeois ideology . . . ideology is experiencing a grave crisis.*

A revolutionary change in the minds of vast masses is a long and complex process. The more victories the world socialist system achieves, the deeper the crisis of world capitalism and the sharper the class struggle, the more important becomes the role of Marxist-Leninist ideas in unifying and mobilising the masses to fight for communism. The ideological struggle is a most important element of the class struggle of the proletariat.

Imperialist reaction mobilises every possible means to exert ideological influence on the masses as it attempts to denigrate communism and its noble ideas and to defend capitalism. The chief ideological and political weapon of imperialism is *anti-communism,* which consists mainly in slandering the socialist system and distorting the policy and objectives of the Communist Parties and Marxist-Leninist theory. Under cover of anti-communism, imperialist reaction persecutes and hounds all

. . . Under *the false slogans* of anti-communism . . .

that is progressive and revolutionary; it seeks to split the ranks of the working people and to paralyse the proletarians' will to fight. Rallied to this black banner today are all the enemies of social progress: the finance oligarchy and the military, the fascists and reactionary clericals, the colonialists and landlords and all the ideological and political vehicles of imperialist reaction. Anti-communism is a reflection of the extreme decadence of bourgeois ideology.

The defenders of the bourgeois system, seeking to keep the masses in spiritual bondage, invent new "theories" designed to mask the exploiting character of the bourgeois system and to embellish capitalism. They assert that modern capitalism has changed its nature, that it has become "people's capitalism" in which property is "diffused" and capital becomes "democratic", that classes and class contradictions are disappearing, that "incomes are being equalised" and economic crises eliminated. In reality, however, the development of modern capitalism confirms the accuracy of the Marxist-Leninist theory of the growing contradictions and antagonisms in capitalist society and of the aggravation of the class struggle within it.

The advocates of the bourgeois state call it a *"welfare state".* They propagate the illusion that the capitalist state opposes monopolies and can achieve social harmony and universal well-being. But the masses see from their own experience that the bourgeois state is an obedient tool of the monopolies and that the vaunted "welfare" is welfare for the magnates of finance capital, and suffering and torture for hundreds of millions of workingmen.

The "theoreticians" of anti-communism describe modern imperial-

. . . describe *the imperialist countries* as . . .

ism as the "free world". In reality the "free world" is a world of exploitation and lack of rights, a world where human dignity and national honour are trampled underfoot, a world of obscurantism and political reaction, of rabid militarism and bloody reprisals against the working people.

Monopoly capital is reviving *fascist ideology*—the ideology of extreme chauvinism and racism. Fascism in power is an overt terroristic dictatorship of the most reactionary, most chauvinistic and most imperialist elements of finance capital. Fascism begins everywhere and always with vicious anti-communism to isolate and rout the parties of the working class, to split the forces of the proletariat and defeat them piecemeal, and then to do away with all the other democratic parties and organisations and turn the people into the blind tool of the policy of the capitalist monopolies. Fascism strikes first of all at the Communist Parties since they are the most consistent, staunch and incorruptible defenders of the interests of the working class and all working people.

Imperialist reaction makes extensive use of *chauvinism* to incite na-
     . . . use of *chauvinism and racism* to incite na-
tionalist *and racial* conflicts, . . .
tionalist conflicts, persecute entire nationalities and national groups
     . . . nationalities *and races*
(anti-Semitism, racial discrimination against Negroes and the peoples of the underdeveloped countries), blunt the class consciousness of the working people and divert the proletariat and its allies from the class struggle.

Clericalism is acquiring ever greater importance in the political and ideological arsenal of imperialism. The clericals do not confine themselves to using the Church and its ramified machinery. They now have their own big political parties which in many capitalist countries are in power. They set up their own trade union, youth, women's and other organisations and split the ranks of the working class and all working people. The monopolies lavishly subsidise clerical parties and organisations, which exploit the religious sentiments of the working people and their superstitions and prejudices.

Bourgeois ideology assumes a variety of forms and uses the most diverse methods and means of deceiving the working people. But they all boil down to the same thing—defence of the declining capitalist system. The ideas running through the political and economic theories of the modern bourgeoisie, through its philosophy and sociology, through its ethics and aesthetics, substantiate monopoly domination, justify exploitation, defame social property and collectivism, glorify militarism and war, whitewash colonialism and racism, and foment enmity and hatred among the peoples.

Anti-communism is becoming the main instrument of reaction in its struggle against the democratic forces of Asia, Africa, and Latin America. It is the meeting ground of imperialist ideology and the ideology of the feudal, pro-imperialist elements and the reactionary groups of the bourgeoisie of the countries which have gained their freedom from colonial tyranny.

The anti-popular circles of those countries seek to tone down the general democratic content of nationalism, to play up its reactionary aspect, to push aside the democratic forces of the nation, to prevent social progress, and to hinder the spread of scientific socialism. At the same time they advance theories of "socialism of the national type", propagate socio-philosophical doctrines that are, as a rule, so many variations of the petty-bourgeois illusion of socialism, an illusion which rules out the class struggle. These theories mislead the people, hamper the development of the national-liberation movement and imperil its gains.

National-democratic, anti-imperialist ideas are becoming widespread in the countries which have liberated themselves from colonial oppression. The Communists and other proponents of these ideas patiently explain to the masses the untenability of the illusion that it is possible to

. . . that *national independence and social progress are possible* without . . .

insure national independence and social progress without an active struggle against imperialism and internal reaction. They come out actively against chauvinism and other manifestations of reactionary ideology, which justifies despotic regimes and the suppression of democracy. At the same time the Communists act as exponents of the socialist ideology, rallying the masses under the banner of scientific socialism.

The ideological struggle of the imperialist bourgeoisie is spearheaded primarily against the working class and its Marxist-Leninist parties. Social-Democracy in the working-class movement and revisionism in the Communist movement reflect the bourgeois influence on the working class.

The contemporary Right-Wing Social-Democrats are the most important ideological and political prop of the bourgeoisie within the working-class movement. They eclectically combine old opportunist ideas with the "latest" bourgeois theories. The Right Wing of Social-Democracy has completely broken with Marxism and contraposed so-called democratic socialism to scientific socialism. Its adherents deny the existence of antagonistic classes and the class struggle in bourgeois society; they forcefully deny the necessity of the proletarian revolution and oppose the abolition of the private ownership of the means of production. They assert that capitalism is being "transformed" into socialism.

The Right-Wing socialists began by advocating social reforms in place of the socialist revolution and went as far as to defend state-monopoly capitalism. In the past they impressed on the minds of the proletariat that their differences with revolutionary Marxism bore not so much on the ultimate goal of the working-class movement as on the ways of achieving it. Now they openly renounce socialism. Formerly the Right-Wing socialists refused to recognise the class struggle to the point of recognising the dictatorship of the proletariat. Today they deny, not only the existence of the class struggle in bourgeois society, but also the very existence of antagonistic classes.

Historical experience has shown the bankruptcy of both the ideology and the policy of Social-Democracy. Even when reformist parties come to power they limit themselves to partial reforms that do not affect the rule of the monopoly bourgeoisie. Anti-communism has brought social reformism to an ideological and political impasse. This is one of the main reasons for the crisis of Social-Democracy.

Marxism-Leninism is winning more and more victories. It is winning them because it expresses the vital interests of the working class, of the vast majority of mankind, which seeks peace, freedom and progress, and because it expresses the ideology of the new society succeeding capitalism.

VIII. Peaceful Coexistence and the Struggle for World Peace

The C.P.S.U. considers that the chief aim of its foreign-policy activity is to provide peaceful conditions for the building of a communist society in the U.S.S.R. and developing the world socialist system, and together with the other peace-loving peoples to deliver mankind from a world war of extermination.

The C.P.S.U. maintains that forces capable of preserving and promoting universal peace have arisen and are growing in the world. Possibilities are arising for essentially new relations between states.

Imperialism knows no relations between states other than those of domination and subordination, of oppression of the weak by the strong. It bases international relations on diktat and intimidation, on violence and arbitrary rule. It regards wars of aggression as a natural means of settling international issues. For the imperialist countries diplomacy has been, and remains, a tool for imposing their will upon other nations and preparing wars. At the time of the undivided rule of imperialism the issue of war and peace was settled by the finance and industrial oligarchy in the utmost secrecy from the peoples.

Socialism contrasts imperialism with *a new type of international relations*. The foreign policy of the socialist countries, which is based on the principles of peace, the equality and self-determination of nations, and respect for the independence and sovereignty of all countries, as well as the fair, humane methods of socialist diplomacy, are exerting a growing influence on the world situation. At a time when imperialism no longer plays a dominant role in international relations, while the socialist system is playing an increasing role, and when the influence of the countries that have won national independence and of the masses of the people in the capitalist countries has grown very considerably, it is becoming possible for the new principles advanced by socialism to gain the upper hand over the principles of aggressive imperialist policy.

For the first time in history, a situation has arisen in which not only the big states, but also the small ones, the countries which have chosen independent development, and all the states which want peace, are in a position, irrespective of their strength, to pursue an independent foreign policy.

The issue of war and peace is the principal issue of today. Imperialism is the only source of the war danger. The imperialist camp is making preparations for the most terrible crime against mankind—a world thermonuclear war that can bring unprecedented destruction to entire countries and wipe out entire nations. The problem of war and peace has become a life-and-death problem for hundreds of millions of people.

The peoples must concentrate their efforts on curbing the imperialists in good time and preventing them from making use of lethal weapons. *The main things is to ward off a thermonuclear war, to prevent it from breaking out*. This can be done by the present generation.

The consolidation of the Soviet state and the formation of the world socialist system were historic steps towards the realisation of mankind's age-old dream of banishing wars from the life of society. In the socialist part of the world there are no classes or social groups interested in starting a war. Socialism, outstripping capitalism in a number of important branches of science and technology, has supplied the peace-loving peoples with powerful material means of curbing imperialist aggression. Capitalism established its rule with fire and sword, but socialism does not require war to spread its ideals. Its weapon is its superiority over the old system in social organisation, political system, economy, the improvement of the standard of living and spiritual culture.

The socialist system is a natural centre of attraction for the peace-loving forces of the globe. The principles of its foreign policy are gaining ever greater international recognition and support. A vast *peace zone* has taken shape on earth. In addition to the socialist countries, it includes a large group of non-socialist countries that for various reasons are not interested in starting a war. The emergence of those countries in the arena of world politics has substantially altered the balance of forces in favour of peace.

There is a growing number of countries that adhere to a policy of neutrality and strive to safeguard themselves against the hazards of participation in military blocs.

ticipation in *aggressive* military blocs.

In the new historical epoch the masses have a far greater opportunity of actively intervening in the settlement of international issues. The peoples are taking the solution of the problem of war and peace into their own hands more and more vigorously. The anti-war movement of the masses, which takes various forms, is a major factor in the struggle for peace. The international working class, the most uncompromising and most consistent fighter against imperialist war, is the great organising force in this struggle of the people as a whole.

It is possible to avert a world war by the combined efforts of the mighty socialist camp, the peace-loving non-socialist countries, the international working class and all the forces championing peace. The growing superiority of the socialist forces over the forces of imperialism, of the forces of peace over those of war, will make it actually possible to banish world war from the life of society even before the complete victory of socialism on earth, with capitalism surviving in a part of the world. The victory of socialism throughout the world will do away completely with the social and national causes of all wars. *To abolish war and establish everlasting peace on earth is a historic mission of communism.*

General and complete disarmament under strict international control is a radical way of guaranteeing a durable peace. Imperialism has imposed an unprecedented burden of armaments on the people. Socialism sees its duty towards mankind in delivering it from this absurd waste of national wealth. The solution of this problem would have historical significance for mankind. By an active and determined effort the peoples can and must force the imperialists into disarmament.

Socialism has offered mankind the only reasonable principle of maintaining relations between states at a time when the world is divided into two systems—the principle of the peaceful coexistence of states with different social systems, put forward by Lenin.

Peaceful coexistence of the socialist and capitalist countries is an *objective necessity* for the development of human society. *War cannot and must not serve as a means of settling international disputes.* Peaceful coexistence or disastrous war—such is the alternative offered by history. Should the imperialist aggressors nevertheless venture to start a new world war, the peoples will no longer tolerate a system which drags them into devastating wars. They will sweep imperialism away and bury it.

Peaceful coexistence implies renunciation of war as a means of settling international disputes, and their solution by negotiation; equality, mutual understanding and trust between countries; consideration for each other's interests; non-interference in internal affairs; recognition of the right of every people to solve all the problems of their country by themselves; strict respect for the sovereignty and territorial integrity of all countries; promotion of economic and cultural co-operation on the basis of complete equality and mutual benefit.

Peaceful coexistence serves as a basis for the peaceful competition between socialism and capitalism on an international scale and constitutes a specific form of class struggle between them. As they consistently pursue the policy of peaceful coexistence, the socialist countries are steadily strengthening the positions of the world socialist system in its competition with capitalism. Peaceful coexistence affords more favourable opportunities for the struggle of the working class in the capitalist countries and facilitates the struggle of the peoples of the colonial and dependent countries for their liberation. Support for the principle of peaceful coexistence is also in keeping with the interests of that section of the bourgeoisie which realises that a thermonuclear war would not spare the ruling classes of capitalist society either. The policy of peaceful coexistence is in accord with the vital interests of all mankind, except the big monopoly magnates and the militarists.

The Soviet Union has consistently pursued, and will continue to pursue, the policy of the peaceful coexistence of states with different social systems.

The Communist Party of the Soviet Union advances the following *tasks in the field of international relations:*

to use, together with the other socialist countries, peaceful states and peoples, every means of preventing war and providing conditions for the complete banishment of war from the life of society;

to pursue a policy of establishing sound international relations, and work for the disbandment of all military blocs opposing each other, the discontinuance of the "cold war" and the propaganda of enmity and hatred among the nations, and the abolition of all air, naval, rocket, and other military bases on foreign territory;

to work for general and complete disarmament under strict international control;

to strengthen relations of fraternal friendship and close co-operation with the countries of Asia, Africa, and Latin America which are fighting to attain or consolidate national independence, with all peoples and states that advocate the preservation of peace;

to pursue an active and consistent policy of improving and developing relations with all capitalist countries, including the United States of America, Great Britain, France, the Federal Republic of Germany, Japan, Italy, and other countries, with a view to safeguarding peace; *Japan and Italy,* [DELETION] with a . . .

to contribute in every way to the militant solidarity of all contingents and organisations of the international working class, which oppose the imperialist policy of war;

steadfastly to pursue a policy of consolidating all the forces fighting against war. All the organisations and parties that strive to avert war, the neutralist and pacifist movements and the bourgeois circles that advocate peace and normal relations between countries will meet with understanding and support on the part of the Soviet Union;

to pursue a policy of developing international co-operation in the fields of trade, cultural relations, science, and technology;

to be highly vigilant with regard to the aggressive circles, which are intent on violating peace; to expose, in good time, the initiators of military adventures; to take all necessary steps to safeguard the security and inviolability of our socialist country and the socialist camp as a whole.

The C.P.S.U. and the Soviet people as a whole will continue to oppose all wars of conquest, including wars between capitalist countries, and local wars aimed at strangling people's emancipation movements, and consider it their duty to support the sacred struggle of the oppressed peoples and their just anti-imperialist wars of liberation.

The Communist Party of the Soviet Union will hold high the banner of peace and friendship among the nations.

Part Two

THE TASKS OF THE COMMUNIST PARTY OF THE SOVIET UNION IN BUILDING A COMMUNIST SOCIETY

Communism—the Bright Future of All Mankind

The building of a communist society has become an immediate practical task for the Soviet people. The gradual development of socialism into communism is an objective law; it has been prepared by the development of Soviet socialist society throughout the preceding period.

What is communism?

Communism is a classless social system with one form of public ownership of the means of production and full social equality of all members of society; under it, the all-round development of people will be accompanied by the growth of the productive forces through continuous progress in science and technology; all sources of public wealth will gush forth abundantly, and the great principle "From each according to his ability, to each according to his needs" will be implemented. Communism is a highly organised society of free, socially conscious working people in which public self-government will be established, a society in which labour for the good of society will become the prime vital requirement of everyone, a necessity recognised by one and all, and the ability of each person will be employed to the greatest benefit of the people.

A high degree of communist consciousness, industry, discipline, and devotion to the public interest are qualities typifying the man of communist society.

Communism ensures the continuous development of social production and high labour productivity through rapid scientific and technological progress; it equips man with the best and most powerful machines, greatly increases his power over nature and enables him to control its elemental forces to an ever greater extent. The social economy reaches the highest stage of planned organisation, and the most effective and rational use is made of the material wealth and labour reserves to meet the growing requirements of the members of society.

Under communism, the classes, and the socio-economic and cultural
. . . communism, *there will be no* classes, . . .

distinctions, and differences in living conditions, between town and countryside disappear completely; the countryside rises to the level of the

tryside *will* disappear . . .

town in the development of the productive forces and the nature of work, the forms of production relations, living conditions and the well-being of the population. With the victory of communism mental and physical labour will merge organically in the production activity of people. The intelligentsia will no longer be a distinct social stratum, since workers by

. . . stratum, *and* workers by

hand will *rise* in cultural . . .

hand will have risen in cultural and technological standards to the level of workers by brain.

Thus, communism puts an end to the division of society into classes and social strata, whereas the whole history of mankind, with the exception of its primitive period, was one of class society in which division into opposing classes led to the exploitation of man by man, class struggle, and antagonisms between nations and states.

Under communism all people will have equal status in society, will stand in the same relation to the means of production, will enjoy equal conditions of work and distribution, and will actively participate in the management of public affairs. Harmonious relations will be established between the individual and society on the basis of the unity of public and personal interests. For all their diversity, the requirements of people will express the sound, reasonable requirements of perfectly developed persons.

The purpose of communist production is to ensure uninterrupted progress of society and to provide all its members with material and cultural benefits according to their growing needs, their individual requirements and tastes. People's requirements will be satisfied from public sources. Articles of personal use will come into the full ownership of each member of society and will be at his disposal.

Communist society, which is based on highly organised production and advanced technology, alters the character of work, but it does not release the members of society from work. It will by no means be a society of anarchy, idleness and inactivity. Everyone will participate in

. . . Every *able-bodied person* will . . .

social labour and thereby ensure the steady growth of the material and spiritual wealth of society. Thanks to the changed character of labour, its better technical equipment and the high degree of consciousness of all members of society, the latter will work willingly for the public benefit according to their own inclinations.

Communist production demands high standards of organisation, precision and discipline, which are ensured, not by compulsion, but through an understanding of public duty, and are determined by the whole pattern of life in communist society. Labour and discipline will not be a burden to people; labour will no longer be a mere source of livelihood—it will be a genuinely creative process and a source of joy.

Communism represents the highest form of organisation of public

Communism *is* the highest . . .

life. All production units and self-governing associations will be harmoniously interlinked by a common planned economy and a uniform rhythm

ously *united* by a common . . .

of social labour.

Under communism the nations will draw closer and closer together in all spheres on the basis of a complete identity of economic, political and spiritual interests, of fraternal friendship and co-operation.

Communism is the system under which the abilities and talents of free man, his best moral qualities, blossom forth and reveal themselves in full. Family relations will be freed from material considerations and

. . . will *finally* be freed . . .

will be based solely on mutual love and friendship.

In defining the basic tasks to be accomplished in building a communist society, the Party is guided by Lenin's great formula: *"Communism is Soviet power plus the electrification of the whole country."*

The C.P.S.U. being a party of scientific communism, proposes and fulfils the tasks of communist construction in step with the preparation and maturing of the material and spiritual prerequisites, considering that it would be wrong to jump over necessary stages of development, and that it would be equally wrong to halt at an achieved level and thus check progress. The building of communism must be carried out by successive stages.

In the current decade (1961-70) the Soviet Union, in creating the material and technical basis of communism, will surpass the strongest and richest capitalist country, the U.S.A., in production per head of population; the people's standard of living and their cultural and technical standards will improve substantially; everyone will live comfortably; all collective and state farms will become highly productive and profitable enterprises; the demand of Soviet people for well-appointed housing will, in the main, be satisfied; hard physical work will disappear; the U.S.S.R. will have the shortest working day.

In the next decade (1971-80) the material and technical basis of communism will be created and there will be an abundance of material and cultural benefits for the whole population; Soviet society will come close to a stage where it can introduce the principle of distribution according to needs, and there will be a gradual transition to one form of ownership—public ownership. Thus, *a communist society will on the whole be built in the U.S.S.R.* The construction of communist society will be fully completed in the subsequent period.

The majestic edifice of communism is being erected by the persevering effort of the Soviet people—the working class, the peasantry and the intelligentsia. The more successful their work, the closer the great goal—communist society.

I. The Tasks of the Party in the Economic Field and in the Creation and Development of the Material and Technical Basis of Communism

The main economic task of the Party and the Soviet people is to create *the material and technical basis of communism* within two decades. This means complete electrification of the country and perfection on this basis of the techniques, technologies, and organisation of social production in *all branches of the national economy;* comprehensive . . .
industry and agriculture; comprehensive mechanisation of production operations and a growing degree of their automation; widespread use of chemistry in the national economy; vigorous development of new, economically effective branches of production, new types of power and new materials; all-round and rational utilisation of natural resources; organic
. . . natural, *material and labour* resources; . . .
fusion of science and production, and rapid scientific and technical progress; a high cultural and technical level for the working people; and substantial superiority over the more developed capitalist countries in productivity of labour, which constitutes a most important prerequisite for the victory of the communist system.

As a result, the U.S.S.R. will possess productive forces of unparalleled might; it will surpass the technical level of the most developed countries and occupy first place in the world in per capita production. This will serve as a basis for the gradual transformation of socialist social relations into communist social relations and for a development of
. . . development of *production*
industry and agriculture that will make it possible to meet in abundance the requirements of society and all its members.

In contrast to capitalism, the planned socialist system of economy combines accelerated technical progress with the full employment of all able-bodied citizens. Automation and comprehensive mechanisation serve as a material basis for the gradual development of socialist labour into communist labour. Technical progress will require higher standards of production and a higher level of the vocational and general education of all working people. The new machinery will be used to improve radically the Soviet people's working conditions, and make them easier, to reduce the length of the working day, to improve living conditions, eliminate hard physical work and, subsequently, all unskilled labour.

The material and technical basis will develop and improve continuously together with the evolution of society towards the complete triumph of communism. The level of development of science and technology, and the degree of mechanisation and automation of production operations, will steadily rise.

The creation of the material and technical basis of communism will call for huge investments. The task is to utilise these investments most rationally and economically, with the maximum effect and gain of time.

1. THE DEVELOPMENT OF INDUSTRY; ITS ... INDUSTRY, CONSTRUCTION AND TRANSPORT: THEIR ROLE ... ROLE IN CREATING THE PRODUCTIVE FORCES OF COMMUNISM

The creation of the material and technical basis of communism, the task of making Soviet industry technologically the best and strongest in the world, calls for the further development of heavy industry. On this basis, all the other branches of the national economy—agriculture, the consumer goods industries, the building industry, transport and communications, as well as the branches directly concerned with services for the population—trade, public catering, health, housing, and communal services—will be technically re-equipped.

A first-class heavy industry, the basis for the country's technical progress and economic might, has been built up in the Soviet Union. The C.P.S.U. will continue to devote unflagging attention to the growth of heavy industry, which ensures the development of the country's produc-
... industry *and its technical progress. The main task of heavy industry is to meet the needs of the country's defence in full, and to develop those branches of the national economy producing consumer goods to meet ever more fully the requirements of the people, the daily needs of Soviet man, and to ensure the development of the country's productive forces.* [NEXT SEVEN LINES DELETED]
tive forces and defence potential. In the new period of the Soviet Union's development, the growth and technological progress of heavy industry must ensure the expansion of consumer goods industries to meet ever more fully the requirements of the people.

Thus, the main task of heavy industry is to meet the needs of the country's defence in full and to satisfy the daily requirements of man, of Soviet society, better and more fully.

With these aims in view, the C.P.S.U. plans the following increases in *total industrial output:*

within the current 10 years, by approximately 150 per cent, exceeding the contemporary level of U.S. industrial output;

ing the [*contemporary* deleted] level . . .

within 20 years, by not less than 500 per cent, leaving the present overall volume of U.S. industrial output far behind.

To achieve this, it is necessary to raise *productivity of labour* in industry by more than 100 per cent within 10 years, and by 300-350 per cent within 20 years. In 20 years' time labour productivity in Soviet industry will exceed the present level of labour productivity in the U.S.A. by roughly 100 per cent, and considerably more in terms of per hour output, due to the reduction of the working day in the U.S.S.R.

Such an intensive development of industry will call for major progressive changes in its *structure.* The role of new branches ensuring the greatest technical progress will grow very considerably. The less effective fuels, types of power, raw and semi-manufactured materials will be increasingly superseded by highly effective ones, and their comprehensive use will increase greatly. The share of synthetic materials, metals and alloys with new properties will increase considerably. New types of automatic and electronic machinery, instruments and apparatus will be rapidly introduced on a large scale.

Electrification, which is the backbone of the economy of communist society, plays a key role in the development of all economic branches and in all modern technological progress. It is therefore important to ensure the priority development of *electric power* output. The plan for the electrification of the country provides for an almost three-fold increase in the use of electricity to equip industrial labour within the present decade; a considerable expansion of industries with a high rate of power consumption through the supply of cheap power; and extensive electrification of transport, agriculture and the household in town and countryside. The electrification of the country will on the whole be completed in the course of the second decade.

The annual output of electricity must be brought up to 900,000-1,000,000 million kilowatt-hours by the end of the first decade, and to 2,700,000-3,000,000 million kwh by the end of the second decade. For this it will be necessary in the course of 20 years to increase accordingly the installed capacities of electric power plants and to build hundreds of thousands of kilometres of high-tension transmission and distribution lines throughout the country. A single power grid for the whole U.S.S.R. will be built and will have sufficient capacity reserves to transmit electric power from the Eastern regions to the European part of the country; it will link up with the power grids of other socialist countries.

As atomic energy becomes cheaper, the construction of atomic power stations will be expanded, especially in areas poor in other power sources, and the use of atomic energy for peaceful purposes in the national economy, in medicine and science will increase.

The further rapid expansion of the output of *metals and fuels,* the basis of modern industry, remains one of the major economic tasks. Within 20 years metallurgy will develop sufficiently to produce about 250 million tons of steel a year. Steel output must cover fully the growing requirements of the national economy in accordance with the technological progress achieved in that period. The output of light, non-ferrous and rare metals will grow very appreciably; the output of aluminium and its use in electrification, engineering, building, and the household will considerably increase. A steady effort will be made to ensure priority output of oil and gas which will be used increasingly as raw materials for the chemical industry. Oil output must meet the requirements

    . . . industry. *Coal, oil and gas* output . . .
of the national economy in full.

    . . . in full. *Wide adoption of the most progressive and economical methods of extracting mineral fuel will be secured.*

One of the most important tasks is the all-round development of the *chemical* industry, and the full use in all economic fields of the achievements of modern chemistry. This provides greater opportunities to increase the national wealth and the output of new, better and cheaper capital and consumer goods. Metal, wood, and other building materials

    . . . other [DELETION] materials
will be increasingly replaced by economical, durable, light synthetic materials. The output of mineral fertilisers and chemical weed and pest killers will rise sharply.

Of primary importance for the technical re-equipment of the entire national economy is the development of *mechanical engineering,* with special stress laid on the accelerated production of automated production lines and machines, automatic, telemechanic and electronic devices and precision instruments. The designing of highly efficient machines consuming less raw materials and power and leading to higher productivity

    . . . productivity *of labour*
will make rapid progress. The requirements of the national economy in all types of modern machines, machine tools, and instruments must be

    . . . tools, *gear, as well as spare parts and* instruments, . . .
met in full.

The development of mechanical engineering in the first decade will serve as the basis for *comprehensive mechanisation* in industry, agriculture, building, transport, loading and unloading operations, and in the

    . . . transport [DELETION] and . . .
municipal economy. Comprehensive mechanisation will exclude manual

    . . . manual
loading and unloading as well as hand labour in the fulfilment of both

basic and auxiliary operations *in production.*
labour from both basic and auxiliary operations.

Within the 20-year period the comprehensive *automation* of production will be effected on a large scale, with more and more shops and plants being fully automated. The introduction of highly efficient auto-
. . . automated, *thus ensuring a high degree of technical-economic efficiency.* The introduction . . .
matic control systems will be accelerated. Cybernetics, computors, and control systems must be introduced on a large scale in industry, research, control systems *will* be introduced on a large scale in *industrial production processes,* the *construction industry, transport,* research . . . designing, planning, accounting, statistics, and management.
. . . accounting [DELETION] and . . .

The vast scope of capital construction calls for the rapid development and technological modernisation of the *building industry,* a sub-
. . . the *building industry, and the industry of building materials to the level which would ensure the needs of the national economy, maximum reduction of the time factor, decrease in cost, and improvement in quality of building through steady industrialization. It calls for accelerated completion of the transition to the building of fully equipped housing units and construction of standardized housing projects and elements of industrial production on a large scale* [REMAINDER OF PARAGRAPH DELETED]
stantial increase in the output of better and cheaper building materials, the maximum acceleration of the rate and reduction of the cost of building through steady industrialisation and the use of prefabricated elements.

The C.P.S.U. will concentrate its efforts on ensuring a rapid increase in the output of *consumer goods.* The growing resources of industry must be used more and more to fully meet all the requirements of Soviet people and to build and equip enterprises and establishments catering to the household and cultural needs of the population. Along with the accelerated development of all branches of the light and food industries, the share of consumer goods in the output of heavy industry will also increase. More electricity and gas will be supplied to the population.

The growth of the national economy will call for the accelerated development of *all transport facilities.* The most important tasks in the sphere of transport are: expansion of transport and road construction to meet in full the requirements of the national economy and the population in all modes of transport; further modernisation of the railways and other transport systems; a considerable increase of the speed of rail, sea and river traffic; the co-ordinated development of all types of transport as components of a single transport network. The share of pipe transport will increase.

A single deep-water system will link the main inland waterways of the European part of the U.S.S.R.

A ramified network of modern roads will be built throughout the country. The automobile fleet will increase sufficiently to fully meet freight and passenger requirements; car hire centres will be organised on a large scale. Air transport will become a means of mass passenger traffic extending to all parts of the country.

Up-to-date *jet* engineering will develop rapidly, above all in air transport, as well as in space exploration.

All means of *communication* (post, radio and television, telephone and telegraph) will be further developed. All regions of the country will
. . . will be *even more* developed . . .
have reliable radio telephone communications and a link-up system of
. . . reliable [DELETION] communications . . .
television stations.

Full-scale communist construction calls for a more rational *geographic distribution* of the industries in order to save social labour and ensure the comprehensive development of areas and the specialisation of their industries, do away with the overpopulation of big cities, facilitate the elimination of essential distinctions between town and countryside, and further even out the economic levels of different parts of the country.

To gain time, priority will be given to developing easily exploited natural resources that provide the greatest economic effect.

The industry in the areas to the *east of the Urals,* where there are immense natural riches, raw material and power resources, will expand greatly.

The following must be achieved within the next 20 years: in Siberia and Kazakhstan—the creation of new large power bases using deposits of cheap coal or the water-power resources of the Angara and Yenisei rivers; the organisation of big centres of power-consuming industries and
. . . industries, [DELETION] the development . . .
the completion, in Siberia, of the country's third metallurgical base, the development of new rich ore and coal deposits; and the construction of a
. . . ore, *oil,* and coal . . .
number of new large machine-building centres; in areas along the Volga, in the Urals, North Caucasus, and Central Asia—the rapid development of the power, oil, gas, and chemical industries and the development of ore deposits. Soviet people will be able to carry out daring plans to
. . . deposits, *together with the development of the existing metallurgical bases in the Urals and the Ukraine, the completion, in Siberia, of the country's third metallurgical base, as well as the building of two new ones, using deposits of iron ore: one in the Central European part of the USSR, the Kursk Magnetic Center, and the other in Kazakhstan.*
Soviet . . .

change the courses of some northern rivers and regulate their discharge for the purpose of utilising vast water resources for the irrigation and watering of arid areas.

The economy in the European part of the U.S.S.R. which contains the bulk of the population and where there are great opportunities for increased industrial output, will make further substantial progress.

The maximum acceleration of scientific and engineering progress is a major national task which calls for daily effort to reduce the time spent on designing new machinery and introducing it in industry. It is necessary to promote in every way the initiative of economic councils, enterprises, social organisations, scientists, engineers, designers, workers and collective farmers in creating and applying technical improvements. Of utmost importance is the material and moral stimulation of mass invention and rationalisation movements, of enterprises, shops, teams, and

. . . shops, *state and collective farms,* teams, . . .

innovators who master the production of new machinery and utilise them skilfully.

The Party will do everything to *enhance the role of science* in the building of communist society; it will encourage research to discover new possibilities for the development of the productive forces, and the rapid and extensive application of the latest scientific and technical achievements; a decisive advancement in experimental work, including research directly at enterprises, and the efficient organisation of scientific and technical information and of the whole system of studying and disseminating progressive Soviet and foreign methods. Science will itself in full measure become a productive force.

The constant *improvement in the technology* of all industries and production branches is a requisite for industrial development. Technological progress will facilitate the substantial intensification and acceler-

. . . will *make the labor of the worker easier, will* facilitate . . .

ation of production operations without putting undue strain on the worker, and will achieve the highest degree of precision, standardisation of mass-produced items and the maximum use of production lines. Machining will be supplemented and, when necessary, replaced by chemical methods, the technological use of electricity, electrochemistry, electric

. . . electrochemistry, [DELETION] etc.; . . .

heat treatment, etc.; radio-electronics, semiconductors and ultrasound will occupy a more and more important place in production techniques. The construction of new, technically up-to-date enterprises will proceed side by side with the reconstruction of those now in existence and the replacement and modernisation of their equipment.

The development of the *specialisation and co-operation of enterprises* is a most important condition for technical progress and the ra-

prises, as well as their expedient combination, is a most . . .

tional organisation of social labour. Articles of similar type should be manufactured mainly at large specialised plants.

. . . plants, *with a view to their most rational distribution.*

New techniques and the reduction of the working day call for *better organisation of work.* Technical progress and better production organisation must be fully utilised to increase labour productivity and reduce production costs at every enterprise. This implies a higher rate of increase in labour productivity as compared with remuneration, better rate-

. . . with *the rate of increase in wages,* better . . . fixing, prevention of loss of working time, and operation on a profitable basis in all sectors of production.

Most important will be systematic improvement of the qualifications of those working in industry and other branches of the economy in connection with technical progress. The planned training, instruction and rational employment of those released from various jobs and transferred to other jobs due to mechanisation and automation are essential.

Existing enterprises will be improved and developed into enterprises of communist society. Typical of this process will be new machinery, high standards of production organisation and efficiency through increased automation of production operations and the introduction of automation into control; an improvement of the cultural and technical standards of the workers, the increasing fusion of physical and mental labour and the growing proportion of engineers and technicians in every industrial enterprise; the expansion of research, and closer links between enterprises and research institutes; promotion of the emulation movement, the application of the achievements of science and the best forms of labour organisation and best methods of raising labour productivity, the extensive participation of workers' collectives in the management of enterprises, and the spreading of communist forms of labour.

2. THE DEVELOPMENT OF AGRICULTURE AND SOCIAL RELATIONS IN THE COUNTRY-SIDE

Along with a powerful industry, a flourishing, versatile and highly productive agriculture is an imperative condition for the building of communism. The Party organises a great development of productive forces in agriculture, which will enable it to accomplish two basic, closely related tasks: (a) to build up an abundance of high-quality food products for the population and of raw materials for industry, and (b) to effect the gradual transition of social relations in the Soviet countryside to communist relations and eliminate, in the main, the distinctions between town and country.

The chief means of achieving progress in agriculture and satisfying the growing needs of the country in farm produce are comprehensive mechanisation and consistent *intensification:* high efficiency of crop farming and stock-breeding based on science and progressive experience in all kolkhozes and state farms, a steep rise in the yielding capacity of all crops and greater output per hectare with the utmost economy of . . . with the *minimum* of labour and funds. On this basis, it is necessary to achieve an unintermittent growth of agricultural production in keeping with the needs of society. Agriculture will approach the level of industry in technical equipment and the organisation of production; farm labour will turn into a variety of industrial labour, and the dependence of agriculture upon the elements will decrease considerably, and ultimately drop to a minimum.

The development of virgin and disused land and establishment of new large-scale state farms, the reorganisation of the machine and tractor stations, the sale of implements of production to the collective farms, and . . . farms, *the introduction of a new planning system,* and the enhancement of material incentives for agricultural workers—all constitute an important stage in the development of agriculture.
. . . agriculture. *The Party will continue to pay its greatest attention to the development of agriculture in the virgin and idle land areas.*

The further advance of the countryside to communism will proceed through the development and improvement of the two forms of socialist farming—the kolkhozes and state farms.

The *kolkhoz system* is an integral part of Soviet socialist society. It is a way charted by V. I. Lenin for the gradual transition of the peasantry to communism; it has stood the test of history and conforms to the distinctive features of the peasantry.

Kolkhoz farming accords in full with the level and needs of the development of modern productive forces in the countryside, and makes possible effective use of new machinery and the achievements of science, and rational employment of manpower. The kolkhoz blends the personal interests of the peasants with common, nation-wide interests, individual with collective interest in the results of production, and offers extensive opportunities for raising the incomes and the well-being of peasants on the basis of growing labour productivity. It is essential to make the most of the possibilities and advantages of the kolkhoz system. By virtue of its organisational structure and its democratic groundwork, which will develop more and more, the kolkhoz is a social economic form which ensures that production is run by the kolkhoz members themselves, that their creative initiative is enhanced and that the collective farmers are educated in the communist spirit. The kolkhoz is a school of communism for the peasantry.

Economic advancement of the kolkhoz system creates conditions for the gradual rapprochement and, in the long run, also for the merging of kolkhoz property and the property of the whole people into one communist property.

The *state farms,* which are the leading socialist agricultural enterprises, play an ever increasing role in the development of agriculture. The state farms must serve the kolkhozes as a model of progressive, scientifically-managed, economically profitable social production, of high efficiency and labour productivity.

The C.P.S.U. proceeds from the fact that the further consolidation of the *unbreakable alliance of the working class and the kolkhoz peasantry* is of crucial political and socio-economic importance for the building of communism in the U.S.S.R.

A. Building up an Abundance of Agricultural Produce

In order fully to satisfy the requirements of the entire population and of the national economy in agricultural produce, the task is to increase the *aggregate volume of agricultural production* in 10 years by about 150 per cent, and in 20 years by 250 per cent. Agricultural output must keep ahead of the growing demand. In the first decade the Soviet Union will outstrip the United States in output of the key agricultural products per head of population.

Accelerated growth of *grain* production is the chief link in the further development of all agriculture and a basis for the rapid growth of stock-breeding. The aggregate grain crops will more than double in twenty years, and their yielding capacity will double. The output of wheat, maize, cereal and leguminous crops will increase substantially.

Livestock breeding will develop at a rapid rate. The output of animal products will rise: meat about threefold in the first ten years and nearly fourfold in twenty years, and milk more than double in the first decade and nearly threefold in twenty years. The planned increase in the output of animal products will be achieved by increasing the cattle and poultry population, improving stock and productivity, and building up reliable fodder resources, chiefly maize, sugar-beet, fodder beans, and other crops.

Productivity of labour in agriculture will rise not less than 150 per cent in ten years, and five- to sixfold in twenty years. The rapid rise of the productivity of farm labour—at a higher rate than in industry—will serve to eliminate the lag of agriculture behind industry and will turn it into a highly-developed branch of the economy of communist society.

The further mechanisation of agriculture, introduction of *compre-*

hensive mechanisation and use of automatic devices and highly efficient and economical machinery adapted to the conditions of each zone will be the basis for the growth of productivity of farm labour. The Party considers rapid *electrification* of agriculture one of the most important tasks. All state farms and kolkhozes will be supplied electric power for production and domestic purposes, from the state power grid and from power stations to be built in the countryside.

The technical re-equipment of agriculture must combine with the most progressive forms and methods of the organisation of labour and production and the maximum improvement of the cultural and technical education of farm workers. Qualified workers with special agricultural training and proficient in the use of new machinery will increasingly
 . . . will *be on the increase* in the kolkhozes . . .
predominate in the kolkhozes and state farms.

To ensure high, stable, steadily increasing harvests, to deliver agriculture from the baneful effects of the elements, especially droughts, to steeply raise land fertility, and to rapidly advance livestock breeding, it is necessary:
[INTERCHANGE ORDER OF NEXT TWO PARAGRAPHS]
 to introduce in all parts of the country *scientific systems of land*
 to introduce *on all collective and state farms scientific* . . .
cultivation and animal husbandry in keeping with local conditions and the specialisation of each farm, ensuring the most effective use of the land and the most economically expedient combination of branches, the best structure of crop acreage with the substitution of high-yielding and valuable crops for crops of little value and those giving low yields; to ensure that every kolkhoz and state farm master the most advanced methods of crop farming with the application of efficient crop rotation and the sowing of high-grade seed only; to build up reliable fodder resources in all districts and to introduce the foremost stock-breeding techniques in kolkhozes and state farms;

 to effect a scientifically expedient distribution of agriculture by natural-economic zones and districts, and a more thorough and stable *specialisation* of agriculture with priority given to the type of farm product where the best conditions for it exist and the greatest saving in outlay is achieved;

 to effect a consistent *introduction of chemicals* in all branches of
 to effect a *rational introduction* . . .
agriculture, to meet all its needs in mineral fertilisers and chemical
 . . . chemical *and biological* means . . .
means of combating weeds, blights, diseases and plant and animal pests, and to ensure the best use of local fertilisers in all kolkhozes;
 . . . fertilisers in all *collective and state farms;*

☆ **81** ☆

to apply broadly biological achievements and microbiology which . . . and *especially* microbiology . . . is assuming ever greater importance, to improve soil fertility;

to carry through a far-flung *irrigation programme,* to irrigate and water millions of hectares of new land in the arid areas and improve existing irrigated farming; to expand field-protective afforestation, building of water reservoirs, irrigation of pastures and melioration of over-moist land; and to combat systematically the water and wind erosion of soil.

. . . soil. *The greatest attention will be paid to the protection and rational utilization of natural resources such as timber and water and their conservation and augmentation.*

The Party will promote the development of *agricultural science,* focus the creative efforts of scientists on the key problems of agricultural progress, and work for the practical application and extensive introduction of the achievements of science and progressive production experience in crop farming and stock-breeding. Research institutions and experimental stations must become important links in agricultural management, and scientists and specialists must become the direct organisers of farm production. Each region or group of regions of the same zonal type should have agricultural research centres, with their own large-scale farms and up-to-date material and technical resources, to work out recommendations for state farms and kolkhozes applicable to the given district. Agricultural research and educational establishments must be . . . educational *institutions and* establishments . . . chiefly located in rural areas and be directly associated with farm production, so that students may learn while working and work while learning.

B. Kolkhozes and State Farms on the Road to Communism; Re-Moulding Social Relations in the Countryside

The economic basis for the development of kolkhozes and state farms lies in the continuous growth and best use of their productive forces, improvement of the organisation of production and methods of management, steady rise of labour productivity, and strict observance of the principle: higher payment for good work, for better results. On this basis the kolkhozes and state farms will become to an increasing degree enterprises of the communist type in production relations, character of labour, and the living and cultural standards of their personnel.

The policy of the socialist state in relation to the kolkhozes is . . . of the *Party* in relation . . . based on blending country-wide interests with the material interest of the kolkhozes and their members in the results of their labour. The state will promote the growth of the productive forces of the kolkhoz system and the economic advancement of all kolkhozes; concurrently, the kolkhoz peasantry must contribute more widely to the building of communist society.

The state will ensure the full satisfaction of the needs of the kolkhozes in modern machinery, chemicals, and other means of production,
. . . machinery, *spare parts,* chemicals, . . .
will train new hundreds of thousands of skilled farm workers, and will considerably increase capital investments in the countryside, in addition to the greater investments by the kolkhozes themselves. The amount of manufactured goods made available to the kolkhoz villages will increase greatly.

Strict observance of their contracted commitments to the state by the kolkhozes and their members is an inviolable principle of their participation in the development of the national economy.

The system of state purchasing must aim at increasing the amount and improving the quality of the agricultural products bought, on the basis of an all-round advancement of kolkhoz farming. It is essential to co-ordinate the planning of state purchases and the production plans of the kolkhozes, with utmost consideration for the interests of agricultural production, its proper distribution and specialisation.

The policy in the sphere of the state purchasing prices of agricultural produce and state selling prices of means of production for the countryside must take account of the interests of extended reproduction in both industry and agriculture and of the need to accumulate funds in the kolkhozes. It is essential that the level of state purchasing prices encourage the kolkhozes to raise labour productivity and reduce production expenses, since greater farm output and lower production costs are the basis of greater incomes for the kolkhozes.

The proper ratio of *accumulation and consumption* in the distribution of incomes is a prerequisite of successful kolkhoz development. The kolkhozes cannot develop without continuously extending their commonly-owned assets for production, insurance, cultural and community needs. At the same time, it must be a standing rule for every kolkhoz to raise its members' incomes from collective farming and to enhance their living standard as labour productivity rises.

Improved methods of rate setting and labour remuneration at kolkhozes, supplementary remuneration of labour, and other incentives are very important for obtaining better production results. Equal economic conditions must be gradually provided to improve the incomes of kolkhozes existing under unequal natural-economic conditions in different zones, and also within the zones, in order to put into effect more consistently the principle of equal pay for equal work on a scale embracing the entire kolkhoz system. Farming on all kolkhozes must be conducted in . . . system. *Production* on all kolkhozes must *take place* in strict accordance with the principle of profitability.

In its organisational work and economic policy, the Party will strive to overcome the lag of the economically weak kolkhozes and to turn all kolkhozes into economically strong, high-income farms in the course of the next few years. The Party sets the task of continuously improving and educating kolkhoz personnel, of ensuring the further extension of kolkhoz democracy and promoting the principle of collectivism in management.

As the kolkhozes develop, their basic production facilities will expand, and modern technical means will become dominant.

The economic advancement of the kolkhozes will make it possible to perfect *kolkhoz internal relations:* to raise the degree to which production is socialised; to bring the rate setting, organisation and payment for labour closer to the level and the forms employed at state enterprises and effect a transition to a guaranteed monthly income; to develop community services more broadly (public catering, kindergartens and nurseries, and other services, etc.).

At a certain point the collective production at kolkhozes will achieve a level at which it will fully satisfy members' requirements. On this basis, supplementary individual farming will gradually become economically unnecessary. When collective production at the kolkhozes is able to replace in full that of the supplementary individual plot of the kolkhoz members, when the collective farmers see for themselves that their supplementary individual farming is unprofitable, they will give it up of their own accord.

As the productive forces increase, inter-kolkhoz production ties will develop and the socialisation of production will transcend the limits of individual kolkhozes. The building, jointly by several kolkhozes, of enterprises and cultural and welfare institutions, state-kolkhoz power stations and enterprises for the primary processing, storage, and transportation of farm products, for various types of building, the manufacture of building materials, etc., should be encouraged. As the commonly- . . . materials, *construction,* etc., should . . . owned assets increase, the kolkhozes will participate more and more in establishing enterprises and cultural and welfare institutions for general public use, boarding-schools, clubs, hospitals and holiday homes. All these developments, which must proceed on a voluntary basis and when the necessary economic conditions are available, will gradually impart to kolkhoz-co-operative property the nature of public property.

The *state farms* have a long way to travel in their development—
                                    . . . development—*con-
tinuing to increase productivity, to improve the quality of the product,
to attain . . .*
to attain high rates of growth of labour productivity, to steadily reduce
production costs and raise farm efficiency. This calls for the economically expedient specialisation of state farms. Their role in supplying food
to the urban population will grow. They must become mechanised and
well-organised first-class factories of grain, cotton, meat, milk, wool,
vegetables, fruit, and other products, and must develop seed farming and
pure-strain animal husbandry to the utmost.

The material and technical basis of the state farms will be extended
and improved and the living and cultural conditions at the state farms
will approach those in towns. State-farm management should follow a
more and more democratic pattern which will allot a greater role to the
personnel, to general meetings and production conferences, in deciding
production, cultural and other community issues.

As the kolkhozes and state farms develop, their production ties with
each other and with local industrial enterprises will grow stronger. The
practice of jointly organising various enterprises will expand. This will
ensure a fuller and more balanced use of manpower and production resources throughout the year, raise the productivity of social labour and
enhance the living and cultural standards of the population. Agrarian-
industrial associations will gradually emerge wherever economically expedient, in which, given appropriate specialisation and co-operation of
agricultural and industrial enterprises, agriculture will combine organically with the industrial processing of its produce.

As production in kolkhozes and state farms develops and social
relations within them advance, agriculture rises to a higher level, afford-
ing the possibility of transition to communist forms of production and
distribution. The kolkhozes will draw level in economic conditions with
the nationally-owned agricultural enterprises. They will turn into highly
developed mechanised farms. By virtue of high labour productivity all
kolkhozes will become economically powerful. Kolkhoz members will be
adequately provided and their requirements fully satisfied out of collective-farm production. They will have the services of catering establishments, bakeries, laundries, kindergartens and nurseries, clubs, libraries,
and sports grounds. The payment of labour will be the same as at
nationally-owned enterprises; they will be provided all forms of social
                    . . . they will *enjoy* all forms . . .
security (pensions, holidays, etc.) out of kolkhoz and state funds.

Gradually, the kolkhoz villages will grow into amalgamated urban communities with modern housing facilities, public amenities and services, and cultural and medical institutions. The rural population will ultimately draw level with the urban population in cultural and living conditions.

Elimination of socio-economic and cultural distinctions between town and country and of differences in their living conditions will be one of the greatest gains of communist construction.

3. MANAGEMENT OF THE NATIONAL ECONOMY AND PLANNING

The building of the material and technical basis of communism calls for a continuous improvement in economic management. Chief emphasis at
. . . management *and planning.* Chief . . .
all levels of planning and economic management must be laid on the most rational and effective use of the material, labour and financial resources and natural wealth and on the elimination of excessive expenditure. The immutable law of economic development is to achieve in penditure *and waste.* The immutable . . .
the interests of society the highest results at the lowest cost.
. . . lowest cost. *The improvement in agricultural leadership must be accompanied by overall simplification and reduction of the management apparatus.*

Planning must at all levels concentrate on the rapid development and introduction of new techniques. It is essential that progressive, scientifically expedient standards for the use of means of production be strictly observed in all sectors of the national economy.

The Party attaches prime importance to the more *effective investment of capital,* the choice of the most profitable and economical trends in capital construction, achievement everywhere of the maximum growth
. . . achievement [DELETION] of the maximum . . .
of output per invested ruble, and reduction of the time lapse between investment and return. It is necessary continuously to improve the structure of capital investments and to expand that portion of them which is spent on equipment, machinery, and machine tools.

[ADDED PARAGRAPH] *Concentration of capital investment in the most important sectors, elimination of too-wide scattering of capital expenses and acceleration of entry into action by builders of enterprises must become unalterable conditions of economic planning and organization.*

Continuous improvement of the *quality of output* is an imperative requirement of economic development. The quality of goods produced by Soviet enterprises must be considerably higher than that of the best

capitalist enterprises. For this purpose it is necessary to apply a wide range of measures, including public control, and to enhance the role of
. . . the role of *production* quality . . .
quality indexes in planning, in the assessment of the work of enterprises and in socialist emulation.

Communist construction presupposes the maximum development of *democratic principles of management* coupled with a strengthening and improvement of *centralised economic management by the state.* The economic independence and the rights of local organs and enterprises will continue to expand within the framework of the single national economic plan. Plans and recommendations made at lower levels, beginning with enterprises, must play an increasing role in planning.

Centralised planning should chiefly concentrate on working out and ensuring the fulfilment of the key targets of the economic plans with the greatest consideration paid to recommendations made at lower levels; on co-ordinating and dovetailing plans drawn up locally; on spreading scientific and technical achievements and advanced production experience; on enforcing a single state policy in the spheres of technical progress, capital investment, distribution of production, payment of labour, prices, and finance, and a unified system of accounting and statistics.

It is essential that the national economy develop on a strictly *proportionate* basis, that economic disproportions are prevented in good time, ensuring sufficient economic reserves as a condition for stable high rates of economic development, uninterrupted operation of enterprises and continuous improvement of the people's well-being.

The growing scale of the national economy, the rapid development of science and technology call for an improvement of the scientific level of planning, accounting, statistics, and industrial designing. A better
. . . planning, *industrial designing, accounting and statistics.* A . . .
scientific, technical and economic basis for the plans will ensure their
. . . plans will *add*
greater stability, which also presupposes timely correction and amendment of plans in the course of their fulfilment. Planning must be continuous, and the annual and long-term plans must be organically integrated.
grated, *and financial, material and technical resources must be secured.*

Firm and consistent discipline, day-to-day control, and determined elimination of elements of parochialism and of a narrow departmental approach in economic affairs are necessary conditions for successful communist construction.

There must be a further expansion of the role and responsibility of *local bodies* in economic management. The transfer of a number of functions of economic management by the all-Union bodies to those of the republics, by republican bodies to those of the regions and by regional bodies to those of the districts should be continued. It is necessary to improve the work of the economic councils as the most viable form of management in industry and building conforming to the present level of the productive forces. The improvement of the work of economic councils within the economic administration areas will also be accompanied by greater co-ordination of the work of other economic bodies, in order better to organise the planned, comprehensive economic development of such major economic areas as the Urals, the Volga area, Siberia, Trans-

. . . Volga area, *Western Siberia, Eastern Siberia, the Far East,* Transcaucasia, . . . caucasia, the Baltic area, Central Asia, etc.

Extension of operative independence and of the *initiative of enterprises* on the basis of the state-plan targets is essential in order to mobilise untapped resources and make more effective use of capital investments, production facilities and finances. It is necessary for enterprises to play a substantially greater part in introducing the latest machinery.

. . . latest *machinery and in the fullest utilization of the production force.*

The selection, training and promotion of people who directly head enterprises and kolkhozes, who organise and manage production, are of decisive importance in economic management. The sphere of material production is the main sphere in the life of society; the most capable people must, therefore, be given leading posts in the sphere of production.

The direct and most active participation of *trade unions* in elaborating and realising economic plans, in matters concerning the labour of factory and office workers, in setting up organs of economic administration and of management of enterprises, must be extended more and more at top level and locally. The role of the collectives of factory and office workers in matters concerning the work of enterprises must be enhanced.

In the process of communist construction economic management will make use of material and moral incentives for high production figures. Proper combination of material and moral labour incentives is a great creative factor in the struggle for communism. In the course of the advance to communism the importance of moral labour incentives, public recognition of achieved results and the sense of responsibility of each for the common cause will become continuously greater.

The entire system of planning and assessing the work of central and local organisations, enterprises and collective farms must stimulate their interest in higher plan targets and the maximum dissemination of progressive production experience. Initiative and successes in finding and using new ways of improving the quantitative and qualitative indexes of production should be specially encouraged.

There must be a continuous improvement in rate setting, the system of labour payments and bonuses, in the financial control over the quantity and quality of work, in the elimination of levelling, and the stimulation of collective forms of incentives raising the interest of each employee in the high efficiency of the enterprise as a whole.

It is necessary in communist construction to make full use of commodity-money relations in keeping with their new meaning in the socialist period. In this, such instruments of economic development as cost accounting, money, price, production cost, profit, trade, credit, and finance play a big part. When the transition to one communist form of people's property and the communist system of distribution is completed, commodity-money relations will become economically outdated and will wither away.

The important role of the budget in distributing the social product and national income will prevail throughout the period of full-scale communist construction. There will be a further strengthening of the monetary and credit system, a consolidation of Soviet currency, a steady rise of the rate of exchange of the ruble by virtue of its growing purchasing power, and an increase in the importance of the ruble in the
. . . and *a strengthening of its role* in the . . .
international arena.

It is necessary to promote profitable operation of enterprises, to work for lower production costs and higher profitability. The price sys-
work *with more economy and frugality for reduction of expenses and for lower* . . .
tem should be continuously improved in conformity with the tasks of communist construction, technical progress, growth of production and consumption, and the reduction of production expenditures. Prices must, to a growing extent, reflect the socially-necessary outlays of labour, ensure return of production and circulation expenditures and a certain profit for each normally operating enterprise. Systematic, economically justified price reductions based on growth of labour productivity and reduction of production costs are the main trend of the price policy in the period of communist construction.

Soviet society possesses immense national assets. For this reason, the role of accounting and control over the maintenance and proper use of the national wealth increases. Thrift, the proper use of every ruble belonging to the people, competent utilisation of funds, the continuous improvement of planning and methods of management, improvement of organisation and conscious discipline, and development of the initiative of the people are powerful means of accelerating the advance of Soviet society to communism.

II. The Tasks of the Party in Improving the Living Standard of the People

The heroic labour of the Soviet people has produced a powerful and versatile economy. There is now every possibility to improve rapidly the living standard of the entire population—the workers, peasants, and intellectuals. The C.P.S.U. sets the historically important task of achieving *in the Soviet Union a living standard higher than that of any of the capitalist countries.*

This task will be effected by: (a) raising the individual payment of
. . . payment [DELETED] according . . .
working people according to the quantity and quality of their work, coupled with reduction of retail prices and abolition of taxes paid by the population; (b) increase of the public funds distributed among members of society irrespective of the quantity and quality of their labour, that is, of society *according to need,* irrespective . . .
free of charge (education, medical treatment, pensions, maintenance of children at children's institutions, transition to cost-free use of public amenities, etc.).

The rise of the real incomes of the population will be outstripped by a rapid increase in the amount of commodities and services, and by extensive construction of dwellings and cultural and service buildings.

Soviet people will be more prosperous than people in the developed capitalist countries even if average incomes will be equal, because in the Soviet Union the national income is distributed fairly among the mem-
. . . fairly *in the interest of all* the mem-
bers of society and there are no parasitical classes as in the bourgeois countries who appropriate and squander immense wealth taken away from millions of working people.

The Party acts upon Lenin's thesis that communist construction must be based upon the principle of material incentive. In the coming twenty years payment according to one's work will remain the principal source for satisfying the material and cultural needs of the working people.

The disparity between high and comparatively low incomes must gradually shrink. Increasingly greater numbers of unskilled personnel will become skilled, and the diminishing difference in proficiency and labour productivity will be accompanied by a steady reduction of disparities in the level of pay. As the living standard of the entire population rises, low income levels will approach the higher, and the disparity between the incomes of peasants and workers, low-paid and high-paid

personnel and the populations of different parts of the country, will gradu-
personnel *and between incomes* of the populations . . .
ally shrink.

At the same time, as the country advances towards communism,
personal needs will be increasingly met out of public consumption funds,
whose rate of growth will exceed the rate of growth of payments for
labour. The transition to communist distribution will be completed after
the principle of distribution according to one's work will outlive itself,
that is, when there will be an abundance of material and cultural wealth
and labour will become a prime necessity of life for all members of
society.

a) **Provision of a high level of income and consumption for
the whole population.**
. . . population. *The development of shopping facilities.*

The national income of the U.S.S.R. in the next ten years will increase nearly 150 per cent, and about 400 per cent in twenty years. The
real income per head of population will increase by more than 250 per
cent in twenty years.

In the course of the coming ten years the real incomes of factory
. . . incomes of *all* factory
and office workers (including public funds) per employed person will, on
the average, be almost doubled, and in twenty years will increase by
. . . doubled, *while the incomes of the factory and
office workers receiving low wages will be approximately trebled. In
this way, already at the end of the next ten years there will be no
groups of factory and office workers receiving low wages in the country.*
[REMAINDER OF PARAGRAPH DELETED]
approximately 200-250 per cent. The increase in the real incomes of
factory, office and professional workers paid relatively lower wages will
be brought to a level at which low-paid brackets throughout the country
will be eliminated within ten years. The real incomes of factory and
office workers receiving the minimum wages will be approximately
trebled (including what they get from public funds) over this period.

By virtue of higher rates of growth of the labour productivity of
collective farmers their real incomes will grow more rapidly than the
incomes of factory workers, and will, on an average per employed person,
more than double in the next ten years and increase more than fourfold
in twenty years.

The wages of such numerically large sections of the Soviet intelligentsia as engineers and technicians, agronomists and stock-breeding ex-
. . . agronomists, *veterinarians* and . . .
perts, teachers, medical and cultural workers, will rise considerably.

As the incomes of the population grow, *the general level of popular consumption will rise rapidly*. The entire population will be able adequately to satisfy its need in high-quality and varied foodstuffs. The share of animal products (meat, fats, dairy produce), fruit, and high-grade vegetables in popular consumption will rise substantially in the near future. The demand of all sections of the population for high-quality consumer goods—attractive clothes, footwear and goods improving and adorning the daily life of Soviet people, such as comfortable modern furniture, up-to-date domestic goods, a wide range of goods for cultural purposes, etc.—will be amply satisfied. Production of motor-cars for the population will be considerably extended.
cars *to serve* the population . . .

Output of consumer goods must meet the growing consumer demand in full, and must conform to its changes. Timely output of goods in accordance with the varied demand of the population, with consideration for local, national and climatic conditions, is an imperative requirement for the consumer industries. Good shopping facilities will be arranged for *all* the consumer industries. [REMAINDER OF PARAGRAPH DELETED] throughout the country, this being a necessary and important condition for the satisfaction of the growing requirements of the population.

[PARAGRAPHS ADDED] *Soviet shopping facilities, a necessary condition for the satisfaction of the growing requirements of the people, will be further developed. Good shopping facilities, with progressive forms of service to the population, will be arranged throughout the country. A network of stores, warehouses, cold-storage houses and vegetable stores will spread the material and technical base of these facilities.*

Consumers' cooperatives will be developed and will be called upon to improve shopping in the villages and to organize the sale of surplus agricultural products. Collective farm markets will preserve their significance. [END OF ADDITION]

The second decade will see an abundance of material and cultural benefits for the whole population, and material prerequisites will be created to complete the transition to the communist principle of distribu-
created *for* the transition . . .
tion according to need in the period to follow.

b) Solution of the housing problem and improvement of living conditions.

The C.P.S.U. sets the task of solving the most acute problem in the improvement of the wellbeing of the Soviet people—the housing problem. [ADDITION] *In the first decade, the national shortage of housing will be eliminated. Families which still live in crowded and inadequate dwellings will receive new apartments.* At the end . . .
At the end of the second decade, every family, including newlyweds,

will have a comfortable flat conforming to the requirements of hygiene and cultural living. Peasant houses of the old type will, in the main, give place to new modern dwellings, or—wherever possible—they will be rebuilt and appropriately improved. In the course of the second decade housing will gradually become rent-free for all citizens.

[ADDED PARAGRAPH] *High standards in urban development, architecture and planning to create industrial, living and public dwellings which will be well built, comfortable and economical in construction and in the utilization of cities and other population centers will acquire great importance. Cities and villages must become rational complex organizations of industrial zones and living sectors, a network of public and cultural establishments, plants, transport, equipment and energy sources safeguarding the conditions under which people work, live and rest.*

An extensive programme of public-services construction and of improvements in all towns and workers' estates will be carried out in the coming period, which will involve completion of their electrification, the necessary gasification, provision of public transport facilities and
. . . gasification, *telephone communication,* provision . . .
waterworks, and measures for the further improvement of sanitary con-
waterworks, *sewer systems* and measures . . .
ditions in towns and other populated localities, including tree planting, pond building, and effective measures to combat air, soil and water pollution. Well-appointed small and middle-size towns will be increasingly developed, making for better and healthier living conditions.

Public transport facilities (tramways, buses, trolley-buses, and subways) will become free in the course of the second decade, and at the end of it such public amenities as water, gas, and heating will also be free.

c) Reduction of working hours and the further improvement of working conditions.

In the coming ten years the country will go over to a *six-hour working day* with one day off a week, or a *34-36-hour working week*
. . . or a *35-hour working week*
with two days off, and in underground and harmful jobs to a five-hour
. . . underground and *similar* jobs *performed under harmful conditions* to a five-hour . . .
working day or a 30-hour five-day working week.

By virtue of a corresponding rise in labour productivity, transition to a still shorter working week will be begun in the second decade.

The Soviet Union will thus have the world's shortest and, concurrently, the most productive and highest-paid working day. Working people will have much more leisure time, and this will add to their opportunities of improving their cultural and technical level.

The length of the annual paid holidays of working people will be increased together with the reduction of the working day. Gradually the minimum length of leave for all industrial, professional and office workers will increase to three weeks and subsequently to one month. Paid holidays will be gradually extended to kolkhoz members.

All-round measures to make working conditions healthier and lighter constitute an important task in improving the well-being of the people. Modern means of labour safety and hygiene designed to prevent occupational injuries and diseases will be introduced at all enterprises. Night shifts will be gradually abolished at enterprises, save those where round-the-clock operation is required by the production process or the need to service the population.

d) Health services and measures for increased longevity.

The socialist state is the only state which undertakes to protect and continuously improve the health of the whole population. This is provided for by a system of socio-economic and medical measures. There will be an extensive programme designed to prevent and sharply reduce diseases, wipe out mass infectious diseases and further increase longevity.

The needs of the urban and rural population in all forms of highly-qualified *medical services* will be met in full. This calls for the extensive building of medical institutions, including hospitals and sanatoria, the equipment of all medical institutions with modern appliances, and regular medical check-ups for the entire population. Special emphasis must be laid on extending in town and country the network of mother-and-child health institutions (maternity homes, medical consultation centres, children's health homes and hospitals, forest schools, etc.).

In addition to the existing free medical services, accommodation of sick persons at sanatoria and the dispensing of medicines will become gratuitous.

In order to afford the population an opportunity to rest in an out-of-town environment, holiday homes, boarding-houses, country hotels, and tourist camps will be built, where working people will be accommodated at a reasonable charge or by way of a bonus, as well as at a discount or gratis.

The Party considers it a most important task to ensure the education from early childhood of a sound young generation harmoniously developed physically and spiritually. This calls for utmost encouragement of all forms of mass sport and physical training, specifically at schools, and for drawing greater and greater sections of the population, particularly the youth, into sports.

e) Improvement of family living conditions and of the position of women. Maintenance of children and incapacitated people at public expense.

The remnants of the unequal position of women in domestic life must be totally eliminated. Social and living conditions must be provided to enable women to combine happy motherhood with increasingly active and creative participation in social labour and social activities, and in scientific and artistic pursuits. Women must be given relatively lighter and yet sufficiently well-paid jobs. Leave of absence from work during confinement will be of longer duration.

It is essential to provide conditions to reduce and lighten the domestic work of women, and later to make possible the replacement of domestic work by public forms of satisfying the daily needs of the family. Up-to-date inexpensive domestic machinery, appliances, and electrical devices will be made extensively available for this purpose; the needs of the population in service establishments will be fully met in the next few years.

The extension of *public catering,* including canteens at enterprises, institutions, and in big dwelling houses, until it meets the demands of the population, calls for special attention. The service at catering establishments and the quality of catering must be radically improved, so that meals at public catering establishments should be tasty and nourishing and should cost the family less than meals cooked at home. Price reductions in public catering will keep ahead of price reductions for foodstuffs in the shops. By virtue of *all* this public catering will be able to take precedence over home cooking within 10-15 years.

The transition to free public catering (midday meals) at enterprises and institutions, and for collective farmers at work, will begin in the second decade.

A happy childhood for every child is one of the most important and noble aspects of communist construction. The development of a ramified network of children's institutions will make it possible for more and more families, and in the second decade for every family, to keep children and adolescents free of charge at children's establishments if they so desire. *The Party considers it necessary to do everything possible so that in the next few years the needs of institutions for children under school age shall be fully satisfied.* [THE NEXT SENTENCE WAS REPLACED BY THE PRECEDING.]
State and community children's institutions will be able to accommodate the bulk of children under school age within the next few years.

In town and country there will be: full and cost-free satisfaction of

[NEXT THREE LINES REVISED] the need *of the population* in kindergartens, playgrounds, nurseries, *schools with extended day,* and young
pioneer camps; the widespread provision of *a network of mass* boarding-schools with free maintenance of children; free hot meals at all
schools, [DELETION] extended . . .
the need in kindergartens, playgrounds, nurseries, and young pioneer
camps; the widespread provision of boarding-schools with free maintenance of children; free hot meals at all schools, introduction of extended
school hours with free dinners for school children, and free issue of school
uniforms and educational aids.

In keeping with the growth of the national income, the state, the
trade unions, and the kolkhozes will in the course of the twenty years
gradually undertake maintenance of all citizens incapacitated through
old age or some disability. Sickness and temporary disability grants and
. . . Sickness and [DELETION] disability . . .
old-age pensions will be extended to kolkhoz members; old-age and disability pensions will be steadily raised. The number of comfortable
homes for old people and invalids providing free accommodation for all
applicants will be greatly increased in town and country.

By fulfilling the tasks set by the Party for the improvement of the
well-being of the people, the Soviet Union will make considerable head-
way towards the practical realisation of the communist principle of distribution according to need.

At the end of the twenty years public consumption funds will total
about half of the aggregate real income of the population. This will make
it possible to provide at public expense:

free maintenance of children at children's institutions and boarding-
schools (if parents wish);

maintenance of disabled people;

free education at all educational establishments;

free medical services for all citizens, including the supply of medicines and the treatment of sick persons at sanatoria;

rent-free housing and also free public services;

free public transport facilities;

free use of some types of communal services;

steady reduction of charges for, and, partially, free use of holiday
homes, boarding-houses, and tourist camps;

. . . boarding-houses, *tourist camps and sport facilities;*

increasingly broad provision of the population with benefits, privileges and scholarships (grants to unmarried mothers, scholarships for
students);

gradual introduction of free public catering (midday meals) at
enterprises and institutions, and for kolkhoz farmers at work.

The Soviet state will thus demonstrate to the world a truly full satisfaction of all the growing material and cultural requirements of man. The living standard of Soviet people will improve all the faster, the faster the productive forces of the country develop and labour productivity grows, and the more broadly the creative energy of the Soviet people comes into play.

The set programme can be fulfilled with success under conditions of peace. Complications in the international situation and the resultant necessity to increase defence expenditures may hold up the fulfilment of the plans for raising the living standard of the people. An enduring normalisation of international relations, reduction of military expenditures and, in particular, the realisation of general and complete disarmament under an appropriate agreement between countries, would make it possible greatly to surpass the plans for raising the people's living standard.

The fulfilment of the grand programme of improving the living standard of the Soviet people will have a world-wide historic impact. The Party calls on the Soviet people to work perseveringly, with inspiration. Every one of the working people of the Soviet Union must do his duty in the building of a communist society and in the struggle to fulfil the programme for the improvement of the people's living standard.

III. The Tasks of the Party in the Spheres of State Development and the Further Promotion of Socialist Democracy

The dictatorship of the proletariat, born of the socialist revolution, has played an epoch-making role by ensuring the victory of socialism in the U.S.S.R. In the course of socialist construction, however, it underwent changes. After the exploiting classes had been abolished, the state function of suppressing their resistance ceased to exist. The chief functions of the socialist state—organisation of the economy, culture and education—have developed in full measure. The socialist state has entered a new phase. The state has begun to grow over into a nation-wide organi-
new *period of its development*. The state . . .
sation of the working people of socialist society. Proletarian democracy is becoming more and more a socialist democracy of the people as a whole.

The working class is the only class in history that does not aim to perpetuate its power. Having brought about the complete and final victory of socialism—the first phase of communism—and the transition of society to the full-scale construction of communism, the dictatorship of the proletariat has fulfilled its historic mission and has ceased to be

indispensable in the U.S.S.R. from the point of view of the tasks of internal development. The state, which arose as a state of the dictatorship of the proletariat, has become a state of the entire people, an organ
. . . become, *in the new contemporary period,* a state . . .
expressing the interests and will of the people as a whole. Since the working class is the foremost and best organised force of Soviet society, it plays a leading role also in the period of the full-scale construction of communism. The working class will have completed its function of
. . . its *role* of
leader of society after communism is built and classes disappear.

The Party holds that the dictatorship of the working class will cease to be necessary before the state withers away. The state as an organisation embracing the entire people will survive until the complete victory of communism. Expressing the will of the people, it must organise the building up of the material and technical basis of communism, and the transformation of socialist relations into communist relations, must exercise control over the measure of work and the rate of consumption, promote welfare, protect the rights and freedoms of Soviet
. . . welfare *of the people,* protect . . .
citizens, socialist law and order and socialist property, instil in the people conscious discipline and a communist attitude to labour, protect socialist property, guarantee the defence and security of the country, promote fraternal co-operation with the socialist countries, uphold world peace, and maintain normal relations with all countries.

Vigorous extension and perfection of socialist democracy, active participation of all citizens in the administration of the state, in the management of economic and cultural development, improvement of the government apparatus, and increased control over its activity by the people constitute the main direction in which socialist statehood develops in the period of the building of communism. As socialist democracy develops, the organs of state power will gradually be transformed into organs of public self-government. The Leninist principle of democratic centralism, which ensures the proper combination of centralised leadership with the maximum encouragement of local initiative, the extension of the rights of the Union Republics and greater creative activity of the masses, will be promoted. It is essential to strengthen discipline, constantly control the activities of all the elements of the administrative apparatus, check the execution of the decisions and laws of the Soviet state and heighten the responsibility of every official for the strict and timely implementation of these laws.

1. THE SOVIETS AND PROMOTION OF THE DEMOCRATIC PRINCIPLES OF GOVERNMENT

The role of the Soviets, which have become an all-inclusive organisation

. . . which *are* an all-inclusive . . .

of the people, the embodiment of their unity, will grow as communist construction progresses. The Soviets, which combine the features of a government body and a social organisation, operate more and more like social organisations, with the masses participating in their work extensively and directly.

The Party considers it essential to perfect the forms of popular representation and promote the democratic principles of the Soviet electoral system.

In nominating candidates for election to the Soviets, it is necessary to guarantee the widest and fullest discussion of the personal and professional qualities of the candidates at meetings and in the press to ensure the election of the worthiest and most authoritative of them.

To improve the work of the Soviets and bring fresh forces into them, it is desirable that at least one-third of the total number of deputies to a Soviet should be elected anew each time so that *more hundreds of thou-*

. . . *so that* new millions . . .

sands and millions of working people may learn to govern the state.

The Party considers *systematic renewal of the leading bodies* necessary to bring a wider range of able persons into them and rule out abuses of authority by individual government officials. It is advisable to introduce the principle that the leading officials of the Union, republican and local bodies should be elected to their offices, as a rule, for not more than three consecutive terms. In those cases when the personal gifts of the official in question are generally believed to make his further activity within a leading body useful and necessary, his re-election may be allowed. His election shall be considered valid, if not a simple majority, but no less than three quarters of the votes are cast in his favour.

The Party regards the perfection of the principles of socialist democracy and their rigid observance as a most important task. It is necessary to develop more and more fully regular accountability of Soviets and Deputies to their constituents and the right of the electorate to recall ahead of term Deputies who have not justified the confidence placed in them; publicity and the free and full discussion of all important questions of government and of economic and cultural development at the meetings of Soviets; regular accountability of executive government bodies to meetings of Soviets—from top to bottom; checking the work of these bodies and control over their activity; systematic discussion by the Soviets of questions raised by Deputies; criticism of shortcomings in the work of government, economic and other organisations.

Every Deputy to a Soviet must take an active part in government affairs and carry on definite work. The role of the standing committees of the Soviets will become greater. The standing committees of the Supreme Soviets must systematically control the activities of ministries, departments, and economic councils; they must actively contribute to the implementation of the decisions adopted by the respective Supreme Soviets. To improve the work of the legislative bodies and increase control over the executive bodies, Deputies shall be periodically released from their official duties for full-time committee work.

An increasing number of questions which now come under the jurisdiction of the departments and sections of executive bodies must be gradually referred to the standing committees of the local Soviets for decision.

The rights of the local Soviets of Working People's Deputies (local self-government) will be extended. Local Soviets will make final decisions on all questions of local significance.

Special attention should be paid to the strengthening of the district bodies. As kolkhoz-co-operative and public property draw closer together, a single democratic body administering all enterprises, organisations and institutions at district level will gradually take shape.

The participation of social organisations and associations of the people in the legislative activity of the representative bodies of the Soviet state will be extended. The trade unions, the Y.C.L. and other mass organisations as represented by their all-Union and republican bodies must be given the right to take legislative initiative, that is, to propose draft laws.

Discussion by the people of draft laws and other decisions of both national and local significance must become the rule. The most important draft laws should be put to a nation-wide referendum.

The C.P.S.U. attaches great importance to improving the work of the government apparatus, which is largely responsible for the proper utilisation of all the resources of the country and the timely settlement of all questions relating to the cultural and everyday needs of the people. The Soviet government apparatus must be simple, qualified, inexpensive, efficient and free of bureaucracy, formalism and red tape.

Constant *state and public control* is an important means of accomplishing this task. In keeping with Lenin's directions, permanent control bodies must function to combine state control with public inspection at the centre and in the localities. The Party regards inspection by people's control bodies as an effective means of drawing large sections of the people into the management of state affairs, and control over the strict observance of legality, as a means of perfecting the government apparatus, eradicating bureaucracy and promptly realising proposals made by the people.

The government apparatus of the socialist state serves the people and is accountable to them. Negligence and abuse of power by an official must be resolutely combated and the official concerned must be severely punished regardless of the position he holds. It is the duty of Soviet people to see to it that legality and law and order are rigidly enforced; they must not tolerate any abuses, and must combat them.

The Party holds that democratic principles in *administration* must be developed further. The principle of electivity and accountability to representative bodies and to the electorate will be gradually extended to all the leading officials of state bodies.

An effort should be made to ensure that the salaried government staffs are reduced, that ever larger sections of the people learn to take part in administration and that work on government staffs eventually cease to constitute a profession.

While every executive must be held strictly and personally responsible for the job entrusted to him, it is necessary consistently to exercise the principle of collective leadership at all levels of the government and economic apparatus.

The broadest democracy must go hand in hand with strict observance of comradely discipline by the working people, which it must promote through control from above and from below. The important thing in the activity of all government bodies is organisational work among the masses, proper selection, testing and appraisal of officials on the strength of their practical work, and control over the actual fulfilment of the assignments and decisions of the leading bodies.

The further *promotion of socialist law and order* and the improvement of legal rules governing economic organisation, cultural and educational work and contributing to the accomplishment of the tasks of communist construction and to all-round development of the individual are very important.

The transition to communism means the fullest extension of personal freedom and the rights of Soviet citizens. Socialism has granted the working people the broadest guaranteed rights and freedoms. Communism will bring the working people further great rights and opportunities.

The Party calls for enforcing strict observance of socialist legality, for eradication of all violations of law and order, for the abolition of crime and the removal of all the causes of crime.

Justice in the U.S.S.R. is exercised in full conformity with the law.

It is based on truly democratic lines: election and accountability of the judges and people's assessors, the right to recall them before expiry of their term, the publicity of court proceedings, and the participation of prosecutors and defenders from the general public in the work of the courts, with the investigating bodies strictly observing legality and all the norms of judicial procedure, the democratic foundations of justice will be developed and improved.

There should be no room for law breakers and criminals in a society building communism. But as long as there are criminal offences, it is necessary severely to punish those who commit crimes dangerous to society, violate the rules of the socialist community and refuse to live by honest labour. Attention should be mainly focussed on crime prevention.

Higher standards of living and culture, and greater social consciousness of the people, will pave the way to the abolition of crime and the ultimate replacement of judicial punishment by measures of public influence and education. Under socialism, anyone who has strayed from the path of the working man can return to useful activity.

The whole system of government and social organisations educates the people in a spirit of voluntary and conscientious fulfilment of their duties and leads to a natural fusion of rights and duties to form the integral rules of communist society.

2. THE FURTHER HEIGHTENING OF THE ROLE OF SOCIAL ORGANISATIONS. THE STATE AND COMMUNISM

The role of social organisations increases in the period of the full-scale construction of communism. The *trade unions* acquire particular importance as schools of administration and economic management, as schools of communism. The Party will help the trade unions to take a growing share in economic management and to make the standing production conferences increasingly effective in improving the work of enterprises and exercising control over production. The trade unions shall:

work constantly to increase the communist consciousness of the masses; organise an emulation movement for communist labour and help the people in learning to manage state and social affairs; take an active part in controlling the measure of labour and rate of consumption;

encourage the activity of factory and office workers, enlisting their aid in the work for continuous technical progress, for higher productivity of labour, for the fulfilment and overfulfilment of state plans and assignments;

work steadfastly for the improvement of the skill of factory and office workers and their working and living conditions; protect the material interests and rights of the working people;

ensure that housing and cultural development plans are fulfilled and that public catering, trade, social insurance, and health resort services are improved;

ensure control over the spending of public consumption funds and over the work of all enterprises and institutions serving the people;

improve cultural services and recreation facilities for the working people; encourage physical training and sports.

The *Young Communist League,* a voluntary social organisation of the youth which helps the Party to educate young people in a communist spirit, enlist them in the practical job of building the new society and train a generation of harmoniously developed people who will live, work and manage public affairs under communism, will play a greater role. The Party regards the youth as a great creative force in the Soviet people's struggle for communism.

The Y.C.L. must display greater initiative in all fields of activity, must encourage the activity and labour heroism of the youth. Y.C.L. organisations must concentrate on educating the youth in a spirit of utmost devotion to their country, the people, the Communist Party and the communist cause, constant preparedness for labour for the good of the country and for overcoming all difficulties and improving the general education and technical knowledge of all young men and women. It is the sacred duty of the Y.C.L. to prepare young people for the defence of their socialist country, to educate them as selfless patriots capable of firmly repelling any enemy. The Y.C.L. educates the youth in a spirit of strict adherence to communist moral principles and standards. Its influence in the schools and Young Pioneer organisations must con-
work in the schools . . .
tribute actively to the moulding of a buoyant, industrious, and physically and morally sound generation.

A greater role will be played by *co-operatives*—kolkhozes, consumers', housing and other co-operative organisations—as a form of drawing the masses into communist construction, as media of communist education and schools of public self-government.

Other social associations of the working people—scientific and scientific-technical societies, rationalisers' and inventors' organisations,
. . . societies, *scientific*-rationalisers' . . .
associations of writers, artists and journalists, cultural-education organisations, and sports societies—will likewise be developed.

The Party regards it as a major task of the social organisations to promote labour emulation in every possible way, and to encourage communist forms of labour to stimulate the activity of working people in

building a communist society, to work for the improvement of the living conditions of the people. Social organisations should be induced to take
. . . people *and the satisfaction of their growing spiritual quest.* Social . . .
a greater part in managing cultural and health institutions; within the
. . . cultural, *health, and social-security institutions;* within . . .
next few years they should be entrusted with the management of theatres and concert halls, clubs, libraries, and other state-controlled cultural-education establishments; they should be encouraged to play a greater
. . . establishments; *these organizations* should . . .
part in promoting law and order, particularly through the people's volunteer squads and comradely courts.

To extend the independent activities of members of social organisations, the Party considers it necessary further to reduce their salaried staffs from top to bottom, to renew each public body by roughly as many as one-half of its members at the regular election and to consider it advisable for the leading functionaries of social organisations not to be elected, as a general rule, for more than two consecutive terms.

As socialist statehood develops, it will gradually become public *communist self-government* which will embrace the Soviets, trade unions, co-operatives, and other mass organisations of the people. This process will represent a still greater development of democracy, ensuring the active participation of all members of society in the management of public affairs. Public functions similar to those performed by the state today in the sphere of economic and cultural management will be preserved under communism and will be modified and perfected as society develops. But the character of the functions and the ways in which they are carried out will be different from those under socialism. The bodies in charge of planning, accounting, economic management, and cultural advancement, now government bodies, will lose their political character and will become organs of public self-government. Communist society will be a highly-organised community of working men. Universally recognised rules of the communist way of life will be established whose observance will become an organic need and habit with everyone.

Historical development inevitably leads to the withering away of the state. To ensure that the state withers away completely, it is necessary to provide both internal conditions—the building of a developed communist society—and external conditions—the final settlement of the
. . . conditions—*the victory and consolidation of socialism in the international arena.* [REMAINDER OF PARAGRAPH DELETED]
contradictions between capitalism and communism in the world arena in favour of communism.

3. THE STRENGTHENING OF THE ARMED FORCES AND THE DEFENCE POTENTIAL OF THE SOVIET UNION

With the wholehearted support of the entire Soviet people, the Communist Party of the Soviet Union steadfastly upholds and defends the gains of socialism and the cause of world peace, and works tirelessly to deliver mankind for all time from wars of aggression. The Leninist principle of peaceful coexistence has been, and remains, the general . . . coexistence *of states with different social systems* has . . . principle of the foreign policy of the Soviet state.

The Soviet Union perseveringly seeks to bring about the realisation of its proposals for general and complete disarmament under strict international control. But the imperialist countries stubbornly refuse to accept these proposals, and feverishly build up their armed forces. They refuse to reconcile themselves to the existence of the world socialist system, and openly proclaim their insane plans for the liquidation of the Soviet Union and the other socialist states through war. This obliges the Communist Party, the Armed Forces, the state security organs and all the peoples of the U.S.S.R. to be keenly vigilant with regard to the aggressive intrigues of the enemies of peace, always to protect peaceful labour, and to be constantly prepared to take up arms in defence of their country.

The Party maintains that as long as imperialism exists the threat of aggressive wars will remain. The C.P.S.U. regards the defence of the socialist motherland, and the strengthening of the defence potential of the U.S.S.R., of the might of the Soviet Armed Forces, as a sacred duty of the Party and the Soviet people as a whole, as a most important function of the socialist state. The Soviet Union sees it as its internationalist duty to guarantee, together with the other socialist countries. the reliable defence and security of the entire socialist camp.

In terms of internal conditions, the Soviet Union needs no army. But since the danger of war coming from the imperialist camp persists, and since complete and general disarmament has not been achieved, the C.P.S.U. considers it necessary to maintain the defensive power of the Soviet state and the combat preparedness of its Armed Forces at a level ensuring the decisive and complete defeat of any enemy who dares to encroach upon the Soviet Union. The Soviet state will see to it that its Armed Forces are powerful, that they have the most up-to-date means of defending the country—atomic and thermonuclear weapons, rockets of every range, and that they keep all types of military equipment and all weapons up to standard.

The Party educates the Communists and all Soviet people in the spirit of constant preparedness for the defence of their socialist country, of love of their armed forces. Defence of the country, and service in the
   . . . forces. *The party will by all means assist the further development and activities of the public defence organisations.* Defence . . .
Soviet Armed Forces, is the lofty and honourable duty of Soviet citizens.

The C.P.S.U. is doing everything to ensure that the Soviet Armed Forces are a well-knit and smoothly operating organism, that they have a high standard of organisation and discipline, carry out in exemplary fashion the tasks assigned them by the Party, the Government and the people, and are prepared at any moment to administer a crushing rebuff to imperialist aggressors. One-man leadership is a major principle of the organisation of the Soviet Armed Forces.

The Party will work indefatigably to train Army and Navy officers and political personnel fully devoted to the communist cause and re-
   . . . political *and technical* personnel . . .
cruited among the finest representatives of the Soviet people. It considers it necessary for the officer corps tirelessly to master Marxist-Leninist theory, to possess a high standard of military-technical training, meet all the requirements of modern military theory and practice, strengthen military discipline. All Soviet soldiers must be educated in the spirit of unqualified loyalty to the people, to the communist cause, of readiness to spare no effort and, if necessary, to give their lives in the defence of their socialist country.

Party leadership of the Armed Forces, and the increasing role and influence of the Party organisations in the Army and Navy are the bedrock of military development. The Party works unremittingly to increase its organising and guiding influence on the entire life and activity of the Army, Air Force and Navy, to rally the servicemen round the Communist Party and the Soviet Government, to strengthen the unity of the Armed Forces and the people, and to educate the soldiers in the spirit of courage, bravery and heroism, of readiness at any mo-
   . . . bravery, *heroism and friendship with the armed forces of the socialist countries,* of readiness . . .
ment to take up the defence of their Soviet country, which is building communism.

IV. The Tasks of the Party in the Field of National Relations

Under socialism the nations flourish and their sovereignty grows stronger. The development of nations does not proceed along lines of strengthening national barriers, national narrow-mindedness and egoism, as it does under capitalism, but along lines of their association, fraternal mutual assistance and friendship. The appearance of new industrial centres, the prospecting and development of mineral deposits, the virgin land development project, and the growth of all modes of transport increase the mobility of the population and promote greater intercourse between the peoples of the Soviet Union. People of many nationalities live together and work in harmony in the Soviet republics. The boundaries between the constituent republics of the U.S.S.R. are increasingly losing their former significance, since all the nations are equal, their life is based on a common socialist foundation, the material and spiritual needs of every people are satisfied to the same extent, and they are all united in a single family by common vital interests and are advancing together to the common goal—communism. Spiritual features deriving from the new type of social relations and embodying the finest traditions of the peoples of the U.S.S.R. have taken shape and are common to Soviet men and women of different nationalities.

Full-scale communist construction constitutes a new stage in the development of national relations in the U.S.S.R. in which the nations will draw still closer together until complete unity is achieved. The building of the material and technical basis of communism leads to still greater unity of the Soviet peoples. The exchange of material and cultural values between nations becomes more and more intensive, and the contribution of each republic to the common cause of communist construction increases. Obliteration of distinctions between classes and the development of communist social relations make for a greater social homogeneity of nations and contribute to the development of common communist traits in their culture, morals and way of living, to a further strengthening of their mutual trust and friendship.

With the victory of communism in the U.S.S.R., the nations will draw still closer together, their economic and ideological unity will increase and the communist traits common to their spiritual make-up will develop. However, the obliteration of national distinctions, and especially of language distinctions, is a considerably longer process than the obliteration of class distinctions.

The Party approaches all questions of national relationships arising in the course of communist construction from the standpoint of proletarian internationalism and firm pursuance of the Leninist national policy. The Party neither ignores nor over-accentuates national characteristics.

The Party sets the following tasks in the sphere of national relations:

(a) to continue the all-round economic and cultural development of *all the Soviet nations,* ensuring their increasingly close fraternal co-op-
. . . *nations and nationalities,* ensuring . . .
eration, mutual aid, unity and affinity in all spheres of life, thus achieving the utmost strengthening of the Union of Soviet Socialist Republics; to make full use of, and advance the forms of, national statehood of the peoples of the U.S.S.R.;

(b) in the economic sphere, it is necessary to pursue the line of comprehensive development of the economies of the Soviet republics, effect a rational geographic location of production and a planned working of natural wealth, and promote socialist division of labour among the republics, unifying and combining their economic efforts, and properly balancing the interests of the state as a whole and those of each Soviet republic. The extension of the rights of the Union Republics in economic management having produced substantial positive results, such measures may also be carried out in the future with due regard to the fact that the creation of the material and technical basis of communism will call for still greater interconnection and mutual assistance between the Soviet republics. The closer the intercourse between the nations and the greater the awareness of the countrywide tasks, the more successfully can manifestations of parochialism and national egoism be overcome.

In order to ensure the successful accomplishment of the tasks of communist construction and the co-ordination of economic activities, inter-republican economic organs may be set up in some zones (notably for such matters as irrigation, power grids, transport, etc.).

The Party will continue its policy ensuring the actual equality of all nations and nationalities with full consideration for their interests and devoting special attention to those areas of the country which are in need of more rapid development. Benefits accumulating in the course of communist construction must be fairly distributed among all nations and nationalities;

(c) to work for the further all-round development of the socialist cultures of the peoples of the U.S.S.R. The big scale of communist construction and the new victories of communist ideology are enriching the cultures of the peoples of the U.S.S.R., which are socialist in content and national in form. The ideological unity of the nations and nationalities is growing, and there is a rapprochement of their cultures. The historical experience of socialist nations shows that national forms do not ossify; they change, advance and draw closer together, shedding all outdated traits that contradict the new living conditions. An international culture common to all the Soviet nations is developing. The cultural treasures of each nation are increasingly augmented by works acquiring an international character.

Attaching decisive importance to the development of the socialist content of the cultures of the peoples of the U.S.S.R., the Party will *promote their further mutual enrichment and rapprochement,* the consolidation of their international basis, and thereby the formation of the future single world-wide culture of communist society. While supporting the progressive traditions of each people, and making them the property of all Soviet people, the Party will in all ways further new revolutionary traditions of the builders of communism common to all nations;

(d) to continue promoting the free development of the languages of the peoples of the U.S.S.R. and the complete freedom for every citizen of the U.S.S.R. to speak, and to bring up and educate his children, in any language, ruling out all privileges, restrictions or compulsions in the use of this or that language. By virtue of the fraternal friendship and mutual trust of peoples, national languages are developing on a basis of equality and mutual enrichment.

The voluntary study of Russian in addition to the native language is of positive significance, since it facilitates reciprocal exchanges of experience and access of every nation and nationality to the cultural gains of all the other peoples of the U.S.S.R., and to world culture. The Russian language has, in effect, become the common medium of intercourse and co-operation between all the peoples of the U.S.S.R.;

(e) to pursue consistently as heretofore the principles of internationalism in the field of national relations; to strengthen the friendship of peoples as one of the most important gains of socialism; to conduct a relentless struggle against manifestations and survivals of nationalism and chauvinism of all types, against trends of national narrow-mindedness and exclusiveness, idealisation of the past and the veiling of social contradictions in the history of peoples, and against obsolete customs
. . . against [DELETION] customs
and habits. The growing scale of communist construction calls for the continuous exchange of trained personnel among nations. Manifestations of national aloofness in the education and employment of workers of different nationalities in the Soviet republics are impermissible. The liquidation of manifestations of nationalism is in the interests of all nations and nationalities of the U.S.S.R. Every Soviet republic can continue to flourish and strengthen only in the great family of fraternal socialist nations of the U.S.S.R.

V. The Tasks of the Party in the Spheres of Ideology, Education, Instruction, Science, and Culture

Soviet society has made great progress in the socialist education of the masses, in the moulding of active builders of socialism. But even after the socialist system has triumphed there persist in the minds and behaviour of people survivals of capitalism, which hamper the progress of society.

In the struggle for the victory of communism, ideological work becomes an increasingly powerful factor. The higher the social consciousness of the members of society, the more fully and broadly their creative activities come into play in the building of the material and technical basis of communism, in the development of communist forms of labour and new relations between people, and, consequently, the more rapidly and successfully the building of communism proceeds.

The Party considers that the paramount task in the ideological field in the present period is to educate all working people in a spirit of ideological integrity and devotion to communism, and cultivate in them a communist attitude to labour and the social economy; to eliminate completely the survivals of bourgeois views and morals; to ensure the all-round, harmonious development of the individual; to create a truly rich spiritual culture. Special importance is attached by the Party to the moulding of the rising generation.

The moulding of the new man is effected through his own active participation in communist construction and the development of communist principles in the economic and social spheres, under the influence of the educational work carried out by the Party, the state, and various social organisations, work in which the press, radio, cinema, and television play an important part. As communist forms of social organisation are created, communist ideas will become more firmly rooted in life and work and in human relations, and people will develop the ability to enjoy the benefits of communism in a rational way. Joint planned labour by the members of society, their daily participation in the management of state and public affairs, and the development of communist relations of comradely co-operation and mutual support, recast the minds of people in a spirit of collectivism, industry, and humanism.

Increased communist consciousness of the people furthers the ideological and political unity of the workers, collective farmers, and intellectuals and promotes their gradual fusion in the single collective of the working people of communist society.

The Party sets the following tasks:

1. IN THE FIELD OF DEVELOPMENT OF COMMUNIST CONSCIOUSNESS

(a) **The Shaping of a Scientific World Outlook.** Under socialism and at a time when a communist society is being built, when spontaneous economic development has given way to the conscious organisation of production and social life as a whole, and when theory is daily translated into practice, the shaping of a scientific world outlook in all working

. . . in all *Soviet* working

people is of prime importance. The ideological basis of this world outlook is Marxism-Leninism, an integral and harmonious system of philosophical, economic and socio-political views. The Party calls for the education of the population as a whole in the spirit of scientific communism and strives to ensure that all working people master the ideas

. . . working people [DELETION] fully understand . . .

of Marxism-Leninism, that they fully understand the course and perspectives of world development, take a correct view of international and domestic events and consciously build their life on communist lines. Communist ideas and communist deeds should blend organically in the behaviour of every person and in the activities of all collectives and organisations.

The theoretical elaboration and timely practical solution of new problems raised by life are essential to the successful advance of society to communism. Theory must continue to illumine the road of practice, and help detect and eliminate difficulties and contradictions hindering

. . . eliminate *obstacles and difficulties* hindering

successful communist construction. The Party regards it as one of its most important duties to further elaborate Marxist-Leninist theory by studying and generalising new phenomena in the life of Soviet society and the experience of the world revolutionary working-class and liberation movements, and creatively to combine the theory and the practice of communist construction.

(b) **Labour Education.** The Party sees the development of a communist attitude to labour in all members of society as its chief educational task. Labour for the benefit of society is the sacred duty of all.

. . . duty of all *able-bodied* persons

Any labour for society, whether physical or mental, is honourable and commands respect. Exemplary labour and management in the social economy should serve to educate all working people.

Everything required for life and human progress is created by labour. Hence everyone must take part in creating the means which are indispensable for his life and work and for the welfare of society. Anyone who received any benefits from society without doing his share of work, would be a parasite living at the expense of others.

It is impossible for a man in communist society not to work, for neither his social consciousness, nor public opinion would permit it. Work according to one's ability will become a habit, a prime necessity of life, for every member of society.

(c) **The Affirmation of Communist Morality.** In the course of transition to communism, the moral principles of society become increasingly important; the sphere of action of the moral factor expands and the importance of the administrative control of human relations diminishes accordingly. The Party will encourage all forms of conscious civic self-discipline leading to the assertion and promotion of the basic rules of the communist way of life.

The Communists reject the class morality of the exploiters; in contrast to the perverse, selfish views and morals of the old world, they promote communist morality, which is the noblest and most just morality, for it expresses the interests and ideals of the whole of working mankind. Communism makes the elementary standards of morality and justice, which were distorted or shamelessly flouted under the power of the exploiters, inviolable rules for relations both between individuals and between peoples. Communist morality encompasses the fundamental norms of human morality which the masses of the people evolved in the course of millenniums as they fought against vice and social oppression. The revolutionary morality of the working class is of particular importance to the moral advancement of society. As socialist and communist construction progresses, communist morality is enriched with new principles, a new content.

The Party holds that *the moral code of the builder of communism* should comprise the following principles:

devotion to the communist cause; love of the socialist motherland and of the other socialist countries;

conscientious labour for the good of society—he who does not work, neither shall he eat;

concern on the part of everyone for the preservation and growth of public wealth;

a high sense of public duty; intolerance of actions harmful to the public interest;

collectivism and comradely mutual assistance: one for all and all for one;

humane relations and mutual respect between individuals—man is to man a friend, comrade and brother;

honesty and truthfulness, moral purity, modesty, and unpretentiousness in social and private life;

mutual respect in the family, and concern for the upbringing of children;

an uncompromising attitude to injustice, parasitism, dishonesty, and careerism;

. . . dishonesty, *careerism and greed;*

friendship and brotherhood among all peoples of the U.S.S.R.; intolerance of national and racial hatred;

an uncompromising attitude to the enemies of communism, peace and the freedom of nations;

fraternal solidarity with the working people of all countries, and with all peoples.

(d) The Promotion of Proletarian Internationalism and Socialist Patriotism. The Party will untiringly educate Soviet people in the spirit of proletarian internationalism and will vigorously promote the international solidarity of the working people. In fostering the Soviet people's love of their country, the Party maintains that with the emergence of the world socialist system the patriotism of the members of socialist society is expressed in devotion and loyalty to their own country and to the entire community of socialist countries. Socialist patriotism and socialist internationalism necessarily imply proletarian solidarity with the working class and all working people of all countries. The Party will continue perseveringly to combat the reactionary ideology of bourgeois nationalism, racism, and cosmopolitanism.

(e) All-Round and Harmonious Development of the Individual. In the period of transition to communism, there are greater opportunities of *educating a new man, who will harmoniously combine spiritual wealth, moral purity and a perfect physique.*

All-round development of the individual has been made possible by historic social gains—freedom from exploitation, unemployment and poverty, from discrimination on account of sex, origin, nationality or race. Every member of society is provided with equal opportunities for education and creative labour. Relations of dependence and inequality between people in public affairs and in family life disappear. The personal dignity of each citizen is protected by society. Each is guaranteed an equal and free choice of occupation and profession with due regard to the interests of society. As less and less time is spent on material production, the individual is afforded ever greater opportunities to develop his abilities, gifts, and talents in the fields of production, science, engineering, literature, and the arts. People will increasingly devote their leisure to public pursuits, cultural intercourse, intellectual and physical development, and artistic endeavour. Physical training and

. . . development, *scientific-technical* and . . .

sports will become part and parcel of the everyday life of people.

(f) **Elimination of the Survivals of Capitalism in the Minds and Behaviour of People.** The Party considers it an integral part of its communist education work to combat manifestations of bourgeois ideology and morality, and the remnants of private-owner psychology, superstitions, and prejudices.

The general public, public opinion, and extensive criticism and self-criticism must play a big role in combating survivals of the past and manifestations of individualism and selfishness. Comradely censure of anti-social behaviour will gradually become the principal means of doing away with manifestations of bourgeois views, customs and habits. The power of example in public affairs and in private life, in the performance of one's public duty, acquires tremendous educational significance.

The Party uses ideological media to educate people in the spirit of a scientific materialist world conception, to overcome religious prejudices without insulting the sentiments of believers. It is necessary to explain
. . . necessary *to conduct systematically broad scientific-atheistic propaganda and* to explain . . .
patiently the untenability of religious beliefs, which were engendered in the past when people were overawed by the elemental forces and social oppression and did not know the real causes of natural and social phenomena. This can be done by making use of the achievements of modern science, which is steadily solving the mysteries of the universe and extending man's power over nature, leaving no room for religious inventions about supernatural forces.

(g) **The Exposure of Bourgeois Ideology.** The peaceful coexistence of states with different social systems does not imply discon-
. . . imply *weakening* of the . . .
tinuance of the ideological struggle. The Communist Party will go on *exposing the anti-popular, reactionary nature of capitalism* and all attempts to paint bright pictures of the capitalist system.

The Party will *steadfastly propagate the great advantages of socialism and communism over the declining capitalist system.*

The Party advances the scientific ideology of communism in contrast to reactionary bourgeois ideology. Communist ideology, which expresses the fundamental interests of the working class and all working people, teaches them to struggle, to live and work for the happiness of all. It is the most humane ideology. Its ideals are to establish truly human relations between individuals and peoples, to deliver mankind from the threat of wars of extermination, and bring about universal peace and a free, happy life for all men on earth.

2. IN THE FIELD OF PUBLIC EDUCATION

The transition to communism implies training that will make people communist-minded and highly-cultured, thus fitting them for both physical and mental labour, for active work in various social, governmental, scientific, and cultural spheres.

The system of public education is so organised as to ensure that the instruction and education of the rising generation are closely bound up with life and productive labour, and that the adult population can combine work in the sphere of production with further training and education in keeping with their vocations and the requirements of society. Public education along these lines will make for the moulding of harmoniously developed members of communist society and for the solution of a cardinal social problem, namely, the elimination of substantial distinctions between mental and physical labour.

The main tasks in the field of instruction and education are:

(a) Introduction of Universal Compulsory Secondary Education. In the next decade compulsory secondary general and polytechnical eleven-year education is to be introduced for all children of school age, and eight-year education for young people engaged in the national economy who have not had the appropriate schooling; in the subsequent decade everyone is to receive a complete secondary education. Universal
. . . everyone *will* receive . . .
secondary education is guaranteed by the development of general and
. . . education *and vocational training are* guaranteed . . .
polytechnical education along with the participation of school children in socially-useful labour to the extent of their physical capacity, as well
. . . capacity, [DELETION] by a considerable . . .
as by a considerable expansion of the network of evening schools, which
. . . network of *all types of schools*
of general education, including evening . . .
provide a secondary education in off-work hours.

Secondary education must furnish a solid knowledge of the fundamentals of the basic sciences, an understanding of the principles of the communist world outlook, and a labour and polytechnical training in accordance with the rising level of science and engineering, with due regard to the needs of society and to the abilities and inclinations of the students, as well as the moral, aesthetic and physical education of a healthy rising generation.

In view of the rapid progress of science and engineering, the system of *vocational and industrial* training . . .
of industrial and vocational training should be improved continuously, so that the skills of those engaged in production may develop together

with their better general education in the social and natural sciences and with the acquisition of specialised knowledge in engineering, agronomy, medicine, and other fields.

(b) The Public Upbringing of Children of Pre-School and School Age. The communist system of public education is based on the public upbringing of children. The educational influence which the family exerts on children must be brought into ever greater harmony with their public upbringing.

The growing number of pre-school institutions and boarding-schools of different types will fully meet the requirements of all working people who wish to give their children of pre-school and school age a public upbringing. The importance of the school, which is to cultivate love of labour and knowledge in children and to raise the younger generation in the spirit of communist consciousness and morality, will increase. An honourable and responsible role in this respect falls to teachers, Y.C.L., and Young Pioneer organisations.

(c) Creation of Conditions for High-Standard Instruction and Education of the Rising Generation. The Party plans to carry out an extensive programme for the construction of schools and cultural-education establishments to meet fully the needs of education and instruction. All schools will be housed in good buildings and will go over to a one-shift time-table. They will all have study workshops and chemical, physical and other laboratories; rural schools will also have their own farming plots; large factories will have production training shops for school children. Modern facilities—cinema, radio, and television—will be widely used in schools.

For physical training and aesthetic education, all schools and extra-scholastic establishments will have gymnasiums, sports grounds and facilities for the creative endeavour of children in music, painting, sculpture, etc. The network of sports schools, sports grounds, tourist camps, skiing centres, aquatic stations, swimming-pools, and other sports facilities will be expanded in town and countryside.

(d) Higher and Secondary Special Education. In step with scientific and technical progress, higher and secondary special education, which must train highly-skilled specialists with a broad theoretical and political background, will be expanded.

Shorter working hours and a considerable improvement in the standard of living of the entire population will provide everyone with an opportunity to receive a higher or secondary special education if he so desires. The number of higher and secondary specialised schools, evening and correspondence schools in particular, as well as higher schools at factories, agricultural institutes on large state farms, people's universi-
. . . farms, [DELETION] studios, . . .
ties, studios, conservatories, etc., must be increased in all areas of the

country with the support of factories and trade unions and other social organisations. The plan is to considerably increase every year the number of students at higher and secondary specialised schools. Special education will be afforded to tens of millions of people.

3. IN THE FIELD OF SCIENCE

Under the socialist system of economy, scientific and technical progress enables man to employ the riches and forces of nature most effectively in the interests of the people, to discover new types of energy and to create new materials, to develop means of weather control, and to master outer space. Application of science in production becomes a decisive factor of rapid growth of the productive forces of society. Scientific progress and the introduction of scientific achievements into the economy will remain an object of special concern to the Party.

Most important are the following tasks:

(a) **Development of Theoretical Investigations.** The further perspectives of scientific and technical progress depend in the present period primarily on the achievements of *the key branches of natural science.* A high level of development in *mathematics, physics, chemistry, and biology* is a necessary condition for the advancement and the effectiveness of the technical, medical, agricultural, and other sciences.

Theoretical investigations will be promoted to the utmost, primarily in such decisive fields of technical progress as electrification of the whole country, comprehensive mechanisation and automation of production, the application of chemistry to the leading branches of the national
tion, *transport and communications,* the application of . . .
economy, industrial uses of atomic energy, transport and communica-
economy, *and* industrial uses of atomic energy [TRANSPOSITION] This . . .
tions. This applies to:

studying the power and fuel balance of the country, finding the best ways and means of utilising the natural sources of power, working out the scientific fundamentals of a single power grid, discovering new power sources and developing methods of direct conversion of thermal, nuclear, solar, and chemical energy into electric power, and solving problems related to control of thermonuclear reactions;

working out the theory and principles of designing new machines, automatic and telemechanical systems, intensively developing radioelectronics, elaborating the theoretical foundations of computing, control and information machines, and technically improving them;

investigating chemical processes, working out new, more efficient technologies and creating inexpensive high-quality artificial and synthetic materials for all branches of the national economy: mechanical engineering, building, the manufacture of household goods and mineral fertilisers, and creating new preparations for use in medicine and agriculture;

improving existing methods and devising new, more effective methods of prospecting minerals and making comprehensive use of natural wealth.

Big advances are to be made in the development of all the biological sciences in order successfully to solve medical problems and achieve further progress in agriculture. The main tasks to be solved by these sciences in the interests of mankind are: ascertainment of the nature of the phenomena of life, study and control of the vital processes, in

. . . life, *research into biological laws of the development of the organic world, study of the physics and chemistry of man, work on the different methods of study* . . .

particular, metabolism and heredity. Medicine must concentrate on

. . . *heredity. Michurin's teaching, which derives from the point of view that the conditions of life are leading conditions in the development of the organic universe, must be developed in breadth and depth in the biological sciences.* Medicine . . .

discovering means of preventing and conquering cancer, virulent, cardiovascular, and other dangerous diseases. It is important to study and extensively use micro-organisms in the economy and the health services, among other things for the production of foods and fodder, vitamins, antibiotics and enzymes, and for the development of new agricultural techniques.

Artificial earth satellites and spaceships have, by enabling man to penetrate into outer space, provided great opportunities of discovering new natural phenomena and laws and of investigating the planets and the sun.

In the age of rapid scientific progress, the elaboration of the philosophical problems of modern natural science on the basis of dialectical materialism, the only scientific world outlook and method of cogni-

. . . scientific [DELETION] method . . .

tion, become still more urgent.

There must be intensive development of research work in the *social sciences,* which constitute the scientific basis for the guidance of the development of society. Most important in this field is the study and theoretical generalisation of the experience gained in communist construction; investigation of the key objective laws governing the economic, political and cultural progress of socialism and its development into communism, and elaboration of the problems of communist education.

The task of economic science is to generalise new phenomena in the economic life of society, and to work out the national economic problems whose solution promotes successful communist construction. Economists must concentrate on finding the most effective ways of utilising material and labour resources in the economy, the best methods of planning and organising industrial and agricultural production, and elaborating the principles of a rational distribution of the productive forces and of the technical and economic problems of communist construction.

The investigation of the problems of world history and contemporary world development must disclose the law-governed process of mankind's advance towards communism, the change in the balance of forces in favour of socialism, the aggravation of the general crisis of capitalism, the break-up of the colonial system of imperialism and its consequences, and the upsurge of the national-liberation movement of peoples.

It is important to study the historical experience of the Communist Party and the Soviet people, tried and proved successful in practice, the objective laws of development of the world socialist system and the world Communist and working-class movement.

[ADDED PARAGRAPH] *Dialectic and historical materialism as a science of all laws of natural development, society and human thought must be further and staunchly advocated and elaborated.*

The social sciences must continue to struggle with determination against bourgeois ideology, against Right-Socialist theory and practice, and against revisionism and dogmatism; they must uphold the purity of the principles of Marxism-Leninism.

(b) **Ties Between Science and Production.** Close ties with the creative labour of the people and practical communist construction are an earnest of a fruitful development of science.

In conformity with the demands of economic and cultural develop-

. . . with the *needs* of economic . . .

ment, it is essential to extend and improve the network of research institutions, including those attached to the central bodies directing economic development and those attached to the economic councils, and the network of research laboratories and institutes at the major industrial plants and in farming areas; to develop research at higher educational establishments; to improve the geographical distribution of research institutions and higher educational establishments, and to ensure the further development of science in all the Union Republics and major economic areas.

The research institutions must plan and co-ordinate their work in the most important trends of research in accordance with the plans of economic and cultural development. The role of the collective opinion of

☆ **119** ☆

scientists in directing scientific work will increase. Free comradely discussions promoting the creative solution of pressing problems are an essential condition for scientific development.

The Party will adopt measures to extend and improve the material facilities of science and to enlist the most capable creative forces in scientific pursuits.

It is a point of honour for Soviet scientists to consolidate the advanced positions which Soviet science has won in major branches of knowledge and to take *a leading place in world science* in all the key fields.

4. IN THE FIELD OF CULTURAL DEVELOP-MENT, LITERATURE AND ART

Cultural development during the full-scale construction of Communist society will constitute the closing stage of a great cultural revolution. At this stage all the necessary ideological and cultural conditions will be created for the victory of communism.

The growth of the productive forces, progress in engineering and in the organisation of production, increased social activity of the working people, development of the democratic principles of self-government, and a communist reorganisation of everyday life depend in very large measure on the cultural advancement of the population.

Communist culture, which will have absorbed, and will develop all the best that has been created by world culture, will be a new, higher the best [DELETION] created . . .

stage in the cultural progress of mankind. It will embody the versatility and richness of the spiritual life of society, and the lofty ideals and humanism of the new world. It will be the culture of a classless society, a culture of the entire people, of all mankind.

a) **All-Round Advancement of the Cultural Life of Society.**

In the period of transition to communism, creative effort in all fields of culture becomes particularly fruitful and accessible to all members of society. Soviet literature, music, painting, cinema and theatre,
. . . cinema, *theatre and television,* and all . . .
and all the other arts, will attain higher standards in their ideological make-up and artistry. People's theatres, mass amateur art, technical invention and other forms of creative endeavour by the people will become widespread. The amateurs will produce new gifted writers,
. . . The *ascendancy of the artistic and creative activity of the masses* will . . .
artists, musicians, and actors. The development and enrichment of the arts are based on a combination of mass amateur endeavour and professional art.

The Party will work unremittingly to ensure that literature, art, and culture flourish, that every individual is given full scope to apply his abilities, that the people are educated aesthetically and develop a fine artistic taste and cultural habits.

      . . . habits. *Art must ever more inspire work and life and ennoble man.*

To provide the material basis for cultural development on a grand scale:

book publishing and the press will be vigorously developed, and the printing and paper industries will be expanded accordingly;

there will be more libraries, lecture halls and reading-rooms, the-atres, clubs, houses of culture, and cinemas;
atres, *houses of culture, clubs,* and cinemas;

the country-wide radio diffusion network will be completed; televi-sion stations covering all industrial and agricultural areas will be built;

people's universities, people's theatrical companies, and other ama-teur cultural organisations will be widely developed;

a large network of scientific and technical laboratories and of art and cinema studios will be provided for the use of all who have the inclination and ability.

The Party considers it necessary to distribute cultural institutions evenly throughout the country in order gradually to bring the cultural standard of the countryside level with that of the town and achieve rapid cultural progress in all the newly-developed areas.

[THE FOLLOWING PARAGRAPH WAS DELETED.]

High standards in urban development, in the architectural treat-ment and planning of towns and rural communities, industrial, cultural and service premises and dwellings acquire great importance. Art will inspire labour, adorn life, and ennoble man to a still greater extent.

(b) Enhancement of the Educational Role of Literature and Art.

Soviet literature and art, imbued with optimism and dynamic com-munist ideas are great factors in ideological education and cultivate in Soviet people the qualities of builders of a new world. They must be a source of happiness and inspiration to millions of people, express their will, their sentiments and ideas, enrich them ideologically and educate them morally.

The highroad of literature and art lies through the strengthening of links with the life of the people, through faithful and highly artistic depiction of the richness and versatility of socialist reality, inspired and vivid portrayal of all that is new and genuinely communist, and exposure of all that hinders the progress of society.

In the art of socialist realism, which is based on the principles of partisanship and kinship with the people, bold pioneering in the artistic depiction of life goes hand in hand with the cultivation and development of the progressive traditions of world culture. Writers, artists, musicians, theatrical workers, and film makers will have better opportunities of displaying creative initiative and skill, using manifold forms, styles, and genres.

The Communist Party shows solicitude for the proper development of literature and art and their ideological and artistic standards, helps social organisations and literary and art associations in their activities.

(c) The Expansion of International Cultural Relations.

The Party considers it necessary to expand the Soviet Union's cultural relations with the countries of the socialist system and with all other countries for the purpose of pooling scientific and cultural achievements and of bringing about mutual understanding and friendship among the peoples.

VI. Communist Construction in the U.S.S.R. and Co-operation of the Socialist Countries

The C.P.S.U. regards communist construction in the Soviet Union as a component of the building of communist society by the peoples of the entire world socialist system.

The fact that socialist revolutions took place at different times and that the economic and cultural levels of the countries concerned are dissimilar, predetermines the non-simultaneous completion of socialist construction in those countries and their non-simultaneous entry into the period of the full-scale construction of communism. Nevertheless, the fact that the socialist countries are developing as members of a single world socialist system and utilising the objective laws and advantages of this system *enables them to reduce the time necessary for the construction of socialism and offers them the prospect of effecting the transition to communism more or less simultaneously, within one and the same historical epoch.*

The first country to advance to communism facilitates and accelerates the advance of the entire world socialist system to communism. In building communism, the peoples of the Soviet Union are breaking new roads for mankind, testing their correctness by their own experience, bringing out difficulties, finding ways and means of overcoming them, and selecting the best forms and methods of communist construction.

Since the social forces—the working class, the co-operative peasantry and the people's intelligentsia—and the social forms of economy (enterprises based on the two forms of socialist property) in the Soviet Union and in the other socialist countries are of one type, there will be common basic objective laws for communist construction in the U.S.S.R. and in those countries, with due allowance made for the historical and national peculiarities of each country.

The construction of communism in the U.S.S.R. promotes the interests of every country of the socialist community, for it increases the economic might and defence potential of the world socialist camp and provides progressively favourable opportunities for the U.S.S.R. to expand its economic and cultural co-operation with the other socialist countries and increase the assistance and support it renders them.

The C.P.S.U. maintains that the existing forms of economic relations between the socialist countries—foreign trade, co-ordination of economic plans, and specialisation and combination of production—will be developed and perfected more and more.

The socialist system makes possible the abolition of the economic and cultural gap between countries inherited from capitalism, the more rapid development of the countries whose economy lagged behind under capitalism, the steady promotion of their economies and cultures with the purpose of evening up the general level of development of the socialist

. . . socialist *commonwealth*. This is . . .

countries. This is ensured by the advantages of the socialist economic system and by equality in economic relations; by mutual assistance and the sharing of experience, specifically, by reciprocal exchanges of scientific and technological achievements and by co-ordinated research; by the joint construction of industrial projects and by co-operation in the development of natural resources. All-round fraternal co-operation benefits every socialist country and the world socialist system as a whole.

It is in the best interest of socialist and communist construction that each socialist country combines the effort to strengthen and develop its national economy with the effort to expand economic co-operation of the socialist camp as a whole. The development and levelling of the economy of the socialist countries must be achieved primarily by every country using its internal resources to the full by improving the forms and methods of economic leadership, steadily applying the Leninist principles and methods of socialist economic management, and making effective use of the advantages of the world socialist system.

Material prerequisites for the construction of communism are created by the labour of the people of the country concerned and by its steadily growing contribution to the common cause—the consolidation of the socialist system. This purpose is served by the application in socialist construction of the law of planned, proportionate development; encouragement of the creative initiative and labour activity of the masses; continuous perfection of the system of the international division of labour through the co-ordination of national economic plans, specialisation and combination of production within the world socialist system on the basis of voluntary participation, mutual benefit and an overall improvement of the level of science and engineering; the study of collective experience; the promotion of co-operation and fraternal mutual assistance; strict adherence to the principles of material incentive and the all-round promotion of moral stimuli to work for the good of society; control over the measure of labour and rate of consumption.

Socialism brings peoples and countries together. In the course of extensive co-operation in all economic, socio-political and cultural fields, the common economic basis of world socialism will be consolidated.
the [DELETION] economic basis . . .

The objective laws of the world socialist system, the growth of the productive forces of socialist society, and the vital interests of the peoples of the socialist countries predetermine an increasing affinity of the various national economies. As Lenin foresaw, tendencies develop toward the future creation of a world communist economy regulated by the victorious working people according to one single plan.

The C.P.S.U. and the Communist Parties of the other socialist countries regard the following as their tasks:

in the *political* field, the utmost strengthening of the world socialist system; promotion of fraternal relations with all the socialist countries on lines of complete equality and voluntary co-operation; political consolidation of the countries of the socialist community in a joint struggle
. . . struggle *against*
imperialist aggression and for universal . . .
for universal peace and for the complete triumph of communism;

in the *economic* field, expansion of trade between the socialist countries; development of the socialist international division of labour; increasing co-ordination of long-range economic plans among the socialist countries envisaging a maximum saving of social labour and an accelerated development of the world socialist economy; the promotion of scientific and technical co-operation;

in the *cultural* field, steady development of all forms of cultural co-operation and intercourse between the peoples of the socialist countries; exchanges of cultural achievements; encouragement of joint creative effort by scientists, writers and artists; extensive measures to ensure the mutual enrichment of national cultures and bring the mode of life and the spiritual cast of the socialist nations closer together.

The C.P.S.U. and the Soviet people will do everything in their power to support all the peoples of the socialist community in the construction of socialism and communism.

VII. The Party in the Period of Full-Scale Communist Construction

As a result of the victory of socialism in the U.S.S.R. and the consolidation of the unity of Soviet society, the Communist Party of the working class has become the vanguard of the Soviet people, a Party of the entire people, and extended its guiding influence to all spheres of social life. The Party is the brain, the honour and the conscience of our epoch, of the Soviet people, the people effecting great revolutionary transformations. It looks keenly into the future and shows the people scientifically motivated roads along which to advance, arouses titanic energy in the masses and leads them to the accomplishment of great tasks.

The period of full-scale communist construction is characterised by a further *enhancement of the role and importance of the Communist Party* as the leading and guiding force of Soviet society.

Unlike all the preceding socio-economic formations, communist society does not develop sporadically, but as a result of the conscious and purposeful efforts of the masses led by the Marxist-Leninist Party. The Communist Party, which unites the foremost representatives of the work-
. . . representatives of the *working class and all* working people and is closely connected with the masses, which enjoys unbounded authority among the people and understands the laws of social development, provides proper leadership in communist construction as a whole, giving it an organised, planned and scientifically based character.

The enhancement of the role of the Party in the life of Soviet society in the new stage of its development derives from:

the growing scope and complexity of the tasks of communist construction, which call for a higher level of political and organisational leadership;

the growth of the creative activity of the masses and the participation of fresh millions of working people in the administration of state affairs and of production;

the further development of socialist democracy, the enhancement of the role of social organisations, the extension of the rights of the Union Republics and local organisations;

the growing importance of the theory of scientific communism, of its creative development and propaganda, the necessity for improving the communist education of the working people and struggling to overcome the survivals of the past in the minds of people.

There must be a new, higher stage in the development of the Party itself and of its political, ideological, and organisational work that is in conformity with the full-scale building of communism. The Party will continuously improve the forms and methods of its work, so that its leadership of the masses, of the building of the material and technical basis of communism, of the development of society's spiritual life will keep pace with the growing requirements of the epoch of communist construction.

Being the vanguard of the people building a communist society, the Party must also be in the van in the organisation of internal Party life and serve as an example and model in developing the most advanced forms of public communist self-government.

Undeviating observance of the Leninist standards of Party life and the principle of collective leadership, enhancement of the responsibility of Party organs and their personnel to the Party rank and file, promotion of the activity and initiative of all Communists and of their participation in elaborating and realising the policy of the Party, and the development of criticism and self-criticism, are a law of Party life. This is an imperative condition of the ideological and organisational strength of the Party itself, of the greater unity and solidarity of Party ranks, of . . . the [DELETION] unity . . . an all-round development of inner-Party democracy and an activisation on this basis of all Party forces, and of the strengthening of ties with the masses.

The cult of the individual, and the violations of collectivism in leadership, of inner-Party democracy and socialist legality arising out of it, are incompatible with the Leninist principles of Party life. The cult of the individual belittles the role of the Party and the masses and hampers the development of the ideological life of the Party and the creative activity of the working people.

In order to effect the Leninist principle of collective leadership consistently, to ensure a greater influx of fresh Party forces into the leading Party organs, to properly combine old and young cadres, and to rule out the possibility of an excessive concentration of power in the hands of individual officials and prevent cases of their getting beyond the control of the collective, the Party considers it necessary to carry out the following measures:

a) To introduce in practice a regular renewal, in certain proportions, of the members of all elected Party bodies—from primary organisations to the Central Committee, at the same time preserving continuity of leadership.

At all regular elections, not less than one-quarter of the members of the Central Committee of the C.P.S.U. and its Presidium shall be renewed. Presidium members shall, as a rule, be elected for not more than three successive terms. Particular Party workers may, by virtue of their generally-recognised authority and high political, organisational and other abilities, be successively elected to the leading bodies for a longer period. In that case, the respective candidate is considered elected, provided not less than three-quarters of the votes are cast for him by secret ballot.

Members of the Central Committees of the Communist Parties of Union Republics, of territorial and regional committees shall be renewed by not less than one-third at each regular election, and those of area, city and district committees, and the committees and bureaus of primary Party organisations shall be renewed by one-half. Furthermore, members of these leading Party bodies may be elected consecutively for not more than three terms, and secretaries of the primary Party organisations for not more than two consecutive terms.

A Party organisation may, in consideration of the political and professional qualities of a person, elect him to its leading body for a longer period. In that case a candidate is considered elected if not less than three-quarters of the Communists attending vote for him.

Party members not re-elected to a leading Party body on the expiration of their term may be re-elected at subsequent elections.

A decision on the removal of a member from the C.C.C.P.S.U. and other leading organs shall be adopted solely by secret ballot, and is valid when not less than two-thirds of the members of the body concerned vote in favour of the decision.

b) To extend the application of the elective principle and that of accountability in Party organisations at all levels, including Party organisations working under special conditions (Army, Navy).

c) To enhance the role of Party meetings, conferences, congresses and plenary meetings of Party committees and other collective bodies. To provide favourable conditions for a free and business-like discussion within the Party of questions concerning its policy and practical activities, for comradely discussions of controversial or insufficiently clear matters.

d) To reduce steadily the salaried Party staffs, enlisting Communists more extensively as non-salaried workers doing voluntary work.

e) To develop criticism and self-criticism to the utmost as a tried and tested method of work and a means of disclosing and rectifying errors and shortcomings and the proper education of cadres.

In the period of full-scale communist construction the role and responsibility of every Party member will steadily increase. It is the duty of a Communist, in production, in social and personal life, to be a model in the struggle for the development and consolidation of communist relations, and to observe the principles and norms of communist morality. The C.P.S.U. will reinforce its ranks with the most politically conscious and active working people, and keep pure and hold high the name of Communist.

The development of inner-Party democracy must ensure greater activity among Communists and enhance their responsibility for the realisation of the noble ideals of communism. It will promote the cultivation in them of an inner organic need to behave and act in all matters in full

. . . need *always* to behave . . .

accordance with the principles of the Party and its lofty aims.

The Party will continue to strengthen the unity and solidarity of its ranks, and to maintain the purity of Marxism-Leninism. The Party preserves such organisational guarantees as are provided by the Rules of the C.P.S.U. against all manifestations of factionalism and group activity incompatible with Marxist-Leninist party principles. *The unshakable ideological and organisational unity of the Party is the most important source of its invincibility, a guarantee for the successful solution of the great tasks of communist construction.*

The people are the decisive force in the building of communism. *The Party exists for the people, and it is in serving the people that it sees the purpose of its activity.* To further extend and deepen the ties between the Party and the people is an imperative condition of success in the struggle for communism. The Party considers it its duty always to consult the working people on the major questions of home and foreign policy, to make these questions an object of nation-wide discussion, and to attract the more extensive participation of non-members in all its work. The more socialist democracy develops, the broader and more versatile the work of the Party among the working people must be, and the stronger will be its influence among the masses.

The Party will in every way promote the extension and improvement of the work of the Soviets, the trade unions, the Y.C.L., and other mass organisations of working people and the development of the creative energy and initiative of the masses, and will strengthen the unity and friendship of all the peoples of the U.S.S.R.

The C.P.S.U. is an integral part of the international Communist and working-class movement. The tried and tested Marxist-Leninist principles of proletarian internationalism will continue to be inviolable principles which the Party will follow undeviatingly.

The Communist Party of the Soviet Union will continue to strengthen the unity of the international Communist movement, to develop fraternal ties with all the Communist and Workers' Parties and to co-ordinate its actions with the efforts of all the contingents of the world Communist movement in the joint struggle against the danger of a new world war, for the interests of the working people, for peace, democracy, and socialism.

* * *

Such is the programme of work for communist construction which the Communist Party of the Soviet Union has mapped out.

The achievement of communism in the U.S.S.R. will be the greatest victory mankind has ever won throughout its long history. Every new step made towards the bright peaks of communism inspires the working masses in all countries, renders immense moral support to the struggle for the liberation of all peoples from social and national oppression, and brings closer the triumph of Marxism-Leninism on a world-wide scale.

When the Soviet people will enjoy the blessings of communism, new hundreds of millions of people on earth will say: "We are for communism!" It is not through war with other countries, but by the example of a more perfect organisation of society, by rapid progress in developing the productive forces, the creation of all conditions for the happiness and well-being of man, that the ideas of communism win the minds and hearts of the masses.

The forces of social progress will inevitably grow in all countries, and this will assist the builders of communism.

The Party proceeds from the Marxist-Leninist proposition: History is made by the people, and communism is a creation of the people, of its energy and intelligence. The victory of communism depends on people, and communism is built for people. Every Soviet man brings the triumph of communism nearer by his labour. The successes of communist construction spell abundance and a happy life to all, and enhance the might, prestige and glory of the Soviet Union.

The Party is confident that the Soviet people will accept the new Programme of the C.P.S.U. as their own vital cause, as the greatest purpose of their life and as a banner of nation-wide struggle for the building of communism. The Party calls on all Communists, on the entire Soviet people—all working men and women, kolkhoz farmers and workers by brain—to apply their energies to the successful fulfilment of the historic tasks set forth in this Programme.

UNDER THE TRIED AND TESTED LEADERSHIP OF THE COMMUNIST PARTY, UNDER THE BANNER OF MARXISM-LENINISM, THE SOVIET PEOPLE HAVE BUILT SOCIALISM.

UNDER THE LEADERSHIP OF THE PARTY, UNDER THE BANNER OF MARXISM-LENINISM, THE SOVIET PEOPLE WILL BUILD COMMUNIST SOCIETY.

THE PARTY SOLEMNLY PROCLAIMS: THE PRESENT GENERATION OF SOVIET PEOPLE SHALL LIVE UNDER COMMUNISM!

1919

PROGRAM OF THE ALL-RUSSIAN COMMUNIST PARTY (BOLSHEVIKS)*

★★★★★★★★★★★★★★★★★★★★★★★★★★★★★★★★★

The October Revolution of October 25 (November 7), 1917, realized the dictatorship of the proletariat, which assisted by poorest peasantry or semi-proletariat, began to lay the foundation of a communist society. The course of development of revolutions in Germany and Austria-Hungary, the growth of the revolutionary movement of the proletariat in all advanced countries, the spreading of the Soviet form of this movement, that is, a form that is directed to the immediate realization of the dictatorship of the proletariat—all this proved that there had begun the era of a world-wide proletarian communist revolution.

This revolution was the inevitable outcome of the development of capitalism which still prevails in the majority of the civilized countries. Our old program, except for the incorrect designation of the party as the Social-Democratic Party, quite correctly characterizes the nature of capitalism and of bourgeois society in the following theses:

"The chief characteristic of such a (capitalist) society is the production of goods on the basis of capital, where the most important and the greatest part of the means of production and ex-

* Adopted at the Eighth Congress March 18-23, 1919. This authentic translation made at the time by the Executive Committee of the Communist International (*Communist Library* No. 6) was widely reprinted. Here it is taken from *Materials for the Study of the Soviet System*, edited by James H. Meisel and Edward S. Kozera, 2nd ed., The George Wahr Publishing Company, Ann Arbor, Michigan, 1953, pp. 100-121, and compared with the original *Programma Rossiiskoi Kommunisticheskai Partii*, Knigoizdat. "Kommunist," Moscow, 1919.

change belong to a numerically small class of people, while all the rest of the population consists of proletarians and semi-proletarians whose economic position compels them permanently or periodically to sell their labor power, i.e., to work for wages for capitalists and to create by their labor the income of the upper classes of society.

"The sphere of domination of the capitalist system of production extends more and more with the development of technical improvements which, increasing the economic importance of large enterprises, leads to the abolition of small independent manufacturers. Some of these are reduced to the state of proletarians; the part played by the remainder in social and economic life is greatly narrowed, and in some cases the small manufacturers are put into a more or less complete, more or less obvious and more or less burdensome dependence upon capital.

"The same technological progress, moreover, gives the capitalists the opportunity to apply in greater dimensions woman and child labor in production and circulation of goods. On the other hand, the development of technical improvements leads to a relative decrease in the demand for human labor on the part of the capitalists, and the supply of labor power exceeds the demand; therefore, the dependence of hired labor upon capital increases, and the degree of exploitation becomes higher.

"Such a state of affairs within bourgeois countries, together with the continual sharpening of their rivalries on the world market, makes the sale of goods, the production of which continually increases, more and more difficult. As a result of over-production industrial crises occur, which are followed by more or less lasitng periods of industrial stagnation. Over-production is the inevitable outcome of the development of productive power in bourgeois society. Crises and the periods of industrial stagnation in their turn ruin the small manufacturers still more, increase the dependence of wage labor upon capital, lead more quickly to a relative and sometimes to an absolute deterioration of the conditions of the working class.

"Thus the improvement of technique, which means an increase in the productivity of labor and the growth of social wealth, in bourgeois society leads to the increase of social inequality, widens the gulf between the rich and the poor, and leads to increased insecurity of existence, unemployment and privation for broader and broader strata of the working masses.

"Just as all these contradictions which are inherent in bourgeois society, grow and develop, so the discontent of the working and the exploited masses with the existing state of things grows also. The number and the solidarity of the proletariat increases and its struggle with the exploiters becomes sharp. At the same time, the development of technique, as a result of which means of production and exchange are concentrated in a few hands and the process of labor in capitalist enterprises becomes more collective, more and more rapidly creates the opportunity for replacing the capitalist system of production by a communist system and for bringing about a social revolution, which is the final aim of the International Communist Party, the conscious expression of the class movement.

"Social revolution, replacing private property by social production and exchange, and introducing the systematic organization of production to secure the welfare and the development of all the members of society, will abolish the division of society into classes and liberate all oppressed humanity. It will put an end to all kinds of exploitation of one section of society by the other.

"The necessary condition for a social revolution is the dictatorship of the proletariat, i.e., the proletariat must seize political power which will enable it to crush all resistance of the exploiters. The International Communist Party, the aim of which is to make the proletariat capable of fulfilling its great historic mission, organizes the proletariat into an independent political party which opposes all the bourgeois parties, leads the workmen in the class struggle, reveals to the proletariat the irreconcilable difference of interests between exploiters and exploited and explains to the proletariat the historic significance and the essential conditions of the approaching social revolution. At the same time, the International Communist Party reveals to all the rest of the toiling and exploited masses the hopelessness of their condition in capitalist society and the necessity for a social revolution for their own liberation from the yoke of capital. The party of the working class, the Communist Party, calls to the toiling and to the exploited masses who have a proletarian point of view, to join its ranks."

At the beginning of the XX century, the process of concentration and centralization of capital, destroying free competition, led to the creation of great capitalist monopolies, syndicates, cartels, trusts—which dominated economic life. The same process brought about the amalgamation of bank capital with highly concentrated industrial capital, and to the increased exportation of capital abroad. The trusts, uniting whole groups of capitalist states, began the economic partition of the world, the territories of which had already been divided between the richest countries. This period of financial capital, in which the struggle between the capitalist countries inevitably grows sharper, is the period of imperialism.

Imperialist wars therefore become inevitable, wars for markets for the sale of goods, (wars) for spheres for investing capital, for raw material and for labor power, i.e., (wars) for world domination and for power over small and weak nations. Such was the nature of the first great imperialist war of 1914-1918.

The exceedingly high stage of development of world capitalism, the replacement of free competition by capitalist, state monopolies, the setting up by banks and also by groups of capitalists of an apparatus for the regulation of production and distribution, the resulting rise in cost of living, the pressure of the combinations on the working class and the oppression of the working class by the imperialist state, the tremendous difficulties for the proletariat to carry on an economic and political struggle, and all the horrors, misery and destruction which an imperialist war brings—all this makes the failure of capitalism and the transition to the higher type of public economy inevitable.

The bourgeois governments could finish the imperialist war neither by the conclusion of a just peace nor of any kind of stable peace. Capitalism has reached the point where an imperialist war must inevitably become transformed, and is becoming transformed, into a civil war between the exploited toiling masses, headed by the proletariat, against the bourgeoisie.

The increasing pressure of the proletariat, particularly its victories in individual countries, strengthens the resistance of the exploiters and compels them to create new forms of international capitalist solidarity (League of Nations, etc.), which by organizing the systematic exploitation of all peoples on a world scale, direct all their efforts to the immediate suppression of the revolutionary movement of the proletariat of all countries.

All this inevitably leads to the blending of civil war within individual countries with the defensive wars of revolutionary countries, and the struggles of oppressed nations against the yoke of imperialist powers.

Under such conditions, the watchwords of pacifism, international disarmament, courts of arbitration, etc., are not merely reactionary utopias, but deception of the toiling classes, directed to the disarming of the proletariat and to diverting it from its own task of disarming the exploiters.

Only the proletarian communist revolution is able to lead

humanity out of the blind alley which was created by the imperialists and imperialist wars. In spite of all the difficulties the revolution will have to face, temporary failures, waves of counter-revolution—the final victory of the proletariat is inevitable.

To attain the victory of the world proletarian revolution, the fullest confidence, the closest unity and co-ordination of all revolutionary activity of the working class in all advanced countries are necessary.

These conditions cannot be realized without a complete break with and bitter opposition to the bourgeois perversion of socialism which has obtained the upper hand in the higher circles of the official social-democratic and socialist parties.

One form of this perversion is the current of opportunism and social chauvinism—socialism in name, but chauvinism in fact, disguising the defense of the interests of the bourgeoisie under the false watchwords of defense of the fatherland, particularly during the imperialist war of 1914-1918. This current of opportunism is due to the opportunities created by the robbery of colonial and weak nations by advanced capitalist states; the surplus profits acquired therefrom by the bourgeoisie enables it to bribe the upper strata of the working class by placing them in a privileged position and guaranteeing them in time of peace a tolerable existence and taking their leaders into its service. The opportunists and the social-chauvinists are the servants of the bourgeoisie and the direct enemies of the proletariat, especially now, when together with the capitalists they are suppressing by armed force the revolutionary movement of the proletariat in their own and in foreign countries.

The other form of perversion is the so-called "Centre," which is also a bourgeois perversion of socialism. This current is observed in equal degrees in all capitalist countries, and fluctuates between social-chauvinists and communists, the latter striving to preserve unity with the former and trying to revive the bankrupt II International. The new III, Communist International alone conducts the struggle of the proletariat for its emancipation, and the All-Russian Communist Party is one of its sections. This International was in fact created when the real proletarian elements of former socialist parties in different countries, particularly in Germany, formed communist parties, and was formally established in March 1919 at the first Congress in Moscow. The Communist International, which is more and more gaining the sympathies of the masses of the proletariat of all countries, not only in words but by deeds, by its political content and idealogy returns to Marxism and realizes the revolutionary teaching of Marx, now cleansed of all bourgeois-opportunistic perversions.

The All-Russian Communist Party, developing the concrete aims of the dictatorship of the proletariat with reference to Russia, the chief characteristic of which is that the majority of the population consists of petty-bourgeois strata, defines these aims as follows:

General Politics

1. A bourgeois republic, even the most democratic, sanctified by such watchwords as "will of the people," "will of the nation," "no class privilege," remains in fact, owing to the existence of private property in land and other means of production, the dictatorship of the bourgeoisie, an instrument for exploitation and oppression of the broad masses of workers by a small group of capitalists. In opposition to this, proletarian or Soviet democracy transformed mass organizations precisely of the classes oppressed by capitalism, of proletarian and poorest peasantry or semi-proletarian, i.e., the vast majority of the population, into a single and permanent basis of the state apparatus, local and central. By this act, the Soviet State realized among other things local and regional autonomy without the appointment of authorities from above, on a much wider scale than is practised anywhere. The aim of the Party is to exert the greatest efforts in order to realize fully this highest type of democracy, which to function accurately requires a continually rising standard of culture, organization and activity on the part of the masses.

2. In contrast to bourgeois democracy, which concealed the class character of the state, the Soviet authority openly acknowledges that every state must inevitably bear a class character until the division of society into classes has been abolished and all government authority disappears. By its very nature, the Soviet state directs itself to the suppression of the resistance of the exploiters, and the Soviet constitution does not stop of depriving* the exploiters of their political rights, bearing in mind that any kind of freedom is a deception if it is opposed to the emancipation of labor from the yoke of the capital. The aim of the Party of the proletariat consists in carrying on a determined suppression of the resistance of the exploiters, in struggling against the deeply rooted prejudicies concerning the absolute character of bourgeois

---

* That is, "hesitate to deprive."

rights and freedom, and at the same time explaining that deprivation of political rights and any kind of limitation of freedom are necessary as temporary measures in order to defeat the attempts of the exploiters to retain or to reestablish their privileges. With the disappearance of the possibility of the exploitation of one human being by another, the necessity for these measures will also gradually disappear and the Party will aim to reduce and completely abolish them.

3. Bourgeois democracy has limited itself to formally extending political rights and freedom, such as the right of combination, freedom of speech, freedom of press, equality of citizenship. In practice, however, particularly in view of the economic slavery of the working masses, it was impossible for the workers to enjoy these rights and privileges to any great extent under bourgeois democracy.

Proletarian democracy on the contrary, instead of formally proclaiming those rights and freedoms, actually grants them first of all to those classes which have been oppressed by capitalism, i.e., to the proletariat and to the peasantry. For that purpose the Soviet state expropriates premises, printing offices, supplies of paper, etc., from the bourgeoisie, placing these at the disposal of the working masses and their organizations. The aim of the All-Russian Communist Party is to encourage the working masses to enjoy democratic rights and liberties, and to offer them every opportunity for doing so.

4. Bourgeois democracy through the ages proclaimed equality of persons, irrespective of religion, race or nationality and the equality of the sexes, but capitalism prevented the realization of this equality and in its imperialist stage developed race and national suppression. The Soviet Government, by being the authority of the toilers, for the first time in history could in all spheres of life realize this equality, destroying the last traces of woman's inequality in the sphere of marriage and the family. At the present moment the work of the Party is principally intellectual and educational with the aim of abolishing the last traces of former inequality and prejudices, especially among the backward sections of the proletariat and peasantry.

The Party's aim is not to limit itself to the formal proclamation of woman's equality, but to liberate woman from all the burdens of antiquated methods of housekeeping, by replacing them by house-communes, public kitchens, central laundries, nurseries, etc.

5. The Soviet Government, guaranteeing to the working

masses incomparably more opportunities to vote and to recall their delegates in the most easy and accessible manner, than they possessed under bourgeois democracy and parliamentarism, at the same time abolishes all the negative features of parliamentarism, especially the separation of legislative and executive powers, the isolation of the representative institutions from the masses, etc.

In the Soviet state not a territorial district, but a productive unit (factory, mill) forms the electoral unit and the unit of the state. The state apparatus is thus brought near to the masses.

The aim of the Party consists in endeavoring to bring the Government apparatus into still closer contact with the masses, for the purpose of realizing democracy more fully and strictly in practice, by making Government officials responsible to, and placing them under the control of, the masses.

6. The Soviet state includes in its organs—the Soviets— workmen and soldiers on a basis of complete equality and unity of interests, whereas bourgeois democracy, in spite of all its declarations, transformed the army into an instrument of the wealthy classes, separated it from the masses, and set it against them, depriving the soldiers of any opportunity of exercising their political rights. The aim of the Party is to defend and develop this unity of the workmen and soldiers in the Soviets and to strengthen the indissoluble ties between the armed forces and the organizations of the proletariat and semi-proletariat.

7. The urban industrial proletariat, being the more concentrated, united and educated section of the toiling masses, hardened in battle, played the part of leader in the whole Revolution. This was evidenced while the Soviets were being created, as well as in the course of development of the Soviets into organs of authority. Our Soviet Constitution reflects this in certain privileges it confers upon the industrial proletariat, in comparison with the more scattered petty-bourgeois masses in the village.

The All-Russian Communist Party, explaining the temporary character of these privileges, which are historically connected with difficulties of socialist organization of the village, must try undeviatingly and systematically to use this position of the industrial proletariat in order closer to unite the backward and the scattered masses of the village proletarians and semi-proletarians, as well as the middle-class peasantry, as a counter-balance to narrow craft professional interests, which were fostered by capitalism among the workmen.

8. The proletarian revolution, owing to the Soviet organi-

zation of the state, was able at one stroke finally to destroy the old bourgeois, official and judicial state apparatus. The comparatively low standard of culture of the masses, the absence of necessary experience in state administration on the part of responsible workers who are elected by the masses, the pressing necessity, owing to the critical situation of engaging specialists of the old school, and the calling up to military service of the more advanced section of city workmen, all this led to the partial revival of bureaucratic practices within the Soviet system.

The All-Russian Communist Party, carrying on a resolute struggle with bureaucratism, suggests the following measures for overcoming this evil:

(1) Every member of the Soviet is obliged to perform a certain duty in state administration.

(2) These duties must change in rotation, so as gradually to embrace all the branches of administrative work.

(3) All the working masses without exception must be gradually induced to take part in the work of state administration.

The complete realization of these measures will carry us in advance of the Paris Commune, and the simplification of the work of administration, together with the raising of the level of culture of the masses, will eventually lead to the abolition of state authority.

Relations of Nationalities

9. With reference to the nationality question the All-Russian Communist Party is guided by the following theses:

(1) The principal aim is to bring into closer relations the proletarians and semi-proletarians of different nationalities, for the purpose of carrying on a general revolutionary struggle for the overthrow of the landlords and the bourgeoisie.

(2) In order to remove mistrust on the part of the working masses of the oppressed countries toward the proletariat of those states which formerly oppressed them, it is necessary to abolish all privileges of any national group, to proclaim the fullest equality of all nationalities and to recognize the rights of colonies and oppressed nations to political separation.

(3) For the same purpose, as a temporary measure toward achieving the unity of nations, the Party suggests a federative combination of all states organized on the Soviet basis.

(4) The All-Russian Communist Party regards the question as to which class expresses the desire of a nation for separation,

from a historical point of view, taking into consideration the level of historical development of the nation, i.e., whether the nation is passing from medievalism toward bourgeois democracy or from bourgeois democracy toward Soviet or proletarian democracy etc.

In any case, particular care and attention must be exercised by the proletariat of those nations which were oppressing nations, toward the prevailing national feelings of the working masses of the oppressed nations, or nations which are limited in their rights. Only by such a policy is it possible to create favorable conditions for a voluntary and real unity of different national elements of the international proletariat, as has been proved by the combination of different national Soviet republics around Soviet Russia.

Military Affairs

10. The aims of the Party with reference to military matters are defined by the following fundamental theses:

(1) In the period when imperialism is decaying and civil war is spreading, it is possible neither to retain the old army nor to construct a new one on a so-called national and non-class basis. The Red Army, as the instrument of the proletarian dictatorship, is compelled to have an undisguised class character, i.e., its ranks must be filled exclusively with proletarians and semi-proletarian sections of the peasantry. Only with the abolition of classes will this kind of army be transformed into national socialist militia.

(2) All proletarians and semi-proletarians must undergo thorough courses of military training. Military training must be introduced into the schools.

(3) The work of military training and of education of the Red Army is conducted on the basis of class solidarity and socialist education. Therefore, political commissaries chosen from devoted and trustworthy communists are as necessary as military chiefs, and communist groups must be organized in all sections of the army, in order to establish class conscious discipline and an intellectual link with the Party.

(4) As a counter-balance to the old order of things in the army, the following changes are necessary: shorter periods of barrack training, barracks to be nearer to the type of military and military-political schools, closer connection between military formations and mills, factories, trade unions and organizations of the poorest peasantry.

(5) Only commanding corps of which at first at least the

lower ranks are drawn from among class-conscious workmen and peasants, can give the necessary organization and stability to the young revolutionary army. Therefore, one of the principal aims in the construction of the army is the training of the most energetic and capable soldiers devoted to the cause of socialism, for the duties of commanders.

(6) It is necessary to make use of, and adopt on a wide scale, the practical and technical experience of the last world war. In connection with this it is necessary to attract military specialists who have gone through the training of the old army, for the organization of the army and for conducting military operations. At the same time this use of military specialists may be made on condition that political guidance and full control over military officials is concentrated in the hands of the working class.

(7) The demand that the commanding corps should be elective had great significance with reference to the bourgeois army where the military commanders were selected and trained to become an instrument of class oppression of soldiers, and through them of the working masses. This demand has no significance with reference to the Red Army, composed of class-conscious workmen and peasants. The possibility of combining the election and appointment of the commanders of the revolutionary class army is determined exclusively by practical considerations, and depends upon the standard of organization attained, the degree of solidarity of the parts of the army, the effective supply of commanders, etc.

Jurisprudence

11. Proletarian democracy, taking power into its own hands and finally abolishing the organs of domination of the bourgeoisie —the former courts of justice—has replaced the formula of bourgeois democracy: "judges elected by the people" by the class watchword: "judges elected from the working masses and only by the working masses," and has applied the latter in the organization of law courts, having extended equal rights to both sexes, both in the election of judges and in the exercise of the functions of judges.

In order to induce the broad masses of the proletariat and the poorest peasantry to take part in the administration of justice, a bench of jury-judges sitting in rotation under guidance of a permanent judge is introduced and various labor organizations and trade unions must impanel their delegates.

The Soviet Government has replaced the former endless series of courts of justice with their various divisions, by a very simplified, uniform system of Peoples' Courts, accessible to the population, and freed of all useless formalities of procedure.

The Soviet Government, abolishing all the laws of the overthrown Governments, commissioned the judges elected by the Soviets to carry out the will of the proletariat in compliance with its decrees, and in cases of absence or incompleteness of decrees, to be guided by socialist conscience.

Constructed on such a basis, the courts of justice have already led to a fundamental alteration of the character of punishment, introducing conditional sentences on a wide scale, applying public censure as a form of punishment by obligatory labor with the retention of freedom, and prisons by institutions for training, and applying the principle of comradely tribunals.

The All-Russian Communist Party, in order to assist the further development of the courts of justice on these lines, will strive to induce all workmen without exception to perform judicial duties and finally replace the system of punishment by measures of an educational character.

Public Education

12. The All-Russian Communist Party in the field of education sets itself the task of bringing to fulfillment the work begun by the October Revolution of 1917, of transforming the school from an instrument of class domination of the bourgeoisie into an instrument for the abolition of the class divisions of society, into an instrument for a communist regeneration of society.

In the period of the dictatorship of the proletariat, i.e., in the period of preparation of conditions suitable for the realization of communism, the school must be not only the conductor of communist principles, but it must become the conductor of the intellectual, organizational and educational influences of the proletariat, to the semi-proletariat and non-proletarian sections of the toiling masses, in order to educate a generation capable of establishing communism. The immediate aim in this direction is at the present time the further development of the following principles of school and educational work, already established by the Soviet Government:

(1) The introduction of free and compulsory general and technical education (instruction in the theory and practice of the principle branches of production) for all children of both sexes up to the age of 17.

(2) The establishment of a system of pre-school institutions: nurseries, kindergartens, homes, etc., to improve the social development of women and assist in their emancipation.

(3) Full realization of the principle of a uniform industrial school with instruction in the native language, with co-education for children of both sexes, free from religious influence; a school where tuition is closely connected with socially useful labor and which prepares members of a communist society.

(4) The supply of all pupils with food, clothes, boots and school appliances at the cost of the state.

(5) The preparation of a new staff of teachers who are imbued with the ideas of communism.

(6) Bringing the toiling masses to take an active part in educational work (the development of councils of public education, mobilization of educated people, etc.).

(7) General state assistance to self-education and the intellectual development of workers and peasants (creation of a system of institutions for education outside of the schools, such as libraries, schools for adults, people's palaces and universities, courses of lectures, cinemas, studios, etc.).

(8) Spreading on a large scale of professional education for persons from the age of 17, in connection with technical knowledge.

(9) Making all universities accessible to all desiring to study, particularly to workmen; attracting all people able to lecture to become instructors in these universities; abolishing all artificial barriers standing in the way of young scientists reaching professional chairs; financial support of students in order to offer the proletarians and the peasants the fullest opportunity to take advantage of the universities.

(10) Opening and making accessible to the toiling classes all the art treasures which were created by the exploitation of their labor, and which were formerly at the exclusive disposal of the exploiters.

(11) The development of the propaganda of communist ideas on a wide scale and for that purpose the utilization of state resources and apparatus.

Religion

13. With reference to religion, the All-Russian Communist Party does not content itself with the already decreed separation of church from state, i.e., measures which are one of the items

of the programs of bourgeois democracy, which was, however, never fulfilled owing to many and various ties binding capital with religious propaganda.

The All-Russian Communist Party is guided by the conviction that only the realization of conscious and systematic social and economic activity of the masses will lead to the disappearance of religious prejudices. The aim of the Party is finally to destroy the ties between the exploiting classes and the organization of religious propaganda, at the same time helping the toiling masses actually to liberate their minds from religious superstitions, and organizing on a wide scale scientific-educational and anti-religious propaganda. It is however, necessary carefully to avoid offending the religious susceptibilities of believers, which leads only to the strengthening of religious fanaticism.

Economics

1. Undeviatingly to continue and finally to realize the expropriation of the bourgeoisie which was begun and which has already been largely completed, the transforming of all means of production and exchange into the property of the Soviet republic, i.e., the common property of all toilers.

2. All possible increase of the productive forces of the country must be considered the fundamental and principal point upon which the economic policy of the Soviet Government is based. In view of the disorganization of the country, everything in other spheres of life must be subordinated to the practical aim immediately and at all costs to increase the quantity of products required by the population. The successful functioning of every Soviet institution connected with public economy must be gauged by the practical results in this direction.

At the same time it is necessary in the first place to pay attention to the following:

3. The decaying imperialist system of economy left to the Soviet state a heritage of chaos in the organization and management of production, which hampered it in the first period of construction. The more imperative therefore becomes the fundamental task of concentrating all the economic activity of the country according to a general state plan; the greatest concentration of production for the purpose of amalgamating it into various branches and groups of branches, and centralizing it in the most productive units, and for the purpose of rapidity in carrying out economic achievements; the most efficient arrangement of the pro-

ductive apparatus and a rational and economical utilization of all material resources of the country.

It is necessary to extend economic co-operation and political ties with other nations, and try at the same time to establish a general economic plan with those which have already adopted the Soviet system.

4. It is necessary to utilize small-scale and handicraft industry to the widest extent by placing Government orders with handicraftsmen; to include handicraft and small-scale industry in the general scheme of supplying raw materials and fuel, as well as financial assistance, on condition that individual handicraftsmen, handicraft associations, productive co-operative societies and small enterprises amalgamate into large productive and industrial units; to encourage such amalgamations by offering them economic privileges, which together with other measures are aimed at defeating the aspirations of the handicraftsmen to become small manufacturers, and thus painlessly replace the backward forms of production by a higher form of large-scale mechanized industry.

5. The organizing apparatus of socialized industry must first of all rest upon the trade unions. The latter must free themselves from their narrow guild outlook and transform themselves into large productive combinations which will unite the majority, and finally all the workmen of a given branch of production.

Trade unions, being already according to the laws of the Soviet Republic and established practice participants in all local and central organs for managing industry, must actully concentrate in their hands the management of the whole system of public economy as an economic unit. The trade unions, thus securing an indissoluble union between the central state administration, the public system of economy and the masses of toilers must induce the latter to take part in the immediate management of production. The participation of trade unions in the management of production and the attraction by them of the broad masses are, moreover, the principal means to carry on a struggle against bureaucracy in the economic apparatus of the Soviet state, and afford the opportunity of establishing a really democratic control over the results of production.

6. A maximum utilization of all labor power existing in the state, its regular distribution and redistribution among various territorial regions as well as among various branches of production, is necessary for the systematic development of public economy, and must be the immediate aim in the economic policy of the Soviet Government. This aim can be attained in closest

co-operation with the trade unions. For the purpose of performing certain social duties, a general mobilization of all capable of work must be carried out by the Soviet Government, aided by the trade unions, on a much wider scale and more systematically than has been done hitherto.

7. In the state of the complete disorganization of the capitalist system of labor, the productive forces of the country can be restored and developed, and a socialist system of production strengthened, only on the basis of the comradely discipline of toilers, maximum activity on their part, responsibility and the strictest mutual control over the productivity of labor.

Persistent systematic effort directed to the re-education of the masses is necessary to attain this aim. This work is now made easier as the masses in reality see the abolition of capitalists, landowners, and merchants, and from their own experience draw the conclusion that the level of their prosperity depends entirely upon the productivity of their own labor.

The trade unions play the principal part in the work of establishing a new socialist discipline. Breaking with old conventions, they must put into practice and try various measures, such as the establishment of control, standards of production, the introduction of responsibility of the workmen before special labor tribunals, etc., for the realization of this aim.

8. Moreover, for the development of the productive forces the immediate wide and full utilization of all specialists in science and technology left to us by capitalism, is necessary, in spite of the fact that the majority of the latter are inevitably imbued with bourgeois ideas and habits. The Party considers that the period of sharp struggle with this group, owing to organized sabotage on their part, is ended as the sabotage is in the main subdued. The Party, in closest contact with the trade unions, will follow its former line of action, i.e., on the one hand it will make no political concessions to this bourgeois section and mercilessly suppress any counter-revolutionary moves on its part, and on the other hand it will carry on a merciless struggle against the pseudo-radical, but in reality, ignorant and conceited opinion that the working class can overcome capitalism and the bourgeois order without the aid of bourgeois specialists or taking advantage of their knowledge, without passing, together with them, through a thorough schooling of hard work.

While striving toward equal remuneration of labor and to realize communism, the Soviet Government does not regard the immediate realization of such equality possible at the moment, when only the first steps are being taken towards replacing capitalism by communism. It is therefore necessary to maintain a higher remuneration for specialists in order that they should work not worse but better than before, and for that purpose it is not possible to abandon the system of bonuses for the most successful, particularly for work of organization.

To the same degree, it is necessary to place the bourgeois experts in a setting of comradely common effort, working hand in hand with the mass of average workers, led by class conscious communists, and thus to assist the mutual understanding and unity between manual and intellectual workers formerly separated by capitalism.

9. The Soviet authority has already adopted a number of measures directed to the development of science and for bringing it into closer contact with production, viz.: the creation of a number of new scientific institutions, laboratories, stations for research and experimental production, in order to verify new technical methods, improvements and inventions, taking stock of and organizing all scientific forces. The All-Russian Communist Party, supporting all these measures, strives to attain their further development and to create more favorable conditions for scientific work in connection with the increase of the productive forces of the country.

Agriculture, Rural Economy

10. The Soviet Government, having carried out the complete abolition of private property in land, has already begun to carry out a series of measures directed to the organization of socialist agriculture on a wide scale. The principal measures are the following: (1) The establishment of Soviet farms, i.e., large socialist economic enterprises; (2) Assistance to societies as well as associations for common land cultivation; (3) Organization by the state of the cultivation of all uncultivated acreage; (4) State mobilization of all agricultural forces for the purpose of taking the most energetic measures to increase agricultural productivity; (5) The support of agricultural communes as absolutely voluntary associations of agricultural laborers for the purpose of conducting a communal system of economy on a large scale.

The All-Russian Communist Party, considering all these measures as the only way toward the absolutely indispensable increase of productivity of agricultural labor, strives to extend them to the more backward regions of the country, and as further steps in this direction the All-Russian Communist Party particularly supports:

(1) All possible encouragement by the state of agricultural co-operative societies engaged in the processing of agricultural products.

(2) The introduction of a system of melioration on a wide scale.

(3) The systematic supply on a wide scale of agricultural implements through special establishments, to the poorest and the middle-class peasantry.

The All-Russian Communist Party, taking into consideration that the small scale system of agriculture will continue for a considerable time, strives to carry out a series of measures directed to the increase of productivity of the peasant enterprise. The measures are: (1) The regulation of the exploitation of land by the peasants (abolition of scattered fields, etc.); (2) The supply to the peasantry of improved seeds and artificial manure; (3) The improvement of the breed of cattle; (4) The dissemination of agricultural information; (5) Agricultural aid to the peasantry; (6) The repair of peasants' agricultural implements in Soviet workshops; (7) The establishment of loan centers, experimental stations, exhibition-fields, etc.; (8) The improvement of peasant lands.

11. The opposition between the town and the village is one of the chief causes of the economic and cultural backwardness of the village. In periods of serious crisis, such as the present, this opposition places the town as well as the village before the immediate danger of degeneration and destruction. The All-Russian Communist Party sees in the abolition of this opposition one of the principal tasks of communist construction, and among other measures considers essential the systematic attraction of industrial workmen to communist construction in agriculture, and greater activity on the part of the already established "Workmen's Committees of Assistance," etc.

12. The All-Russian Communist Party in its work in the village, as formerly, looks for support to the proletarian and semi-proletarian groups in it, and in the first place organizes these into an independent force, creating Party circles in the village, organizations of the rural poor, special types of trade unions of village proletarians and semi-proletarians, and so on, bringing them into closer contact with the urban proletarians, freeing them from the influence of the rural bourgeoisie and the interests of small property-holders.

The relation of the All-Russian Communist Party to the rural bourgeois elements is one of carrying on a resolute struggle against their attempts at exploitation, and suppressing their resistance to the Soviet policy.

The policy of the All-Russian Communist Party with reference to the middle-class peasantry consists in gradually and systematically attracting it to the work of socialist construction. The Party's aim is to separate this section from the kulaks (rich peasants), by giving consideration to its needs, to bring it over to the side of the proletariat, to struggle against its backwardness by means of education and not by means of suppression, in all cases where the vital interests of this section are involved to come to an agreement with it, making concessions to it on questions related to method of realizing socialist reorganization.

Distribution

13. In the field of distribution, the task of the Soviet Government at the present time is undeviatingly to replace private trade by a systematic distribution of products on a national scale. The aim is to organize the population into a single network of consumers' communes, which will be able with the greatest rapidity, systematically, economically and with the least expenditure of labor, to distribute all necessary products, strictly centralizing the whole apparatus for distribution.

The already existing general and workmen's co-operative societies, which are the largest organizations of consumers and which the development of capitalism has made a most efficient apparatus for distribution on a large scale, will become the basis of the communes of consumers and their groupings.

The All-Russian Communist Party, considering more correct on principle the further communist development of the co-operative apparatus and not its abolition, must systematically continue its policy: to make the work in co-operative societies obligatory for all members of the Party, to conduct them with the aid of trade unions on a communist basis, to develop among the workers in co-operative societies initiative and discipline, to strive toward the aim that the whole population belong to co-operative societies, combined into one co-operative embracing all Soviet Russia and finally—and most essential—to see that the influence of the proletariat on other groups of toilers should always prevail, and introduce measures facilitating and realizing the transformation of petty-bourgeois co-operatives of the old capitalist type into communes of consumers conducted by the proletariat and semi-proletariat.

Money and Banking

14. The Soviet Government in Russia, avoiding the mistakes of the Paris Commune, immediately expropriated the State Bank, then proceeded to the nationalization of private commercial banks and combined the nationalized banks and saving banks with the State Bank, thus laying the foundation of a single national bank of the Soviet Republic and transforming the banks from an instrument of economic domination of financial capital and of the political domination of exploiters, into an organ of power of the workers, and a lever of economic revolution. The All-Russian Communist Party considers its aim to be the final accomplishment of the work begun by the Soviet Government and regards the following principles as paramount:

(1) The monopolization of all banking by the Soviet State.

(2) A complete alteration and simplification of bank transactions by transforming the banks into an apparatus for uniform accounting and general bookkeeping of the Soviet Republic. The organization of a systematic public economy will lead to the abolition of the bank and to the transformation of it into a central bookkeeping department of the communist society.

15. In the first period of transition from capitalism to communism, while communist production and distribution of products is not yet organized, it is impossible to abolish money. Under such conditions the bourgeois sections of society are able to utilize money, which still remains private property, for the purpose of speculation, profiteering and robbery of the toilers. The All-Russian Communist Party strives toward the adoption of a series of measures which will render it possible to extend the field of operations without the aid of money and which will lead to the abolition of money, such as the compulsory depositing of money in the public bank; the introduction of budget books; the replacing of money by checks, short-term tickets for procuring products, and so on.

Finance

16. In the period of the beginning of the socialization of the means of production expropriated from the capitalists, the state ceases to be a parasitic apparatus ruling the process of produc-

tion: it begins to become transformed into an organization performing the function of managing the economic system of the country, and to that extent the state budget becomes the budget of public economy as a whole.

Under such circumstances the balancing of state revenues and expenditures can be realized on the condition that state production and distribution of products are arranged in the most efficient manner. The All-Russian Communist Party with reference to the covering of immediate state expenditure in the period of transition, defends the transition from the system of levies imposed on the capitalists which was historically necessary and legal in the period of social revolution, to the progressive income and property tax. As this tax becomes obsolete, owing to the general expropriation of the propertied class, state expenditure must be met by the direct conversion of a part of the income derived from the various state monopolies, into state revenue.

Housing

17. The Soviet Government, in trying to solve the housing problem which was particularly sharpened during the war, has expropriated completely all the houses of capitalist owners, and handed them over to the municipal Soviets; has removed in mass the workmen from the suburbs into bourgeois houses; handed over the best houses to the workmen's organization, undertaking the maintenance of these at the expense of the State; and has arranged for the supply of furniture to workmen's families.

The aim of the All-Russian Communist Party is to exert the greatest effort for the improvement of the housing conditions of the toiling masses without infringing on the interests of non-capitalist home-ownership; the abolition of over-crowding in unsanitary quarters; the abolition of inadequate housing, the rebuilding of old and the building of new houses which will be in conformity with the new conditions of life of the working masses, and the rational resettlement of the working masses.

Protection of Labor and Social Security

The establishment of the dictatorship of the proletariat for the first time made it possible to realize fully the minimum program of all socialist parties in the sphere of the protection of labor.

The Soviet Government has introduced by legislative enactment and ratified in the "Code of Labor Laws" a maximum eight-
hour day for all workmen, and a six-hour day for persons under
18 years of age and those working in unhealthy branches of production, and for miners; a 42-hour uninterrupted rest every week
for all toilers; the prohibition of continuous overtime; the prohibition of employment of young persons under 16; the prohibition
of night work, particularly in harmful branches of production, for
all women and males under 18; the exemption from work of preg-
nant women 8 weeks before and 8 weeks after confinement, with
the maintenance of full wages together with free medical assistance and medicine; permission to working women of not less
than half an hour every three hours for nursing their babies, and
supplementary subsidies to all nursing mothers; factory and sanitary inspection elected by the trade union councils.

The Soviet Government by legislative enactment has introduced complete social maintenance of all workmen not exploiting
the labor of others, and in all cases of loss of capacity for work,
and for the first time in the world has introduced unemployment
insurance of workmen at the cost of employers and of the state,
granting complete self-administration to those who are maintained
and with the participation of trade unions.

Moreover, the Soviet Government in some respects has gone
further than the minimum program and provided in the same
"Code of Labor Laws" for the participation of the workmen's organizations in the discussion of questions referring to the hiring
and discharging of workmen; a month's holiday for all workmen
who have worked continually for not less than a year, with the
maintenance of wages; the state regulation of wages according to
rates worked out by trade unions; the duty of certain organs such
as the Soviet and trade union departments for the distribution
and regulation of labor power, to provide work for unemployed
workmen.

The extreme destruction caused by the war and the pressure of world imperialism have compelled the Soviet Government
to depart from the code in the following instances: to allow
overtime in exceptional cases, but not exceeding 50 days in the
course of one year; to permit youths between 14 and 16 to work,
but the length of their working day not to exceed 4 hours; tem-
porarily to reduce holidays from a month to a fortnight; to increase the hours of night work to 7.

The All-Russian Communist Party must carry on an extensive propaganda for the participation of all workmen in the reali-

zation of all these measures for the protection of labor, for which purpose it is necessary:

(1) To make the work of organization and extension of labor inspection more intensive by choosing and preparing for that purpose active workers from among the workmen and to extend inspection to small-scale and home industry.

(2) To abolish completely child labor and further to decrease the working hours for young persons.

In addition the All-Russian Communist Party's task is to establish:

(1) With the general increase of productivity of labor the six-hour working day as a maximum without reduction of wages, but on condition that all workers must devote two hours' overtime without pay to the study of the theory of trade and industry, to practical training for state administration and to military drill.

(2) The introduction of the premium bonus system for the increase of labor productivity.

The All-Russian Communist Party in the sphere of social security strives to organize on a large scale the state support not only of war victims and victims of various catastrophes, but the victims of abnormal social relations. The Party also conducts a struggle against parasitism and idleness and sets itself the task of bringing back to a life of work any who have been dislodged from work.

Protection of Public Health

The All-Russian Communist Party proposes as the starting point in its work for the protection of public health, the realization of sanitary measures on a large scale for the purpose of preventing the spreading of disease. The dictatorship of the proletariat has already made it possible to carry out a series of measures, the realization of which was impossible in bourgeois society: the nationalization of drug stores, of large private medical institutions, of health resorts, compulsory work for all medical men and women, and so on.

In conformity with the above the All-Russian Communist Party sets as its immediate task:

(1) To carry out in the interests of the toilers, sanitary measures on a large scale, such as:

(a) Sanitation of centers of population (guarding of soil, water and air).

(b) Setting up communal feeding on a scientific and hygienic basis.

(c) The organization of measures preventing the development and spreading of infectious diseases.

(d) The introduction of sanitary legislation.

(2) The struggle with social diseases (consumption, venereal diseases, alcoholism, etc.).

(3) Free trained medical assistance and medical supplies accessible to all.

1961

RULES OF THE COMMUNIST PARTY OF THE SOVIET UNION*

✶✶✶✶✶✶✶✶✶✶✶✶✶✶✶✶✶✶✶✶✶✶✶✶✶✶✶✶✶✶✶✶✶✶

The Communist Party of the Soviet Union (CPSU) is the tried and tested militant vanguard of the Soviet people, which unites, on a voluntary basis, the more advanced, the politically more conscious section

* Embassy of the Union of Soviet Socialist Republics, Press Department, Washington, D.C. Press Release No. 176, August 7, 1961. Changes made at the XXII Congress of the CPSU on October 31, 1961, are those reported in *Izvestiia* on November 3, 1961, and translated by the Editor of this book for incorporation into this text. **Changes are indicated by interlinear insertions.**

✶✶✶✶✶✶✶✶ **1961**▲ 　　▼**1952** ✶✶✶✶✶✶✶✶

1952 (1956)

RULES OF THE COMMUNIST PARTY OF THE SOVIET UNION*

✶✶✶✶✶✶✶✶✶✶✶✶✶✶✶✶✶✶✶✶✶✶✶✶✶✶✶✶✶✶✶✶✶✶

I. The Party, Party Members, Their Duties and Rights

1. The Communist Party of the Soviet Union is a voluntary militant union of like-minded people, Communists, consisting of members of the working class, working peasants and working intellectuals.

The Communist Party of the Soviet Union, having organized

* Adopted at the XIX Congress of the Communist Party of the Soviet Union in 1952. Foreign Language Publishing House, Moscow, 1953. Amended at the XX Party Congress in 1956. *Pravda*, February 25, 1956.

of the working class, collective-farm peasantry and intelligentsia of the USSR.

Founded by V. I. Lenin as the vanguard of the working class, the Communist Party has travelled a glorious road of struggle, and brought the working class and the working peasantry to the victory of the Great October Socialist Revolution and to the establishment of the dictatorship of the proletariat in the USSR. Under the leadership of the Communist Party, the exploiting classes were abolished in the Soviet Union, and the moral and political unity of Soviet society has taken shape and grown in strength. Socialism has triumphed completely and finally. The Communist Party, the party of the working class, has today become the party of the Soviet people as a whole.

The Party exists for, and serves, the people. It is the highest form of socio-political organization, and is the leading and guiding force of Soviet society. It directs the great creative activity of the Soviet people, and imparts an organized, planned, and scientifically-based character to their struggle to achieve the ultimate goal, the victory of communism.

The CPSU bases its work on the unswerving adherence to the Leninist standards of Party life—the principle of collective leadership, the promotion, in every possible way, of inner-party democracy, the activity and initiative of the Communists, criticism and self-criticism.

Ideological and organizational unity, monolithic cohesion of its ranks, and a high degree of conscious discipline on the part of all Communists are an inviolable law of the CPSU. All manifestations of fac-

******** **1961** ▲   ▼ **1952** ********

an alliance of the working class and the labouring peasantry, achieved, as a result of the Great October Socialist Revolution of 1917, the overthrow of the power of the capitalists and landlords, the establishment of the dictatorship of the proletariat, the elimination of capitalism and the abolition of the exploitation of man by man, and ensured the building of a socialist society.

The principal objects of the Communist Party of the Soviet Union today are to build a communist society through gradual transition from socialism to communism, continuously to raise the living and cultural standards of society, to educate the members of society in the spirit of internationalism and fraternal ties with the working people of all countries, and to strengthen to the utmost the active defence of the Soviet Motherland against aggressive actions on the part of its enemies.

tionalism and group activity are incompatible with Marxist-Leninist Party principles, and with Party membership.

In all its activities, the CPSU is guided by Marxist-Leninist theory and the Program based on it, which defines the fundamental tasks of the Party for the period of the construction of communist society.

In creatively developing Marxism-Leninism, the CPSU vigorously combats all manifestations of revisionism and dogmatism, which are profoundly alien to revolutionary theory.

The Communist Party of the Soviet Union is an integral part of the international communist and working-class movement. It firmly adheres to the tried and tested Marxist-Leninist principles of proletarian internationalism; it actively promotes the unity of the international communist movement as a whole, and of the fraternal ties with the great army nist *and workers'* movement . . .*
of the Communists of all countries.

I. Party Members, Their Duties and Rights

1. Membership in the CPSU is open to any citizen of the Soviet Union who accepts the Program and Rules of the Party, takes an active part in communist construction, works in one of the Party organizations, carries out all Party decisions, and pays membership dues.

2. It is the duty of a Party member:

(A) to work for the creation of the material and technical basis of communism; to serve as an example of the communist attitude toward labor; to raise labor productivity; to take the initiative in all that is new and progressive; to support and propagate advanced methods; to

* Interlinear passages give the changes from the draft version of the Rules.

******** **1961** ▲　　▼ **1952** ********

2. Membership of the Communist Party of the Soviet Union is open to any working citizen of the Soviet Union who does not exploit the labour of others, accepts the Party's Program and Rules, actively helps to carry them into effect, works in one of the organizations of the Party and fulfils all Party decisions.

Party members shall pay the established membership dues.

3. It is the duty of a Party member:

a. To protect the unity of the Party might and main, as the chief requisite for its power and strength;

b. To be an active fighter for the implementation of **Party**

☆　**156**　☆

master techniques, to improve his skills; to protect and increase socialist social property, the mainstay of the might and prosperity of the Soviet country; [cf. Art. 3.c, 1952 Rules]

(B) to put Party decisions firmly and steadfastly into effect; to explain the policy of the Party to the masses; to help strengthen and multiply the Party's bonds with the people; to be considerate and attentive to people; to respond promptly to the needs and requirements of the working people;

(C) to take an active part in the political affairs of the country, in the administration of state affairs, and in economic and cultural development; to set an example in the fulfillment of his public duty; to assist in developing and strengthening communist social relations; [cf. Art. 3.d, 1952 Rules]

(D) to master Marxist-Leninist theory, to improve his ideological knowledge, and to contribute to the molding and education of the man of communist society; to combat all manifestations of bourgeois ideology,

. . . combat *decisively* all . . .

remnants of a private-property psychology, and other survivals of the

. . . psychology, *religious prejudices*, and . . .

past; to observe the rules of communist morality, and to give public interests precedence over his own; [cf. Art. 3.e, 1952 Rules]

✶✶✶✶✶✶✶ **1961** ▲   ▼ **1952** ✶✶✶✶✶✶✶

decisions. It is not enough for a Party member merely to agree with Party decisions; it is incumbent upon him to strive actively to have them put into effect. A passive and formal attitude on the part of Communists towards Party decisions undermines the Party's efficiency and is therefore incompatible with continuance in its ranks;

c. To set an example in work, to master the technique of his job, constantly to improve his trade or professional skill, and assiduously to protect and fortify socialist social property as the sacred and inviolable foundation of the Soviet system;

d. Constantly to strengthen the ties with the masses, promptly to respond to the needs and requirements of the working people, and to explain to the non-party masses the policy and decisions of the Party, always remembering that the strength and invincibility of our Party lies in its vital and unbreakable bond with the people;

e. To raise his level of political understanding and to broaden his knowledge of the principles of Marxism-Leninism;

☆ **157** ☆

(E) to be an active proponent of the ideas of socialist internationalism and Soviet patriotism among the masses of the working people; to
combat survivals of nationalism and chauvinism; to contribute by word
and by deed to the consolidation of the friendship of the peoples of the
USSR and the fraternal bonds linking the Soviet people with the peoples of the socialist countries, with the proletarians and other working
people in all countries;

(F) vigorously to protect the ideological and organizational unity
(F) vigorously to *strengthen* the . . .
of the Party; to safeguard the Party against the infiltration of people
unworthy of the lofty name of Communist; to be truthful and honest
with the Party; to display vigilance, to guard Party and state secrets;
[cf. Art. 3.a, i, j, 1952 Rules]

(G) to develop criticism and self-criticism, boldly to lay bare shortcomings and strive for their removal; to combat ostentation, conceit,
complacency and parochial tendencies; firmly to rebuff all attempts at
suppressing criticism; to resist all actions injurious to the Party and the

✶✶✶✶✶✶✶✶ **1961** ▲   ▼ **1952** ✶✶✶✶✶✶✶✶

f. To observe Party and state discipline, which is equally
binding on all Party members. There cannot be two disciplines in
the Party—one for leaders, the other for rank-and-file members.
The Party has one discipline, one law for all Communists, irrespective of their past services or the positions they occupy. Violation of Party or state discipline is a serious evil, which is detri-
mental to the Party and therefore incompatible with continuance
in its ranks;

g. To develop self-criticism and criticism from below, to bring
to light shortcomings in work and to strive to eliminate them, to
combat every tendency to make a pretence of all being well and
to indulge in raptures over achievements in work. Suppression
of criticism is a grave evil. He who stifles criticism, who substitutes
ostentatious parade and adulation for it, can have no place in the
ranks of the Party;

h. To inform leading Party bodies, up to and including the
Central Committee, of shortcomings in work, irrespective of person. A Party member has no right to conceal an abnormal state
of affairs, to close his eyes to reprehensible actions which injure
the interests of the Party or the state. He who hinders a Party
member in the performance of this duty should be sternly punished as a violator of the will of the Party;

state, and to give information about them to Party bodies, up to and including the Central Committee of the Communist Party of the Soviet Union (CC CPSU); [cf. Art. 3.g,h, 1952 Rules]

(H) to implement undeviatingly the Party's policy with regard to the proper selection of personnel according to their political and professional qualifications; to be uncompromising whenever the Leninist principles of the selection and education of personnel are infringed on;

(I) to observe Party and state discipline, which is equally binding on all Party members. The Party has one discipline, one law, for all Communists, irrespective of their past services or the positions they occupy. [cf. Art. 3.f, 1952 Rules]

[ADDED PARAGRAPH] (J)

(J) vigorously to assist in the strengthening of the defensive might of the USSR in order that the USSR may lead the tireless struggle for peace and friendship among nations.

3. A Party member has the right:

(A) to elect and be elected to Party bodies; [cf. Art. 4.c, 1952 Rules]

******** **1961** ▲   ▼**1952** ********

i. To be truthful and honest with the Party and not conceal or distort the truth. Untruthfulness or deception practised by a Communist towards the Party is a grave evil and is incompatible with continuance in the Party's ranks;

j. To guard Party and state secrets and to display political vigilance, always remembering that vigilance on the part of Communists is essential on all sectors and in all circumstances. Divulgence of Party or state secrets is a crime against the Party and incompatible with continuance in its ranks;

k. In any post entrusted to him by the Party, undeviatingly to observe the Party's injunction regarding the proper selection of personnel on the basis of their political and professional qualifications. Infringement of this injunction, selection of personnel from considerations of friendship, personal loyalty, home town ties or kinship, is incompatible with continuance in the ranks of the Party.

4. A Party member has the right:

a. To take part in the free and businesslike discussion at Party meetings or in the Party press of questions of Party policy;

(B) to discuss freely questions of the Party's policies and practical activities at Party meetings, conferences and congresses, at the meetings of Party committees and in the Party press; to table* motions; openly to express and uphold his opinion as long as the organization concerned has not adopted a decision; [cf. Art. 4.a, 1952 Rules]

(C) to criticize any Communist, irrespective of the position he holds, at Party meetings, conferences and congresses and at the plenary meetings of Party committees. Those who commit the offense of suppressing criticism or victimizing anyone for criticism are responsible to and will be penalized by the Party, to the point of expulsion from the CPSU. [cf. Art. 4.b, 1952 Rules]

(D) to attend in person all Party meetings and all bureau and committee meetings that discuss his activities or conduct;

(E) to address any question, statement or proposal to any Party body, up to and including the CC CPSU, and to demand an answer on the substance of his address.

4. Applicants are admitted to Party membership only individually. Membership in the Party is open to politically conscious and active work-

. . . active *workers, peasants, and members of the intelligentsia devoted to the communist cause.* New . . .

ing people devoted to the communist cause from among the workers, peasants and intellectuals. New members are admitted from among the candidate members who have passed through the established probationary period. Persons may join the Party on attaining the age of eighteen. Young people up to the age of twenty may join the Party only through the Young Communist League (YCL). [cf. Art. 5.c, 1952 Rules]

* *Table:* that is, propose, put on the table for the attention of the meeting.—Editor

******** **1961** ▲ ▼ **1952** ********

b. To criticize any Party worker at Party meetings;

c. To elect and be elected to Party bodies;

d. To demand to be present in person whenever decisions are taken regarding his activities or conduct;

e. To address any question or statement to any Party body, up to and including the Central Committee of the Communist Party of the Soviet Union.

5. Members are admitted to the Party only individually. New members are admitted from among the candidate members who have been through the specified probationary period. Member-

The procedure for the admission of candidate members to full Party membership is as follows:

(A) applicants for Party membership must submit recommendations from three Party members who have a Party standing of not less than three years and who know the applicants from having worked with them, professionally and socially, for not less than one year.

Note 1. In the case of members of the YCL applying for membership in the Party, the recommendation of a district committee of the . . . district *or city* committee . . . YCL is equivalent to the recommendation of one Party member.

Note 2. Members and alternate members of the CC CPSU shall refrain from giving recommendations.

(B) Applications for Party membership are discussed and a decision is taken by the general meeting of the primary Party organization; the decision of the latter takes effect after endorsement by the district Party committee, or by the city Party committee in cities with no district divisions.

✸✸✸✸✸✸✸ **1961** ▲　　　▼ **1952** ✸✸✸✸✸✸✸

ship of the Party is open to politically conscious and active workers, peasants and intellectuals who are devoted to the cause of communism.

Persons may join the Party on attaining the age of eighteen.

The procedure of admission of candidate members to full Party membership is as follows:

a. Applicants for Party membership must submit recommendations from three Party members who have a Party standing of not less than three years and who know the applicants from having worked with them for not less than one year.

Note 1. In the case of members of the Leninist Young Communist League applying for membership of the Party, the recommendation of a district committee of the Y.C.L. is equivalent to the recommendation of one Party member.

Note 2. Members and alternate members of the Central Committee of the Communist Party of the Soviet Union shall refrain from giving recommendations.

b. Applications for Party membership are discussed and decided by the general meeting of the primary Party organization, whose decision takes effect after endorsement by the district Party committee, or by the city Party committee in cities with no district divisions.

The presence of those who have recommended an applicant for Party membership at the discussion of the application concerned is optional;

(C) Citizens of the USSR who formerly belonged to the Communist or Workers' Party of another country are admitted to membership of the Communist Party of the Soviet Union in conformity with the rules established by the CC CPSU.

Former members of other parties are admitted to membership of the CPSU in conformity with the regular procedure, except that their admission must be endorsed by a regional or territorial committee or the CC of the Communist Party of a union republic.

5. Communists recommending applicants for Party membership are responsible to Party organizations for the impartiality of their description of the professional and political qualifications of those they recom-
. . . the *political, professional, and moral* qualifications . . .
mend.

6. The Party standing of those admitted to membership dates from the day when the general meeting of the primary Party organization decides to accept them as full members.

7. The procedure of registering members and candidate members

******** **1961** ▲   ▼ **1952** ********

The presence of the recommenders at the discussion of applications for Party membership is not essential.

c. Persons up to the age of twenty inclusive may join the Party only through the Young Communist League.

d. Former members of other parties require for admission to the Party the recommendations of five Party members; three of ten years' Party standing and two of prerevolutionary Party standing. They may be admitted only through a primary Party organization, and the endorsement of the Central Committee of the Communist Party of the Soviet Union is essential.

6. Persons recommending applicants for admission to the Party are responsible for the soundness of their recommendations.

7. The Party standing of a candidate member admitted to full membership dates from the day of the decision of the general meeting of the primary Party organization to adopt him as full member.

8. A member of one Party organization who moves to the locality of another Party organization shall be entered on the membership rolls of the latter.

of the Party, and their transfer from one organization to another is determined by the appropriate instructions of the CC CPSU.

8. If a Party member or candidate member fails to pay membership dues for three months in succession without sufficient reason, the matter shall be discussed by the primary Party organization. If it is revealed as a result that the Party member or candidate member in question has virtually lost contact with the Party organization, he shall be regarded as having ceased to be a member of the Party; the primary Party organization shall pass a decision thereon and submit it to the district or city committee of the Party for endorsement.

9. A party member who fails to fulfill his duties as laid down in the Rules, or commits other offenses, shall be called to account, and may be subjected to the penalty of admonition, reprimand (or severe reprimand), with entry in the registration card. The highest Party penalty is expulsion from the Party.

Should the necessity arise, a Party organization may, as a Party penalty, reduce a Party member to the status of candidate member for a

******** **1961** ▲   ▼**1952** ********

Note. The transfer of Party members from one organization to another is effected in accordance with regulations laid down by the Central Committee of the Communist Party of the Soviet Union.

9. A Party member or candidate member who fails to pay membership dues for three months in succession without sufficient reason is regarded as having automatically ceased to be a member of the Party; the primary Party organization shall pass a decision to this effect, which shall be subject to endorsement by the district or city Party committee.

[10. See below, following Art. 14.]

14. When the question of expelling a member from the Party is discussed, the maximum caution and comradely consideration must be exercised, and the grounds for the charges preferred against him must be thoroughly investigated.

In the case of minor offences, measures of Party education and influence should be applied (admonition, reprimand, etc.), and not expulsion from the Party, which is the supreme Party penalty.

Should the necessity arise, Party organizations may, as a Party penalty, demote members to the status of candidate member for a period of not more than one year. The decision of the pri-

period of up to one year. The decision of the primary Party organization reducing a Party member to candidate membership is subject to endorsement by the district or city Party committee. On the expiration of his period of reduction to candidate membership his readmission to full membership of the Party will follow the regular procedure, with retention of his former Party standing.

In the case of insignificant offenses, measures of Party education and influence should be applied—in the form of comradely criticism, Party censure, warning, or reproof.

When the question of expelling a member from the Party is dis-
. . . expelling a *Communist* from . . .
cussed, the maximum prudence and attention must be shown, and the grounds for the charges preferred against him must be thoroughly investigated.

10. The decision to expel a Communist from the Party is made by the general meeting of a primary Party organization. The decision of the primary Party organization expelling a member is regarded as adopted if not less than two-thirds of the Party members attending the meeting have voted for it, and takes effect after endorsement by a regional or ter-
. . . and *is endorsed by a district or city Party Committee.*
The decision of the district or city Party Committee expelling a member from the Party takes . . .
ritorial committee or the CC of the Communist Party of a union republic.

Until such time as the decision to expel him is endorsed by a re-

✶✶✶✶✶✶✶✶ **1961** ▲ ▼ **1952** ✶✶✶✶✶✶✶✶

mary Party organization demoting a Party member to candidate membership requires the endorsement of the district or city Party committee. On the expiration of his period of demotion to candidate membership he shall be admitted to full membership of the Party in accordance with the regular procedure, but he shall retain his former Party standing.

[15. See below, following Art. 13.]

10. The question of the expulsion of a Communist from the Party is decided by the general meeting of the primary Party organization to which he belongs and must be endorsed by the district or city Party committee. The decision of a district or city committee to expel a member takes effect only when endorsed by the regional or territorial Party committee, or by the Central Committee of the Communist Party of a Union Republic.

Until such time as the decision to expel him is endorsed by

gional or territorial Party committee or the CC of the Communist Party of a union republic, the Party member retains his membership card and . . . membership *or candidate membership card,* and . . . is entitled to attend closed Party meetings.

An expelled Party member retains the right to appeal, within the period of two months, to the higher Party bodies, up to and including the CC CPSU.

11. The question of calling a member or alternate member of the CC of the Communist Party of a union republic, of a territorial, regional, area, city or district Party committee, or of an auditing commission, to account before the Party is discussed by primary Party organizations.

Party organizations pass decisions imposing penalties on members or alternate members of the said Party committees, or on members of auditing commissions, in conformity with the regular procedure.

A Party organization which proposes expelling a Communist from the CPSU communicates its proposal to the Party committee of which he is a member. A decision to expel from the Party a member or alternate member of the CC of the Communist Party of a union republic or a territorial, regional, area, city or district Party committee, or a member of an auditing commission, is taken at the plenary meeting of the committee concerned by a majority of two-thirds of the membership.

✶✶✶✶✶✶✶ **1961**▲ ▼**1952** ✶✶✶✶✶✶✶

the regional or territorial Party committee or the Central Committee of the Communist Party of a Union Republic, the Party member retains his membership card and is entitled to attend closed Party meetings.

11. A primary Party organization cannot pass a decision on the expulsion of a Communist from the Party, or on his demotion to the status of candidate member, if he is a member of the Central Committee of the Communist Party of the Soviet Union, or of the Central Committee of the Communist Party of a Union Republic, or of a territorial, regional, area, city or district Party committee.

The expulsion of a member of the Central Committee of the Communist Party of a Union Republic, or of a territorial, regional, area, city or district Party committee from the given committee or from the Party, or his demotion from full membership to candidate membership, is decided at a plenary meeting of the committee concerned, and only if the necessity for it is recognized by two thirds of the votes.

The decision to expel from the Party a member or alternate member of the CC CPSU, or a member of the Central Auditing Commission, is made by the Party congress, and in the interval between two congresses, by a plenary meeting of the Central Committee, by a majority of two-thirds of the membership.

12. Should a Party member commit an indictable offense, he shall be expelled from the Party and prosecuted in conformity with the law.

13. Appeals against expulsion from the Party or against the imposition of a penalty, as well as the decisions of Party organizations on expulsion from the Party shall be examined by the appropriate Party bodies within not more than one month from the date of their receipt.

II. Candidate Members

14. All persons joining the Party must pass through a probationary
14. *Those* joining . . .

******** **1961** ▲   ▼ **1952** ********

12. The expulsion of a member of the Central Committee of the Communist Party of the Soviet Union from the Central Committee or from the Party, or his demotion to candidate membership, is decided by the Party Congress, or, in intervals between congresses, by the Plenum of the Central Committee of the Communist Party of the Soviet Union, the assent of a two-thirds majority of the members of the C.C. Plenum being required. The expelled member of the Central Committee is automatically replaced by an alternate member of the C.C., in the order established by the Congress when electing the C.C. alternate members.

13. Should a Party member commit an offence punishable by court of law, he shall be expelled from the Party and the administrative or judicial authorities informed of the offence.

[**14.** See above, following Art. 9.]

15. Appeals against expulsion from the Party, and also decisions of Party organizations to expel members from the Party, must be examined by the appropriate Party bodies within not more than twenty days from date of their receipt.

II. Candidate Members

16. All persons desirous of joining the Party must pass

period as candidate members in order to familiarize themselves with the Program and Rules of the CPSU and prepare for admission to full membership of the Party. Party organizations must assist candidates to prepare for admission to full membership of the Party, and test their personal qualities. Probationary membership shall be one year. [Cf. Art. 18, 1952 Rules.]

15. The procedure for the admission of candidate members (individual admission, submission of recommendations, decision of the primary organization as to admission, and its endorsement) is identical with the procedure for the admission of Party members.

16. On the expiration of a candidate member's probationary period the primary Party organization discusses and passes a decision on his application for admission to full membership. Should a candidate member fail, in the course of his probationary period, to show his worthiness, and should he prove, by his personal qualities, to be unfit for admission

. . . qualities, *that he cannot be admitted*

******** **1961** ▲   ▼**1952** ********

through a probationary period as candidate members, the object of which is to give them an opportunity to familiarize themselves with the Program, Rules and tactics of the Party and to enable the Party organizations to test the personal qualities of the candidates.

17. The procedure of admission of candidate members (individual admission, submission of recommendations and their verification, decision of the primary organization as to admission and its endorsement) is identical with the procedure of admission of Party members.

18. The period of probationary membership shall be one year.

It is the duty of Party organizations to assist candidates to prepare for admission to the Party. On the expiration of a candidate member's probationary period the Party organization shall discuss his fitness for admission at a general meeting. If a candidate was unable to prove his fitness for reasons which the primary Party organizations considers sufficient, it may prolong his probationary period for a term of not more than one year. Should it be found in the course of his probationary period that a candidate member does not possess the personal qualities warranting his admission to the Party, the Party organization shall pass a decision to remove him from the list of candidate members. A decision of a primary Party organization to prolong the probationary period of a candidate member, or to remove him from the

to membership in the CPSU, the Party organization shall pass a decision rejecting his admission to membership in the Party; after endorsement of that decision by the district or city Party committee, he shall cease to be considered a candidate member of the CPSU.

17. Candidate members of the Party must participate in all the activities of their Party organizations; they shall have a consultative voice at Party meetings. They may not be elected to any leading Party body, nor may they be elected delegates to a Party conference or congress.

18. Candidate members of the CPSU pay membership dues at the same rate as full members.

III. Organizational Structure of the Party. Inner-Party Democracy

19. The guiding principle of the organizational structure of the Party is democratic centralism, which signifies:

(A) election of all leading Party bodies, from the lowest to the highest;

(B) periodic reports of Party bodies to their Party organizations and to higher bodies;

******** **1961** ▲   ▼ **1952**   ********

list of candidate members, takes effect after it has been endorsed by the district or city Party committee.

19. Candidate members attend the meetings of the organization to which they are attached, and have a voice but no vote.

20. Candidate members pay the usual membership dues to the local Party committee.

III. Structure of the Party: Inner-Party Democracy

21. The guiding principle of the organizational structure of the Party is democratic centralism, which signifies:

a. Election of all leading Party bodies, from the highest to the lowest;

b. Periodical reports of the Party bodies to their Party organizations;

(C) strict Party discipline and subordination of the minority to the majority;

(D) that the decisions of higher bodies are obligatory for lower bodies.

20. The Party is built on the territorial-industrial principle: Primary organizations are established wherever Communists are employed, and are associated territorially in district, city, etc., organizations. An organization serving a given area is higher than any Party organization serving part of that area.

21. All Party organizations are autonomous in the decision of local questions, unless their decisions conflict with Party policy.

22. The highest leading body of a Party organization is the general meeting (in the case of primary organizations); the conference (in the case of district, city, area, regional or territorial organizations); or the congress (in the case of the Communist Parties of union republics and the Communist Party of the Soviet Union).

23. The general meeting, conference or congress elects a bureau or committee which acts as its executive body and directs all the current work of the Party organization.

******** 1961 ▲   ▼1952 ********

c. Strict Party discipline and subordination of the minority to the majority;

d. Absolutely binding character of the decisions of higher bodies upon lower bodies.

22. The Party is built on the territorial-industrial principle: a Party organization serving a given area is regarded as higher than any Party organization serving part of that area; and a Party organization serving a whole branch of work is regarded as higher than any Party organization serving part of that branch of work.

23. All Party organizations are autonomous in the decision of local questions, provided that their decisions do not conflict with decisions of the Party.

24. The highest governing body in each Party organization is the general membership meeting (in the case of primary organizations), conference (e.g., in the case of district or regional organizations), or congress (in the case of Communist Parties of Union Republics and the Communist Party of the Soviet Union).

25. The general meeting, conference or congress elects a bureau or committee which acts as its executive body and directs all the current work of the given organization.

24. The election of Party bodies shall be effected by secret ballot. In an election, all Party members have the unlimited right to challenge candidates and to criticize them. Each candidate shall be voted upon separately. A candidate is considered elected if more than one half of those attending the meeting, conference or congress has voted for him.

25. The principle of systematic renewal of the composition of Party bodies and of continuity of leadership shall be observed in the election of those bodies.

At each regular election, not less than one-quarter of the composition of the CC CPSU and its Presidium shall be renewed.* Members of the Presidium shall not, as a rule, be elected for more than three successive terms. Particular Party officials may, by virtue of their generally recognized prestige and high political, organizational and other qualities, be successively elected to leading bodies for a longer period. In that case, a candidate is considered elected if not less than three-quarters of the votes are cast for him by secret ballot.

The composition of the Central Committees of the Communist Parties of the union republics, and of the territorial and regional Party committees shall be renewed by not less than one-third at each regular election; the composition of the area, city and district Party committees and of the committees or bureaus of primary Party organizations, by one half. Furthermore, members of these leading Party bodies may be elected successively for not more than three terms, and the secretaries of primary Party organizations, for not more than two terms.

A Party organization may, in consideration of the political and pro-
A meeting, conference, or congress may, . . .
fessional qualities of a person, elect him to a leading body for a longer period. In such cases a candidate is considered elected if not less than three-quarters of the Communists attending vote for him.

      * *Be renewed:* be newly elected; that is, be persons who have not been members of the body during the immediately preceding period.— Editor

✶✶✶✶✶✶✶✶ **1961** ▲   ▼**1952** ✶✶✶✶✶✶✶

26. Voting by lists of candidates in the election of Party bodies is forbidden. Each candidate shall be voted upon separately, every Party member being ensured the unlimited right to challenge the candidates and to criticize them. Voting of candidates shall be by secret ballot.

[27. See below, following Art. 28.]

Party members not re-elected to a leading Party body on the expiration of their term may be re-elected at subsequent elections.

26. A member or alternate member of the CC CPSU must by his entire activity justify the great trust placed in him by the Party. A member or alternate member of the CC CPSU who does not uphold his honor and dignity may not remain a member of the Central Committee. The question of the removal of a member or alternate member of the CC CPSU from that body shall be decided by a plenary meeting of the Central Committee by secret ballot. The decision is regarded as adopted if not less than two-thirds of the membership of the CC CPSU vote for it.

The question of the removal of a member or alternate member of the CC of the Communist Party of a union republic, or of a territorial, regional, area, city or district Party committee from the Party body concerned is decided by a plenary meeting of that body. The decision is regarded as adopted if not less than two-thirds of the membership of the committee in question vote for it by secret ballot.

A member of the Central Auditing Commission who does not justify the great trust placed in him by the Party shall be removed from that

. . . from *the*

body. This question shall be decided by a meeting of the Central Audit-

Commission. This . . .

ing Commission. The decision is regarded as adopted if not less than two-thirds of the membership of the Central Auditing Commission vote

. . . Commission *have voted*

by secret ballot for the removal from that body of the member or alternate member concerned.

The question of the removal of a member from the auditing commission of a republican, territorial, regional, area, city or district Party organization shall be decided by a meeting of the appropriate commission according to the procedure established for members and alternate members of Party committees.

27. The free and business-like discussion of questions of Party policy in individual Party organizations or in the Party as a whole is the inalienable right of every Party member and is an important principle of inner-Party democracy. Only on the basis of inner-Party democracy

✶✶✶✶✶✶✶✶ **1961** ▲　　▼ **1952** ✶✶✶✶✶✶✶✶

28. The free and businesslike discussion of questions of Party policy in individual organizations or in the Party as a whole is the inalienable right of every Party member and logically follows from inner-party democracy. Only on the basis of inner-party

is it possible to develop criticism and self-criticism and to strengthen Party discipline, which must be conscious and not mechanical.

Discussion of controversial or insufficiently clear issues may be held within the framework of individual organizations or the Party as a whole.

Party-wide discussion is necessary:

(A) if the necessity is recognized by several Party organizations at regional or republican level;

(B) if there is not a sufficiently solid majority in the Central Committee on major questions of Party policy;

(C) if the CC CPSU considers it necessary to consult the Party as a whole on any particular questions of policy.

Wide discussion, especially discussion on a countrywide scale, of questions of Party policy must be held so as to ensure for Party members the free expression of their views and preclude attempts to form fac-

******** **1961** ▲   ▼ **1952** ********

democracy is it possible to develop self-criticism and to strengthen Party discipline, which must be conscious and not mechanical.

But wide discussion, especially discussion on a national scale, of questions of Party policy must be so organized as to prevent it leading to attempts by an insignificant minority to impose their will upon the majority of the Party, or to attempts to form factional groupings, which break the unity of the Party, attempts to cause splits, which may shake the strength and stability of the socialist system. [cf. Art. 27(c), 1961 Rules]

Wide discussion on a national scale can be regarded as necessary only:

a. If this necessity is recognized by at least several local Party organizations of regional or republican scale;

b. If there is not a sufficiently solid majority in the Central Committee of the Communist Party of the Soviet Union on important questions of Party policy;

c. If, in spite of the existence of a solid majority in the Central Committee holding a definite opinion, the Central Committee deems it necessary to test the correctness of its policy by means of a discussion in the Party.

Only compliance with these conditions can safeguard the Party against abuse of inner-party democracy by anti-Party elements, only these conditions can give the assurance that inner-Party democracy will be beneficial and not be used to the detriment of the Party and the working class.

tional groupings destroying Party unity, attempts to split the Party. [cf. Art. 28, paragraph 2, 1952 Rules]

28. The highest principle of Party leadership is collectivism, which is an absolute requisite for the normal functioning of Party organizations, the proper education of personnel, and the promotion of the activity and initiative of Communists. The cult of the individual and the violations of inner-Party democracy resulting from it must not be tolerated in the Party; they are incompatible with the Leninist principles of Party life.

Collective leadership does not exempt persons in office from their responsibility for the job entrusted to them.

29. The Central Committees of the Communist Parties of union republics, and territorial, regional, area, city and district Party committees shall systematically inform Party organizations of their work.
shall, *in the period between congresses and conferences,* systematically . . .

[Cf. Art. 43, 1952 Rules.]

30. Meetings of the most active members of district, city, area, regional and territorial Party organizations and of the Communist Parties of union republics shall be held to discuss major decisions of the Party and to work out practical measures for their execution, as well as to examine questions of local significance.

IV. Higher Party Organs

31. The supreme organ of the CPSU is the Party congress. Con-

********* 1961 ▲   ▼ 1952 *********

[29. See below, following Art. 27.]

27. In cities and district centres, meetings of active members of the city and district Party organizations shall be convened for the discussion of the more important decisions of the Party and the government. They shall be convened not for parade and the formal and ceremonial approval of the decisions, but for their genuine discussion.

[28. See above, following Art. 26.]

IV. Higher Party Organs

29. The highest organ of the Communist Party of the Soviet

gresses are convened at least once in four years. The convocation of a Party congress shall be announced at least six weeks before the congress. Extraordinary congresses are convened by the Central Committee of the Party on its own initiative or on the demand of not less than one-third of the total membership represented at the preceding Party congress. Extraordinary congresses shall be convened within two months. A congress is considered properly constituted if not less than one half of the total Party membership is represented at it.

The rates of representation at a Party congress are determined by the Central Committee.

32. Should the Central Committee of the Party fail to convene an extraordinary congress within the period specified in article 31, the organizations which demanded it have the right to form an organizing committee which shall enjoy the powers of the Central Committee of the Party with respect to the convocation of the extraordinary congress.

33. The congress:

(A) hears and approves the reports of the Central Committee, of

✷✷✷✷✷✷✷ 1961 ▲   ▼ 1952 ✷✷✷✷✷✷✷

Union is the Party congress. Ordinary congresses are convened at least once in four years. Extraordinary congresses are convened by the Central Committee of the Party on its own initiative or at the demand of not less than one third of the total membership represented at the preceding Party Congress. The convocation of a Party congress and its agenda shall be announced at least six weeks before the Congress. Extraordinary congresses shall be convened within two months.

A congress is regarded as properly constituted if not less than one half of the total Party membership represented at the last ordinary congress are represented at it.

The basis of representation at a Party congress is determined by the Central Committee.

30. Should the Central Committee of the Party fail to convene an extraordinary congress within the period specified in Article 29, the organizations which demanded it have the right to form an Organization Committee which shall enjoy the powers of the Central Committee of the Party as regards the convocation of the extraordinary congress.

31. The Congress:

a. Hears and acts on the reports of the central Committee of the Central Auditing Commission, and of the other central organizations;

(B) reviews, amends and endorses the Program and the Rules of the Party;

(C) determines the line of the Party in matters of home and foreign policy, and examines and decides the most important questions of communist construction;

(D) elects the Central Committee and the Central Auditing Commission.

34. The number of members to be elected to the Central Committee and to the Central Auditing Commission is determined by the congress. In the event of vacancies occurring in the Central Committee, they are filled from among the alternate members of the CC CPSU elected by the congress.

35. Between congresses the CC CPSU directs the activities of the Party, the local Party bodies, selects and appoints leading functionaries, directs the work of central government bodies and social organizations of working people through the Party groups in them, sets up various Party organs, institutions and enterprises and directs their activities,

******** **1961** ▲   ▼ **1952** ********

the Party, of the Central Auditing Commission, and of the other central organizations;

b. Revises and amends the Program and Rules of the Party;

c. Determines the tactical line of the Party on major questions of current policy;

d. Elects the Central Committee of the Communist Party of the Soviet Union and the Central Auditing Commission.

32. The number of members to be elected to the Central Committee of the Party and to the Central Auditing Commission is determined by the Congress. In the event of members falling out of the Central Committee, their places are filled from among the alternate members elected by the congress.

[33-35. See below, following Art. 39.]

36. The Central Committee of the Communist Party of the Soviet Union directs the entire work of the Party in the interval between Congresses, represents the Party in its relations with other parties, organizations and institutions, sets up various Party institutions and directs their activities, appoints the editors of central press organs under its control and confirms the appointment of the editors of the Party organs of big local organizations, organizes and manages enterprises of a public character, distributes

appoints the editors of the central newspapers and journals operating under its control, and distributes the funds of the Party budget and controls its execution.

The Central Committee represents the CPSU in its relations with other parties.

36. The CC CPSU shall keep the Party organizations regularly informed of its work.

37. The Central Auditing Commission supervises the expeditious and proper handling of business by the central bodies of the Party, and audits the accounts of the treasury and the enterprises of the CC CPSU.

38. The CC CPSU shall hold not less than one plenary meeting every six months. Alternate members of the Central Committee shall at-

******** **1961** ▲   ▼ **1952** ********

the forces and resources of the Party, and manages the central funds.

The Central Committee guides the work of the central Soviet and public organizations through the Party groups within them.

37. In order to strengthen leadership and political work, the Central Committee of the Party has the right to create Political Departments and to assign Party Organizers of the Central Committee to individual sectors of socialist construction which have acquired special importance for the national economy and the country in general; and, in the measure that the Political Departments complete their tasks, to abolish them or to convert them into ordinary Party bodies on the industrial-territorial principle.

The work of the Political Departments is governed by special instructions endorsed by the Central Committee.

38. The Central Committee of the Communist Party of the Soviet Union keeps the Party organizations regularly informed of its work.

39. The Central Auditing Commission (a) investigates whether affairs are handled expeditiously and properly by the central bodies of the Party and whether the apparatus of the Secretariat of the Central Committee is working smoothly, and (b) audits the accounts of the treasury and the enterprises of the Central Committee of the Party.

[40. See below, following Art. 43.]

33. The Central Committee of the Communist Party of the Soviet Union holds not less than one plenary meeting every six

tend its plenary meetings with consultative voice.

39. The CC CPSU elects a Presidium to direct the work of the CC between plenary meetings and a Secretariat to direct current work, chiefly the selection of personnel and the verification of the fulfillment of Party decisions, and sets up a Bureau of the CC CPSU for the Russian Soviet Federative Socialist Republic (RSFSR).

40. The CC CPSU organizes the Party Control Committee of the CC.

The Party Control Committee of the CC:

. . . of the CC *of the CPSU:*

(A) verifies the observance of Party discipline by members and candidate members of the CPSU, and takes action against Communists who violate the program and the Rules of the Party, and Party or state discipline, and against violators of Party ethics;

(B) considers appeals against decisions of Central Committees of the Communist Parties of union republics or of territorial and regional Party committees to expel members from the Party or impose Party penalties upon them.

******** **1961** ▲   ▼ **1952** ********

months. Alternate members of the Central Committee attend its plenary meetings with voice but no vote.

34. The Central Committee of the Communist Party of the Soviet Union sets up a Presidium to direct the work of the Central Committee between plenary meetings, and a Secretariat to direct the current work, chiefly the organization of verification of fulfillment of Party decisions, and selection of personnel.

35. The Central Committee of the Communist Party of the Soviet Union sets up a Party Control Committee of the C.C.

The Party Control Committee of the C.C.:

a. Verifies how Party members and candidate members observe Party discipline, and takes action against Communists who violate the Program and Rules of the Party, or Party and state discipline, and against violators of Party ethics (against those who deceive the Party or are dishonest and insincere with it, against slanderers or bureaucrats, against persons guilty of moral delinquency in private life, etc.);

b. Reviews appeals against decisions of Central Committees of Communist Parties of Union Republics, or of territorial and regional Party committees, expelling members from the Party or imposing Party penalties upon them.

[36-39. See above, following Art. 32.]

V. Republican, Territorial, Regional, Area, City and District Organizations of the Party

41. The republican, territorial, regional, area, city and district Party organizations and their committees take guidance in their activities from the Program and the Rules of the CPSU, conduct all work for the implementation of Party policy and organize the fulfillment of the directives of the CC CPSU within the republics, territories, regions, areas, cities and districts concerned.

[Cf. Art. 40, 1952 Rules.]

42. The basic duties of republican, territorial, regional, area, city and district Party organizations, and of their leading bodies, are:

(A) political and organizational work among the masses, mobilization of the masses for the fulfillment of the tasks of communist construction, for the maximum development of industrial and agricultural production, for the fulfillment and over-fulfillment of state plans; solicitude for the steady improvement of the material and cultural standards of the working people;

(B) organization of ideological work, propaganda of Marxism-Leninism, promotion of the communist awareness of the working people, guidance of the local press, radio and television, and control over the

******** **1961** ▲ ▼ **1952** ********

V. Provincial, Territorial, and Republican Party Organizations

[40-42. See below, following Art. 43.]

43. The provincial committees, territorial committees and Central Committees of the Communist Parties of Union Republics organize various Party institutions within their particular province, territory or republic and direct their activities; ensure faithful observance of Party directives, development of criticism and self-criticism, and education of Communists in a spirit of intolerance of shortcomings; direct the study of Marxism-Leninism by Party members and candidate members; organize the communist education of the working people; appoint the editors of the provincial, territorial or republican Party press organ which works under their control; guide the activities of the provincial, territorial or republican Soviet and public organizations through the Party groups within them, organize and manage their own enterprises

activities of cultural and educational institutions;

(C) guidance of Soviets, trade unions, the YCL, the cooperatives and other public organizations through the Party groups in them, and increasingly broader enlistment of working people in the activities of these organizations, development of the initiative and activity of the masses as an essential condition for the gradual transition from socialist statehood to public self-government under communism.

Party organizations must not act in place of government, trade-union, cooperative or other public organizations of the working people; they must not allow either the merging of the functions of Party and other bodies or undue parallelism in work;

(D) selection and appointment of leading personnel, their education in the spirit of communist ideas, honesty and truthfulness, and a high sense of responsibility to the Party and the people for the work entrusted to them;

(E) large-scale enlistment of Communists in the conduct of Party activities as non-staff workers, as a form of social work;

(F) organization of various institutions and enterprises of the Party within the bounds of the respective republic, territory, region, area, city or district, and guidance of their activities; distribution of Party funds within the given organization; systematic information of the higher Party body and accountability to it for their work.

Leading Bodies of Republican, Territorial and Regional Party Organizations

43. The highest body of regional, territorial and republican Party organizations is the respective regional or territorial Party conference or the congress of the Communist Party of the union republic, and in

✸✸✸✸✸✸✸✸ **1961** ▲   ▼ **1952** ✸✸✸✸✸✸✸✸

of general importance in the particular province, territory or republic; distribute within the limits of their organization the forces and resources of the Party; manage the Party funds of the province, territory or republic; send regular information to the Central Committee of the Party and at fixed intervals present reports to it on their activities.

[**44.** See below, following Art. 42.]

40. The highest organ of a provincial, territorial or republican Party organization is the provincial or territorial Party Conference or the Congress of the Communist Party of the Union Republic,

the interim between their meetings the regional committee, territorial committee or the Central Committee of the Communist Party of the union republic.

44. Regional and territorial Party conferences, and congresses of the Communist Parties of union republics, are convened by the respective regional or territorial committees or the CC of the Communist Parties of union republics once every two years, and extraordinary conferences and congresses are convened by decision of regional or territorial committees, or the CC of the Communist Parties of union republics, or on the demand of one-third of the total membership of the organizations belonging to the regional, territorial or republican Party organization. Congresses of Communist Parties of those union republics divided into regions (the Ukraine, Byelorussia, Kazakhstan and Uzbekistan) may be convened once in four years.

The rates of representation at regional and territorial conferences

******** **1961** ▲ ▼ **1952** *******

and, in the interval between them, the provincial committee, territorial committee or Central Committee of the Communist Party of the Union Republic. They guide themselves in their activities by the decisions of the Communist Party of the Soviet Union and its leading bodies.

41. Ordinary provincial and territorial conferences and congresses of the Communist Parties of Union Republics are convened once every two years* by the particular provincial or territorial committee or Central Committee of the Communist Party of the Union Republic. Extraordinary conferences or congresses are convened by decision of the particular provincial committee, territorial committee or Central Committee of the Communist Party of the Union Republic, or at the demand of one third of the total membership of the organization belonging to the provincial, territorial or republican Party organization.

The basis of representation at provincial and territorial conferences and congresses of Communist Parties of Union Republics

* Congresses of Communist Parties in the Union Republics which have provinces (Ukraine, Byelorussia, Kazakhstan, and Uzbekistan) are held every four years.—Editor

and at congresses of Communist Parties of union republics are determined by the respective Party committees.

Regional and territorial conferences and congresses of the Communist Parties of union republics hear and act upon the reports of the respective regional or territorial committee, or the CC of the Communist Party of the union republic, and of the Auditing Commission; discuss at their own discretion other matters of Party, economic and cultural development, and elect the regional or territorial committee, the Central Committee of the union republic, the Auditing Commission and the delegates to the congress of the CPSU.

45. The regional and territorial committees, and the Central Committees of the Communist Parties of union republics elect bureaus, which

******** **1961** ▲　　▼ **1952** ********

is determined by the particular provincial committee, territorial committee or Central Committee of the Communist Party of the Union Republic.

Provincial and territorial conferences and congresses of Communist Parties of Union Republics hear and act on the reports of the respective provincial or territorial committee or Central Committee of the Communist Party of the Union Republic, of the auditing commission and of other provincial, territorial or republican organizations, discuss questions of Party, Soviet, economic and trade union work in the particular province, territory or republic, and elect a provincial committee, territorial committee or Central Committee of the Communist Party of the Union Republic, as the case may be, an auditing commission and delegates to the Congresses of the Communist Party of the Soviet Union.

42. The provincial and territorial committees and Central Committees of the Communist Parties of Union Republics each elect an executive body, consisting of not more than eleven members, including secretaries,* the appointment of the latter being subject to the confirmation of the Central Committee of the Party. The secretaries must have a Party standing of not less than five years.

The provincial committees, territorial committees and Central Committees of Communist Parties of Union Republics each set up

---

* The number of secretaries allocated to the various Party committees is determined by the Central Committee of the Communist Party of the Soviet Union.—Editor

also include secretaries of the committees. The secretaries must have a Party standing of not less than five years. The plenary meetings of the committees also confirm the chairmen of Party commissions, heads of departments of these committees, editors of Party newspapers and journals.

Regional and territorial committees and the Central Committees of the Communist Parties of union republics may set up secretariats to examine current business and verify the execution of decisions.

46. The plenary meetings of regional and territorial committees and the Central Committees of the Communist Parties of union republics shall be convened at least once every four months.

47. The regional and territorial committees and the Central Committees of the Communist Parties of union republics direct the activities of area, city and district Party organizations, inspect their work and regularly hear reports of area, city and district Party committees.

Party organizations in autonomous republics, and in autonomous and other regions forming part of a territory or union republic, function under the guidance of the respective territorial committees or Central Committees of the Communist Parties of union republics.

******** **1961** ▲   ▼ **1952** ********

a secretariat for the examination of current questions and for verification of fulfilment. The secretariats report the decisions they adopt to the bureaus of their respective provincial or territorial Party committees or Central Committees of the Communist Parties of Union Republics.

[43. See above, preceding Art. 40.]

44. Plenary meetings of provincial committees, territorial committees and Central Committees of the Communist Parties of Union Republics are convened at least once every four months.

45. Party organizations in autonomous republics and in national and other provinces forming part of a territory or Union Republic work under the direction of their particular territorial committee or Central Committee of the Communist Party of the Union Republic, and guide their internal life by the regulations set forth in Section V of the Party Rules relating to provincial, territorial and republican organizations.

VI. Regional Party Organizations

46. Regional Party organizations are formed in provinces, territories and republics which have regions.

The highest organ of a regional Party organization is the regional Party Conference, which is convened by the regional Party committee at least once in two years; extraordinary conferences are convened by decision of the regional Party committee or at the demand of one third of the total membership of the organizations belonging to the regional organization.

The regional conference hears and acts on the reports of the regional committee, of the auditing commission and of other regional Party organizations, and elects the regional Party committee, the auditing commission, and delegates to provincial or territorial conferences and to congresses of the Communist Party of the Union Republic.

47. Each regional committee elects a bureau, consisting of not more than nine persons, including secretaries of the regional committee. The secretaries must have a Party standing of not less than three years. Secretaries of regional committees must be confirmed by the provincial committee, territorial committee or Central Committee of the Communist Party of the Union Republic, as the case may be.

Plenary meetings of regional committees are convened not less than once in three months.

48. A regional committee organizes various Party institutions within its particular region and directs their activities; ensures faithful observance of Party directives, development of criticism and self-criticism, and education of Communists in a spirit of intolerance of shortcomings; directs the study of Marxism-Leninism by Party members and candidate members; organizes the communist education of the working people; appoints the editors of the regional Party press organ which works under its direction and control; guides the activities of the regional Soviet and public organizations through the Party groups within them; organizes its own enterprises of general importance to the region; distributes the forces and resources of the Party within the limits of its region, and manages the regional Party funds.

✴✴✴✴✴✴✴✴   ▲ **1952**   ✴✴✴✴✴✴✴✴

Leading Bodies of Area, City and District (Urban and Rural) Party Organizations

48. The highest body of an area, city or district Party organization is the area, city and district Party conference or the general meeting of Communists convened by the area, city or district committee at least once in two years, and the extraordinary conference convened by decision of the respective committee or on the demand of one-third of the total membership of the Party organization concerned.

The area, city or district conference (general meeting) hears reports of the committee and auditing commission, discusses at its own discretion other questions of Party, economic and cultural deveolpment, and elects the area, city and district committee, the auditing commission and delegates to the regional and territorial conference or the congress of the Communist Party of the union republic.

[ADDED PARAGRAPH] *The rates of representation at area, city and district conferences are determined by the respective Party Committees.*

49. The area, city or district committee elects a bureau, including the committee secretaries, and confirms the appointment of heads of

✶✶✶✶✶✶✶ 1961▲　　▼1952 ✶✶✶✶✶✶✶

VII. City and District (Rural and Urban) Party Organizations

49. City and district Party conferences are convened by the city and district committees at least once a year;* extraordinary conferences are convened by decision of the particular city or district committee, or at the demand of one third of the total membership of the organizations in the city or district.

The city or district conference hears and acts on the reports of the city or district committee, of the auditing commission and of other city or district organizations, and elects the city or district committee, the auditing commission and the delegates to territorial or provincial conferences or congresses of the Communist Party of the Union Republic.

50. Each city or district committee elects a bureau consisting of from seven to nine persons, including secretaries of the city or

* Party conferences in cities that are divided into boroughs meet every two years.—Editor

committee departments and newspaper editors. The secretaries of the area, city and district committees must have a Party standing of at least three years. The committee secretaries are confirmed by the respective regional or territorial committee, or the Central Committee of the Communist Party of the union republic.

50. The area, city and district committee organizes and confirms the primary Party organizations, directs their work, regularly hears reports concerning the work of Party organizations, and keeps a register of Communists.

51. The plenary meeting of the area, city and district committee is convened at least once in three months.

52. The area, city and district committee has non-staff instructors, sets up standing or ad hoc commissions on various aspects of Party

********** **1961** ▲   ▼ **1952** **********

district committee. Secretaries of city or district committees must have a Party standing of not less than three years. Their appointment is subject to the confirmation of the provincial committee, territorial committee, or Central Committee of the Communist Party of the Union Republic.

51. A city or district committee organizes and confirms the primary Party organizations in industrial enterprises, state farms, repair tractor stations, collective farms and offices, directs their activities and keeps a register of Communists; ensures the observance of Party directives, development of criticism and self-criticism, and education of Communists in a spirit of intolerance of shortcomings; organizes the study of Marxism-Leninism by Party members and candidate members; conducts the communist education of the working people; appoints the editors of the city or district Party press organ which works under its direction and control; guides the activities of the city or district Soviet and public organizations through the Party groups within them; distributes the forces and resources of the Party in the city or district, and manages the city or district Party funds. The city or district committee submits to the provincial committee, territorial committee or Central Committee of the Communist Party of the Union Republic reports on its activities at the times and in the form established by the Central Committee of the Party.

52. Plenary meetings of city or district committees are convened not less than once every three months.

work and uses other ways to draw Communists into the activities of the Party committee on social lines.

[Cf. Art. 51, 1952 Rules.]

VI. Primary Party Organizations

53. The primary Party organizations are the basis of the Party.

Primary Party organizations are formed at the places of work of Party members—in factories, on state farms and at other enterprises, collective farms, units of the Soviet Army, offices, educational establishments, etc., wherever there are not less than three Party members. Primary Party organizations may also be organized on the residential principle in villages and at house administrations.

54. Shop, sectional, farm, team departmental, etc., Party organizations may be formed as units of the general primary Party organization,

******** **1961** ▲   ▼ **1952** ********

53. In big cities, district organizations subordinate to the city committees may be set up with the permission of the Central Committee of the Communist Party of the Soviet Union.

VIII. Primary Party Organizations

54. The primary Party organizations are the basis of the Party.

Primary Party organizations are formed in mills, factories, state farms, repair tractor stations and other economic enterprises, in collective farms, units of the Soviet Army and Navy, in villages, offices, educational establishments, etc., where there are not less than three Party members.

In enterprises, candidate member groups or Party and Young Communist League groups are formed, headed by a Party organizer appointed by the district or city Party committee or by the Political Department.

Primary Party organizations are confirmed by the district or city committees or by the competent Political Departments.

The highest organ of a primary Party organization is the general meeting of its members which is convened not less than once a month.

55. In factories, offices, collective farms, etc., where there are over fifty Party members and candidate members, shop, sectional,

with the sanction of the area, city or district committee, at enterprises, collective farms and institutions with over 50 Party members and candidate members.

Within shop, sectional, etc., organizations, and also within primary Party organizations having less than 50 members and candidate members, Party groups may be formed in the teams and other production units.

55. The highest organ of the primary Party organization is the Party meeting, which is convened at least once a month. [Art. 54, 1952 Rules.]

In large Party organizations with a membership of more than 300 Communists a general Party meeting is convened when necessary at times fixed by the Party committee or on the demand of a number of shop or departmental Party organizations. [Art. 56, 1952 Rules.]

56. For the conduct of current business the primary, shop or departmental Party organization elects a bureau for the term of one year. The number of its members is fixed by the Party meeting. Primary, shop and departmental Party organizations with less than 15 Party members do not elect a bureau. Instead, they elect a secretary and deputy secretary of the Party organization.

Secretaries of primary, shop and departmental Party organizations must have a Party standing of at least one year.

✶✶✶✶✶✶✶ 1961▲ ▼1952 ✶✶✶✶✶✶✶

departmental, etc., Party organizations may be formed within the general primary Party organization covering the whole factory, office, etc., subject to the approval in each particular case of the district or city committee or of the competent Political Department.

Within shop, sectional, etc., organizations, and also within primary Party organizations having less than fifty members and candidate members, Party groups may be formed in the brigades or units of the establishment.

[56-58. See below, following Art. 59.]

59. For the conduct of its current business each primary Party organization elects a bureau consisting of not more than eleven persons for a term of one year.

Bureaus of primary Party organizations are formed if the organization has not less than fifteen Party members.

In Party organizations having less than fifteen Party members, no bureaus are formed, but a secretary of the primary Party organization is elected.

Primary Party organizations with less than 150 Party members shall have, as a rule, no salaried functionaries released from their regular work.

57. In large factories and offices with more than 300 members and candidate members of the Party, and in exceptional cases in factories and offices with over 100 Communists by virtue of special production conditions and territorial dispersion, subject to the approval of the regional committee, territorial committee or Central Committee of the Communist Party of the union republic, Party committees may be formed, the shop and departmental Party organizations at these factories and offices being granted the status of primary Party organizations.

The Party organizations of collective farms may set up Party committees if they have a minimum of 50 Communists.

The Party committees are elected for the term of one year. Their numerical composition is fixed by the general Party meeting or conference.

58. In its activities the primary Party organization takes guidance

✴✴✴✴✴✴✴✴ **1961** ▲ ▼ **1952** ✴✴✴✴✴✴✴✴

With the object of rapidly training and educating Party members in collective leadership, a shop Party organization having not less than fifteen and not more than one hundred Party members has the right to elect a bureau of the shop Party organization consisting of from three to five persons; a shop organization having over one hundred Party members may elect a bureau of from five to seven persons.

In primary Party organizations having not more than one hundred Party members, the persons who conduct the Party work are as a rule not exempted from their regular work.

Secretaries of primary and shop Party organizations must have a Party standing of not less than one year.

[60. See below, following Art. 63.]

56. In large factories and offices where there are over three hundred Party members and candidate members, Party committees may be formed with the sanction in each particular case of the provincial Party committee, the territorial Party committee, or the Central Committee of thte Communist Party of the Union Republic, the shop Party organizations in such establishments being granted the rights of primary Party organizations.

57. A primary Party organization connects the mass of the

from the Program and the Rules of the CPSU. It conducts its work directly among the working people, rallies them around the Communist Party of the Soviet Union, organizes the masses to carry out the Party policy and to work for the building of communism.

The primary Party organization:

(A) enrolls new members to the CPSU;

(B) educates Communists in a spirit of loyalty to the Party cause, ideological staunchness and communist ethics;

(C) organizes the study by Communists of Marxist-Leninist theory in close connection with the practice of communist construction and opposes all attempts to introduce revisionist distortions into Marxism-Leninism and its dogmatic interpretation; [cf. Art. 57.c, 1952 Rules]

(D) ensures the vanguard role of Communists in the sphere of labor and in the socio-political and economic activities of enterprises, collective farms, institutions, educational establishments, etc.;

(E) acts as the organizer of the working people for the performance of the current tasks of communist construction; heads the socialist emulation movement for the fulfillment of state plans and undertakings;

. . . undertakings *of the working people;* rallies the masses to disclose and make the best use of untapped re-

✶✶✶✶✶✶✶ **1961**▲   ▼**1952** ✶✶✶✶✶✶✶

workers, peasants and intellectuals with the leading organs of the Party. Its task is:

a. To conduct agitational and organizational work among the masses for the carrying out of Party calls and decisions, and to ensure direction of the primary press (printed bulletins, wall newspapers, etc.);

b. To recruit new members for the Party and to take care of their political training;

c. To organize the political education of Party members and candidate members and to see that they acquire an essential minimum knowledge of Marxism-Leninism;

d. To assist the district committee, city committee or Political Department in all its practical work;

e. To mobilize the efforts of the masses in factory, state farm, collective farm, etc., for the fulfilment of the production plan, for the strengthening of labour discipline and for the development of socialist emulation;

f. To combat inefficiency and mismanagement in factory, state farm and collective farm, and to show a daily concern for the im-

sources at enterprises and collective farms, and on a broad scale to apply in production the achievements of science, engineering and the experience of front-rankers; works for the strengthening of labor discipline, the steady increase of labor productivity and improvement of the quality of production, and shows concern for the protection and increase of social wealth at enterprises, state farms and collective farms; [cf. Art. 57.e, 1952 Rules]

(F) conducts agitational and propaganda work among the masses, educates them in the communist spirit, helps the working people to acquire proficiency in administering state and social affairs; [cf. Art. 57.a, 1952 Rules]

(G) on the basis of extensive criticism and self-criticism, combats cases of bureaucracy, parochialism, and violations of state discipline, thwarts attempts to deceive the state, acts against negligence, waste and extravagance at enterprises, collective farms and offices; [cf. Art. 57.g, 1952 Rules]

(H) assists the area, city and district committees in their activities and is accountable to them for its work. [cf. Art. 57.d, 1952 Rules]

The Party organization must see to it that every Communist should observe in his own life and cultivate among working people the moral principles set forth in the Program of the CPSU:

. . . the CPSU—*the moral code of a builder of communism:*

— loyalty to the communist cause, love of his own socialist country, and of other socialist countries;

— conscientious labor for the benefit of society: He who does not work, neither shall he eat;

— concern on everyone's part for the protection and increase of social wealth;

— a lofty sense of public duty, intolerance of violations of public interests;

— collectivism and comradely mutual assistance: one for all, and all for one;

******** **1961**▲   ▼**1952** ********

provement of the living and cultural standards of factory and office workers and collective farmers;

g. To develop criticism and self-criticism and to educate Communists in a spirit of intolerance of shortcomings;

h. To take an active part in the economic and political life of the country.

— humane relations and mutual respect among people: Man is to man a friend, comrade and brother;

— honesty and truthfulness, moral purity, unpretentiousness and modesty in public and personal life;

— mutual respect in the family circle and concern for the up-bringing of children;

— intolerance of injustice, parasitism, dishonesty and careerism;

. . . dishonesty, *careerism, and profiteering;*

— friendship and fraternity among all peoples of the USSR, intolerance of national and racial hostility;

— intolerance of the enemies of communism, the enemies of peace and those who oppose the freedom of the peoples;

— fraternal solidarity with the working people of all countries, with all peoples.

59. Primary Party organizations of industrial enterprises and trading establishments; state farms, collective farms; and design organizations, drafting offices and research institutes directly related to production enjoy the right to control the work of the administration.

The Party organizations at ministries, state committees, economic councils and other central and local government or economic agencies and departments, whose function is not that of controlling the administration, must actively promote improvement of the apparatus, cultivate among the personnel a high sense of responsibility for work entrusted to them, work for the strengthening of state discipline and for the better servicing of the population, firmly combat bureaucracy and red tape,

✶✶✶✶✶✶✶ **1961** ▲   ▼**1952** ✶✶✶✶✶✶✶

58. In order to enhance the role of the primary Party organizations in production and trading establishments, including state farms, collective farms and repair tractor stations, and their responsibility for the state of the work in their enterprises, these organizations have the right to exercise control over the activities of the management of their particular enterprise.

It is the duty of Party organizations of Ministries, which, owing to the specific nature of the work in government institutions, cannot exercise functions of control, to draw attention to defects in the work of their institutions, to be alive to shortcomings in the work of the Ministry and of any of its personnel and to communicate their information and opinions to the Central Committee and to the heads of the Ministry.

Secretaries of primary Party organizations of Ministries are inform the appropriate Party bodies in good time of shortcomings in the work of the respective offices and individuals, regardless of what posts the latter may occupy.

VII. The Party and the YCL

60. The Leninist YCL of the Soviet Union is a voluntary social organization of young people, an active helper and reserve of the Party. The YCL helps the Party educate the youth in the communist spirit, draws it into the work of building a new society, trains a rising generation of harmoniously developed people who will live and work and administer public affairs under communism.

61. YCL organizations enjoy the right of broad initiative in discussing and submitting to the appropriate Party organizations questions related to the work of enterprises, collective farms and offices. They must be really active in the implementation of Party directives in all spheres of communist construction, especially where there are no primary Party organizations.

******** **1961** ▲   ▼**1952** ********

confirmed by the Central Committee of the Party.

All Communists working in the central apparatus of a Ministry belong to one general Party organization of that Ministry.

[59. See above, following Art. 55.]

[60-61. See below, following Art. 63.]

IX. The Party and the Young Communist League

62. The Y.C.L. is an active assistant of the Party in all state and economic affairs. The Y.C.L. organizations must be in effect active vehicles of the Party's directives in all spheres of socialist construction, especially where there are no primary Party organizations.

63. Y.C.L. organizations enjoy wide initiative in discussing and submitting to the appropriate Party organizations all questions designed to remove shortcomings in the work of the particular factory, collective farm, state farm or office, and in helping them to improve the work, in organizing socialist emulation, in conducting mass campaigns, etc.

62. The YCL conducts its activities under the guidance of the Communist Party of the Soviet Union. The work of the local YCL organizations is directed and controlled by the appropriate republican, territorial, regional, area, city and district Party organizations.

63. Members of the YCL who have become members or candidate
. . . YCL, *admitted to the CPSU*, cease . . .
members of the Party cease to belong to the YCL the moment they join the Party, provided they do not hold leading posts in YCL organizations.

VIII. Party Organizations in the Soviet Army

64. Party organizations in the Soviet Army take guidance in their work from the Program and the Rules of the CPSU and operate on the basis of instructions issued by the Central Committee.

The Party organizations of the Soviet Army carry through the policy of the Party in the Armed Forces; rally servicemen around the Communist Party; educate them in the spirit of Marxism-Leninism and

******** **1961** ▲   ▼ **1952** ********

60. The Leninist Young Communist League conducts its activities under the guidance of the Communist Party of the Soviet Union. The Central Committee of the Y.C.L., as its leading body, is subordinated to the Central Committee of the Communist Party of the Soviet Union. The activities of the local organizations of the Y.C.L. are directed and controlled by the appropriate republican, territorial, provincial, city and district organizations of the Party.

61. Members of the Y.C.L. shall retire from that body from the moment they become members or candidate members of the Party, provided they do not hold leading posts in Y.C.L. organizations.

[62-63. See above, preceding Art. 60.]

X. Party Organizations in the Soviet Army and Navy and in the Transport Services

64. The guidance of Party work in the Soviet Army and Navy is exercised by the Chief Political Administrations of the Soviet Army and the Soviet Navy, and in the transport services by the

boundless loyalty to the socialist homeland; actively further the unity of the army and the people; work for the strengthening of discipline; rally servicemen to carry out the tasks of military and political training and acquire skill in the use of new techniques and weapons, and irreproachably to perform their military duty and the orders and instructions of the command.

65. The guidance of Party work in the Armed Forces is exercised by the Central Committee of the CPSU through the Chief Political Administration of the Soviet Army and Navy, which functions as a department of the CC CPSU.

The chiefs of the political administrations of military areas and fleets, and chiefs of the political administrations of armies must be Party members of five-years' standing, and the chiefs of political departments of military formations must be Party members of three years' standing.

66. The Party organizations and political bodies of the Soviet Army maintain close contact with local Party committees, and keep them informed about political work in the military units. The secretaries of military Party organizations and chiefs of political bodies participate in the work of local Party committees.

✶✶✶✶✶✶✶✶ **1961** ▲ ▼ **1952** ✶✶✶✶✶✶✶✶

Political Administrations of the Ministry of Railways of the U.S.S.R., the Ministry of Merchant Marine of the U.S.S.R., and the Ministry of Inland Water Transport of the U.S.S.R., which function as departments of the Central Committee of the Communist Party of the Soviet Union.*

Party organizations in the Soviet Army and Navy and in the transport services work on the basis of special instructions confirmed by the Central Committee.

65. The chiefs of the political administrations of military regions, fleets and armies, and the chiefs of the political departments of the railways must be Party members of five years' standing, and the chiefs of political departments of divisions and brigades Party members of three years' standing.

66. The political organs must maintain close contact with the local Party committees through constant participation of the heads of the political organs in the local Party committees, as well as through regular reports made at meetings of the Party committees

* Amendments to the Party Statutes in 1956 deleted all references to transport services in this section.—Editor

IX. Party Groups in Non-Party Organizations

67. At congresses, conferences and meetings and in the elective bodies of Soviets, trade unions, cooperatives and other mass organizations of the working people, having at least three Party members, Party groups are formed for the purpose of strengthening the influence of the Party in every way and carrying out Party policy among non-Party people, strengthening Party and state discipline, combatting bureaucracy and verifying the fulfilment of Party and government.

68. The Party groups are subordinate to the appropriate Party bodies: CC CPSU, the Central Committees of the Communist Parties of union republics, territorial, regional, area, city or district Party committees.

In all matters the groups must strictly and unswervingly abide by decisions of the leading Party bodies.

******** **1961** ▲   ▼ **1952** ********

by the chiefs of the political organs on political work in the military units and through reports by the political departments in the transport services.

XI. Party Groups in Non-Party Organizations

67. At all congresses and conferences and in all elective bodies of Soviet, trade union, cooperative and other mass organizations having not less than three Party members, Party groups are formed whose task is to strengthen the influence of the Party in every way and to carry out the Party policy among the non-party people, to strengthen Party and state discipline, to combat bureaucracy, and to verify fulfilment of Party and Soviet directives. Each such group elects a secretary to conduct its current work.

68. The Party groups are subordinated to the appropriate Party organizations (Central Committee of the Communist Party of the Soviet Union, Central Committee of the Communist Party of the Union Republic, territorial, provincial, regional, city or district Party committee).

In all questions the groups must strictly and unswervingly govern themselves by the decisions of the leading Party bodies.

X. Party Funds

69. The funds of the Party and its organizations are derived from membership dues, income from Party enterprises and other revenue.

70. The monthly membership dues for Party members and candidate members are as follows:

*Monthly Earnings**	*Dues*	
up to 50 rubles	10 kopeks	
from 51 to 100 rubles	0.5 per cent	
from 101 to 150 rubles	1.0 per cent	of the
from 151 to 200 rubles	1.5 per cent	monthly
from 201 to 300 rubles	2.0 per cent	earnings
from 201 to 250 rubles	*2.0 per cent*	
from 251 to 300 rubles	*2.5 per cent*	
over 300 rubles	3.0 per cent	

71. An entrance fee of 2 per cent of monthly earnings is paid on acceptance into the Party as a candidate member.

* In new rubles (one new ruble equals 10 old rubles).—Editor

******** 1961 ▲　▼ 1952 ********

XII. Party Funds

69. The funds of the Party and its organizations consist of membership dues, income from Party enterprises and other revenues.

70. The membership dues payable monthly by Party members and candidate members are as follows (per cent of earnings):

Monthly Earnings	Dues
Up to 500 rubles	½ per cent
From 501 to 1,000 rubles	1 per cent
From 1,001 to 1,500 rubles	1½ per cent
From 1,501 to 2,000 rubles	2 per cent
Over 2,000 rubles	3 per cent

71. Candidate members upon admission pay an entrance fee amounting to 2 per cent of their monthly earnings.